Timothy Phillips was born and grew up in Northern Ireland. He has studied at the universities of Oxford and Helsinki and has travelled widely in the former Soviet Union, including the Caucasus. In 2005 he completed a doctoral thesis on the development of holiday and health resorts in Russia. He has worked extensively as a translator, and was the principal translator for the BBC on their Beslan documentaries. This is his first book.

BESLAN

THE TRAGEDY OF SCHOOL NO. 1

TIMOTHY PHILLIPS

Granta Books

London

Granta Publications, 12 Addison Avenue, London W11 4QR

First published in Great Britain by Granta Books 2007
This edition published by Granta Books 2008

A CIP catalogue record for this book
is available from the British Library.

1 3 5 7 9 10 8 6 4 2

ISBN 978 1 86207 993 9

Printed and bound in Great Britain by
CPI Bookmarque, Croydon, CR0 4TD

CONTENTS

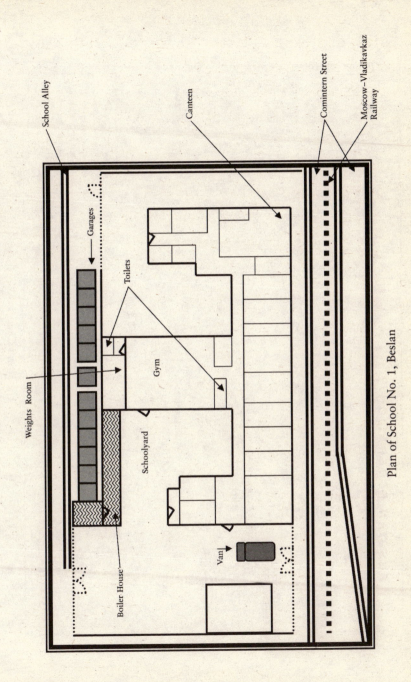

Plan of School No. 1, Beslan

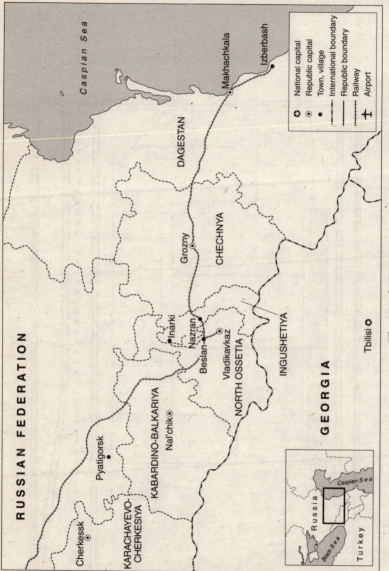

The North Caucasus

FOREWORD

I was born in Northern Ireland, a beautiful place, but like the North Caucasus famous for its troubles. The farmland of County Down is green and rolling; its farmhouses and bungalows afford views of the Mourne Mountains. I spent my first eighteen years there and was happy. But for most of that time I was also learning about the nature of the problems I lived amongst: in part rebelling against them, in part growing into them.

When I was four, I started at the local Protestant primary school. Mum or Dad drove me to the end of the lane every morning and I waited for the school bus to take me into the village. We shared the bus with the pupils from St Mary's, the local Catholic primary. By an unwritten rule we always sat in separate parts of the bus. It was a quiet, rural area and we never fought, but we hardly spoke to each other either. Somehow, we understood implicitly that we were strangers.

A few years later – I was seven or eight – I got into trouble for something I said on the bus. Two of the Catholic children were called Áine and Fionnuala, outlandish names I had never heard before. Although they lived just a mile away on a farm much like our own, they might as well have been from another planet. I suppose I thought their names were stupid and that the girls were stupid too; I started calling them Onion and Vanilla and telling other people to do the same. This bullying can't have gone on for very long – a couple of days at most. Fionnuala started to cry and Áine told the bus driver what I was doing. My parents got to know of my behaviour. I was punished and was probably made to apologize (I can't remember).

In my early teens, I was walking through a park in Belfast one afternoon. I was wearing my grammar school uniform, on my way home from rugby practise. From out of nowhere, a group of three boys came up in front of me and one asked cockily, 'Are you a Prod or a Taig?'

I was frightened and I could see from their blazer pockets that they were from a nearby Catholic school. 'I'm a Taig,' I said.

'No you're not; you're a Prod.'

One of them kicked me in the stomach. It didn't hurt that much, but I fell to the ground crying nonetheless. They took the bag with my sports kit off me and emptied its contents across the grass. One of them stood on my Parker pen – which had been a Christmas present – and they ran off holding my rugby boots in the air.

I'm not sure, looking back, how much we understood about what lay behind the insults we traded with each other. Intolerance and hatred seem to have a life of their own: everyone plays their small part, but no one is really responsible. At times it seems like these kinds of difference – tribal, religious, linguistic, ethnic – are little more than friendly rivalry, a source of local humour. At others, as in Beslan, they can cause truly horrific atrocities. All the while, the dead, long lists of their names stretching through time and across the globe, do not remember their religion or ethnicity.

EASTER SUNDAY

I stood still and looked straight ahead. There it was, set in bright grass, dandelion-speckled and overlooked by trees: a building deeply at odds with its surroundings. Swallows and thrushes darted about. I could hear children playing in nearby streets and gardens.

The building spoke for itself. It bore witness to the wrongs done inside its walls. The mangled roof appeared jagged against the blue sky. Crimson curtains billowed out of empty window frames. Bullet holes and bloodstains drew my eye away from the flowers. Torn and sodden textbooks lay where they had fallen months before. Graffiti promised those who had not survived that they would be remembered and avenged.

This place had been at the forefront of my mind for many months, but now, on its threshold at last, I didn't know what to do. It had taken my breath away: something heavy was pressing on my chest, but there were no readily definable emotions to go with it. I held back the tears because I wanted my thoughts to catch up with my body's physical reflexes. Later, I regretted this because, when I eventually thought that I should cry, I could not.

Slowly I started to walk around the school building. At first,

I thought to remain outside looking in, but this was no more respectful to the dead than walking around inside. I stepped over the low remnant of a wall that had once stood twenty feet high. The inarticulate build-up of emotion that I felt was fed by each new sign of destruction: broken chairs, mangled pipes, lopsided posters on classroom walls, abandoned class registers, blood. All of the walls were still coated in a sickly shade of institutional blue, except where the plaster had been blown off, exposing the brickwork underneath. A sign hanging on the wall in one of the classrooms announced that 4+2=6 and 6-2=4. On the floor there was a board with a heading in Russian which reads 'They Studied in Our School'. It must once have carried pictures of notable former pupils, but these have all now gone. To limit my reaction to all of this I took photographs and thought about how they would be useful for this book.

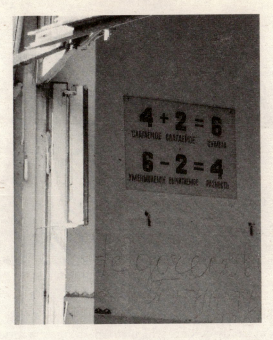

The dining hall or canteen, from where the terrorists mounted their final resistance, was the most damaged part of the school, but the gymnasium was the most affecting. I entered through the fire exit and stood looking up at the sky through charred rafters. My first thought was that if this had been anywhere in Western Europe or America, the structure would have been declared unsafe and access forbidden. What was left of the roof looked like it might still collapse at any moment. A large ventilation pipe had fallen on top of one of the basketball hoops. Everywhere inside there was evidence of fire damage. Months of snow and rain had not washed the soot from the walls. Wooden climbing frames, blackened but still solid, looked as if they might yet be hot to the touch. In some places I could see where the intense heat had blistered the paint on the walls.

Small bunches of dead flowers were dwarfed by large plastic wreaths in gaudy colours which stood, evergreen, around the four walls. Here and there cut flowers had been placed in plastic bottles filled with water. A poster sent by people in a neighbouring region, bearing the words 'We Are Crying Along With You', lay slumped against a radiator, and, hanging from one of the climbing frames, a banner sent by the pupils of a Middle School in North Carolina proclaimed in English 'You Are Not Alone'. On top of the rusted radiators cuddly toys stared vacantly, cheerily out. Across the hall three teddy bears faced a collection of stuffed rabbits, ducks and frogs.

This is what remains of School No. 1 in the small town of Beslan in the far south of Russia. For three days at the beginning of September 2004 more than 1,300 men, women and children had been crammed into a space not much bigger than a tennis court. They were held hostage by a gang of terrorists, many of whom lived only a few miles down the road. After enduring extremes of fear, hunger and thirst, many of them

did not leave the building alive. Others suffered terrible physical injuries and lasting mental trauma. Their plight attracted unprecedented media attention in a world which has often ignored or passed over Russia's troubles. Though very local, the event struck a chord with people across the globe and, for a short time, the previously unknown town was at the top of every news programme.

Inevitably, news of the siege and its aftermath disappeared from view as other atrocities and tragedies clamoured for attention. As Beslan became a memory, many issues remained unexplored and questions were left unanswered. I had come to the town to try to understand more about the terrible event that had occurred there and about the circumstances that had caused it. But standing at the epicentre of the attack, the whole thing seemed more, not less, incomprehensible. My mind, though focused entirely on the death and destruction that human beings had caused in that place, was utterly inarticulate. My thoughts could find neither form nor structure and I felt a strong desire to leave; the form and structure that now fix these memories have been imposed retrospectively.

On the point of leaving, I saw a small group of people. They came quietly but confidently into the gym. They stepped carefully between the different memorials, stopping to look more closely at only a few – the ones that had appeared most recently. One of them, a man in his late fifties, stood still with his head back and took a deep breath. Spotting me for the first time, he came over. We made polite introductions and he told me that a monk at a local monastery had suggested he visit the school. The sight of the gym would help him to come to terms with what had happened there, the monk said. It would help him to feel able to celebrate Easter. The man's granddaughter had died in the school and, despite his courteous exterior, he looked destroyed. He wasn't capable of having a long conversation, despite his natural desire to be hospitable to a visitor. There are many others like him in the houses and flats that surround the school, their lives marked for ever. I too was relieved that our conversation was brief, and I said goodbye and left.

'THE HAPPIEST DAY OF MY YEAR'

To every thing there is a season, and a time to every purpose under the heaven: a time to be born, and a time to die; a time to plant, and a time to pluck up that which is planted; a time to kill, and a time to heal; a time to break down, and a time to build up; a time to weep, and a time to laugh; a time to mourn, and a time to dance.

Ecclesiastes, 3:1–4

On the morning of 1 September 2004, children and teachers all over Russia were getting ready for the first day of the new school year. Across the country, schools were preparing to celebrate the Day of Knowledge and, in particular, the Ceremony of the First Bell. Children had new uniforms and uncomfortable new shoes. New schoolbags held pristine exercise books and pencil cases, and new lunchboxes were filled with sandwiches and fizzy drinks. Those going to school for the first time had their own mixture of excitement and fear; as did their parents. Teachers, too, had their own preoccupations. Some worried about how the ceremonies they had planned for the opening of the new school year would go. Others thought about their new classes, the new names and faces to be committed to memory. More than a few felt regret at the start of another year in a badly paid career.

At 6.15 a.m., before many other people were awake, Alik Tsagolov was already making his way through the streets of Beslan. He was heading for the gymnasium of School No. 1 to do his morning exercise routine. It was a place that the fifty-four-year-old knew well; he had spent much of his working life there as the school's P.E. teacher. He said, 'I got there about half past six to do my exercises. I had been coming every morning during the summer holidays as well. I went in and opened the windows in the main gym, to air it, and walked through to the little room on the other side, where we kept the weights and equipment. I did my normal workout and then headed back home at about twenty to eight. That was my morning constitutional.' As soon as he got home, Alik started getting ready for the school day ahead and the opening ceremony.

Only a few minutes after he left the school, seventy-two-year-old Lydia Tsalieva arrived and made her way to her office. As headmistress, she felt that it was her duty to be there earlier than everyone else. School No. 1 was her life; its staff and pupils her family. She was happy to see the long summer holiday finally at an end. As ever, she had been anticipating the return to school for many weeks. But she had had to spend the days running up to the start of term in meetings and now felt worried that she had not given the celebrations sufficient attention. In the short time that remained, she was determined to do all she could to ensure that they ran smoothly and felt a shiver of nerves at the thought that something might go wrong. She said, 'The first of September was always the happiest day of my year. It was a genuine celebration. Children, teachers and parents alike all loved it. *I* loved it.'

Leaving her things in her office, Lydia set out to walk around the school and check that everything was in place: 'The schoolyard was absolutely spotless. The school was so clean it was as if it had been sterilized. You could smell the new paint. It was a delight to behold.' By eight o'clock some pupils had already started arriving. Lydia was relieved because it meant that word had spread of her last-minute change of plan. At a meeting of the school's teaching staff a couple of days earlier, one of her teachers had suggested that they should start proceedings an hour earlier than usual, at nine o'clock rather than ten so that the ceremony would not run on into the hottest part of the day. This was to avoid a repeat of what had happened on the last day of the school year in May, when one girl had fainted because of the intensity of the heat and other people had gone home with sunstroke. Though she thought the suggestion sensible, Lydia had feared that it might be impossible to inform all the parents and pupils in time. Her staff had insisted that a few strategic phone calls to parents in each year group would be enough and it now seemed they had been right.

'The children all looked so smart as they walked in wearing their school uniforms,' she said. 'It took me nine years to bring in school uniforms, but almost all the pupils – really, almost all of them – were wearing them that day. White aprons and white ribbons and blue dresses. They looked so lovely. I thought I'd never seen such beautiful and handsome-looking children as I stood at my window watching them arriving.'

Among the first to arrive were Alana Lolaeva and her grandmother Felisa Batagova. Alana was ten years old; her brother Khetag was also due back at school that day but, being thirteen, he didn't want to be too early and had waited at home for his friends. Felisa recalled how she heard that the timing of the opening ceremony had changed: 'I got a phone call from Alana's class teacher the evening before to say that we should be there ready for the line-up to start at nine. Alana's year was to do some kind of presentation and the teacher told me that I should buy some balloons. She said that they had to have five balloons each. I sent Alana out to buy them from the shop; I told her to get more than five if she needed them.' Balloons in hand, Felisa and Alana got to school as early as they could.

'The school was still empty,' Felisa remembered. 'I went in with my granddaughter but all the classrooms were still locked. I wasn't meaning to go to the ceremony that day – I had actually been planning to go into the city – but little Alana insisted that I went with her. She tied her balloons to a radiator and we started to wait for the teachers and everyone else to arrive. Then one of Alana's teachers came along and said that Alana's new textbooks were ready for her. She took us up the stairs and opened her classroom up. We got the new books and I said to the teacher that I would nip home and bring her the ones from last year that Alana hadn't returned. I live really near the school. I left Alana with the teacher and went to get the books.'

Svetlana Dzherieva and her daughter had also been told to arrive as early as possible. Like all the seven-year-olds present, Dana was going to school for the first time and would have a particularly important role to play in the festivities. She had already met her new class on a couple of occasions: first, when her teacher had invited them and their parents into school in the hope of making the real first day a less daunting experience, and again, just the previous day. The teacher had told them about the change of timetable and said they should arrive no later than half past eight. Svetlana said, 'I asked her why she needed us to be there so early. She told me that Dana was one of five pupils in the class who she had taught in the reception class at the Activities Club during the previous year, and that she wanted those five to recite some poems and sing a couple of songs. I think she wanted time to give them a little rehearsal before the parade started.'

Like Alana, Dana had been told to bring balloons. When

Svetlana asked why, she was told that they were to be released at the climax of the ceremony. She arranged to meet another young mother and her child at a local shop, where they could blow up their balloons before going to the school. 'I left the house with my daughter at eight o'clock. We walked along the side of the railway tracks, like we did when I had taken Dana to nursery school. Every morning, when we got to the pedestrian crossing, we'd see the car from the traffic police parked there. I remember being surprised that morning, because it wasn't there.' Svetlana met her friend and, after blowing up their balloons, they headed for the school. 'There was hardly a soul in the schoolyard. Our teacher was talking to someone. Anya Karaeva was standing over to one side with her daughter and husband. I remember we said hello to each other. Then our teacher invited us to go inside to Dana's classroom. We went in – the corridors were empty – and we sat down and waited for the rest to arrive.'

Many families were still at home at this time. Some were less heedful of the teachers' last-minute change of plan; others hadn't heard about it or, like Elvira Tuaeva, were simply running late. She was due to attend the Day of Knowledge celebrations along with her twelve-year-old daughter Karina and ten-year-old son Khetag but was still fast asleep when, at twenty to nine, Karina came in, woke her up and told her off for being lazy. 'I got dressed really quickly and we all got in a taxi to get to the school on time. We'd never had to be there so early for the start of the new school year in the past. I'll never forgive myself. We didn't even stop to have any breakfast.'

The three of them got out of the taxi and started walking towards the school. At the gates Karina stopped in her tracks and said, 'I'm scared of going to school.' Elvira took her by the hand: 'I told her that there was absolutely nothing to be frightened of. She said that she didn't know why, but she was afraid of something all the same. It's strange when you look back.' Still rushing, Elvira took Karina to her class and, seeming to forget about her fears, her daughter ran off to talk with friends. After waiting for a few moments, Elvira then took her son to his classroom. Despite getting up so late, they had all made it just in time.

At 8.30 a.m., fourteen-year-old Tamerlan Mamitov was standing in Beslan's hospital, waiting for his mother Larisa, a forty-five-year-old doctor, who was just coming off a night shift in casualty. Behind her thick glasses Larisa's eyes looked tired but, by prior arrangement, Tamerlan was to meet her here to walk the short distance to School No. 1 together. Larisa said, 'If I'm honest, Tamerlan didn't really like those kinds of events – the Day of Knowledge, the Ceremony of the Last Bell and things like that. To start with, he told me that he wasn't going to go that year.' Like many boys of his age, Tamerlan found such occasions cringe-worthy – the juxtaposition of parents and children; the boredom of the speeches; the artificial jollity of it all. Larisa had talked him round the previous evening, before she went on her shift. 'One of the little girls who lives beside us was going to school for the first time and I wanted to see her taking part in the ceremony. Her dad had hired a camcorder and I remember telling Tamerlan that, if he came, he might even get to appear on film.' Grudgingly he had agreed, which made Larisa happy. She sensed that, underneath the hardening veneer of aloof adolescence, part of him still wanted to attend.

Larisa met her son in the hospital reception and, after quickly changing her clothes, they set out for the school. They walked until they got to Comintern Street, which ran along the front of the school, with an exposed railway track and a small stream up the middle of it. As they approached the zebra crossing right outside School No. 1, they noticed that the traffic police weren't there. 'They always had a car there in the mornings during the school term to make sure that the traffic stopped to let the children cross to get into school,' said Larisa. 'I remember turning to Tamerlan and saying, as we walked through the school gates, "I wonder why they haven't come today, Tam."'

By 8.30 a.m., most of the school staff had arrived. Some went straight to their classrooms to meet their new pupils; others smoked a last cigarette before starting the day's work. Forty-four-year-old Nadehzda Gurieva had lots on her mind. The history teacher's classroom was closest to the school's main entrance. As she had done for as long as she could remember, Nadezhda was overseeing the removal of her desks and chairs to the schoolyard, where they would be used in the celebrations. She was thinking about her fourteen-year-old son Boris, who was sick with a temperature. Instead of staying in bed, he had struggled into school to perform a dance with his younger sister in front of the new first-year pupils. She had made him agree that he would go back home as soon as the event was over. Once all the furniture was outside, Nadezhda helped one of her daughters to change into her costume and headed upstairs to the assembly hall, where her colleague, Elena Kosumova, was checking the microphones and speakers. Suddenly aware that it was already 8.45, she began to worry that she hadn't seen many of her final-year pupils, whose role in the festivities was so critical.

Washed and breakfasted after his early morning exercises, Alik Tsagolov, the P.E. teacher, was back in school by a quarter to nine. Just after that, he heard the school bell ring three times in quick succession, the signal that all classes, except for the new first-years, were to assemble in the schoolyard. He recalled, 'Within the space of a few minutes, everyone was lined up outside, except for a few stragglers who continued to arrive in dribs and drabs.'

Intensive-care nurse Larisa Tomaeva was hurrying her eleven-year-old son and nine-year-old daughter through the school gates at exactly this time. She could see pupils being led out into the schoolyard. Larisa was running behind schedule and felt flustered: 'I was late. I always am. I have another little child as well. He was a year and three months back then. I'd had to leave him at home because we were late. I got the two older children out of the house and we ran to the corner, but there were no buses in sight. Then I saw a neighbour and he agreed to drive us to school in his car. We ran into the school-yard and my son's class – Year 6 – had already formed up outside. I took him over to join them and then headed into the school with my daughter.'

Another straggler was twenty-seven-year-old Madina Khuzmieva. A clerk at the local courthouse, she had taken the morning off to watch her seven-year-old son Alex's first day. Because it was such a special occasion she had got her hus-band Murat to arrange leave as well. 'First thing that morning, I had to go into Vladikavkaz to pick up a bouquet of flowers that I had ordered. My mother lives near School No. 1 and so I left Alex with her. When the time came, she took him to school along with his sister and his aunt. I was still on the way back from the city with my dad in the car. We had to stop to buy balloons as well, I remember.' When she finally got to the school, Madina had to make her way through the groups of people assembled in the yard and into the building itself, where her son Alex was sitting in the class-room with the other new first-years.

When nineteen-year-old Zarina Daurova woke up that 1 September it was the first time for eleven years that she did not have to get ready to go to School No. 1. She had finished her education a few months earlier, on that sweltering day in May at the Ceremony of the Last Bell when one of the pupils had fainted. In a few weeks' time she was going to study tax-ation in Moscow. Her younger brother Zaur was still at the school and she had heard him leaving earlier that morning.

The family home was just a couple of hundred yards from the school and, as 9 a.m. approached, she heard the music starting up in the schoolyard. 'I went out onto the balcony of our flat. The sun was so bright and the music from the school was so loud. I spotted my neighbour and she asked me if I wanted to go to the celebrations. I said, "Why not?" The two of us and her mum hurried over there. All the children were already standing out in the yard and we went and positioned ourselves by the boiler house. The first-years were still to come out – they were standing just inside the door waiting – and the headmistress was still to step up to the microphone to make her speech.'

'START DIGGING YOUR OWN GRAVES'

Some hours earlier, before even P.E. teacher Alik Tsagolov was awake, another group of men and women were up preparing for the day ahead. They had slept the night in an Ingush forest just a few dozen miles to the north-east of Beslan. Waking just before dawn, some of them prayed while others took care of more mundane concerns, cleaning and checking weapons and preparing a quick breakfast. This was their second camp. Their green lorry had halted there the previous evening under cover of darkness. There were at least thirty-two of them. Some had been living in the forest for weeks; others had only joined the band the night before. Though it can never be verified, it seems that a few were there against their will and many knew very little of what was planned for the rest of the day.

Almost everyone in the camp was either Chechen or Ingush. Their leader was Ruslan Khuchbarov. In 1998 he had murdered two Armenian men during a dispute over a woman. Since then, he had turned to religion, channelling his aggression into what he believed to be a holy war. He was known as the Colonel. Twenty-eight-year-old Vladimir Khodov was effectively the Colonel's deputy. Half-Ukrainian, half-Ossetian, he too had a background in 'ordinary' violence – in

1998 he had raped a woman – but, like the Colonel, had channelled his love of violence into the pursuit of political and religious ends. Though born a Christian, Khodov followed his younger brother in converting to Islam and went on to fight against Russian sovereignty in the North Caucasus. Already in 2004 he had been involved in the bombing of a train near Beslan and the detonation of a car bomb outside a North Ossetian police academy.

Little is known about many of the other people in the group; in some cases, their very identities remain a mystery. Some were refugees from Chechnya, living a more or less transient existence in camps or poor rented accommodation in nearby regions like Ingushetia. Others had still been living in Chechnya until a few days earlier, trying to evade capture by the Russians. Plenty of them had previous form. Twenty-three-year-old Issa Torshkhoev had been arrested for robbery and given a suspended sentence. Almost exactly a year earlier, Mairbek Chabirkhanov had successfully ambushed a detachment of Russian soldiers in Chechnya, killing six and wounding seven.

All but two were men. These women's identities are still uncertain. They spent the final minutes before their departure attaching explosive belts around their waists. If the Russian authorities' analysis of DNA samples is to be trusted, their names were Roza Nagaeva and Mariam Taburova. Both in their mid-twenties, they came from the countryside but had been renting a flat in central Grozny – the capital of Chechnya – for most of 2004. They were living with Roza's sister, Amnat, and another friend, Satsita. Until very recently, they had all earned a living in the city's main market, selling children's clothes which they bought whole-sale in Azerbaijan once a month. But by the end of the summer all four women had turned towards violence. On 22 August, they left Chechnya supposedly to travel to Baku, the

Azerbaijani capital, to buy new stock. Their relatives say that the women would have been intending to purchase school uniforms to sell to parents for the new school year. The trip to Baku was a ruse, it seems, and instead of heading south the women split into pairs and set out on two deadly missions. Roza and Mariam joined the Colonel at the camp in the forest. Now, on the morning of 1 September, their friends Amnat and Satsita were already dead. They had travelled to Moscow where they had tickets to travel on two separate passenger flights on 24 August. Shortly after each plane had taken off the women had blown themselves up.

Only one of these thirty-two people was to survive the event that the Colonel and his masters had planned. Twenty-four-year-old Nurpashi Kulaev was thinking about everything that had happened to him during the preceding twelve hours. If his version of events is to be believed he was then very frightened about what the future held. For all that his is a convenient story, much of it has a ring of truth about it and it has withstood tests of time and robust interrogation.

The previous afternoon, he had been in the wrong place at the wrong time and had been kidnapped by the Colonel's men. As he was leaving a shop in the Ingush village where he lived, a white car had pulled up alongside driven by Issa Torshkhoev; the occupants had demanded to know the whereabouts of his brother, Khanpasha. Two of the four men in the car were wearing masks and camouflage. They said that they suspected that Khanpasha had become a spy for the government and that they needed to see him immediately. They named a place and time later that day and told Nurpashi to pass the message on.

Khanpasha was at home with his friend Mairbek Chabirkhanov when Nurpashi got back. Khanpasha seemed to understand the importance of the message. He asked Nurpashi to repeat the names of the men in the car and then got ready to go and meet them. Khanpasha had a long history of involvement with the Chechen rebels. In 2001, he had been arrested during an attack in which he lost an arm. The names – perhaps those of old comrades or people to whom he owed favours – were familiar to him. He took his friend Mairbek with him to the appointed place. After about twenty minutes they returned home, where they found Nurpashi with his friend Islam. Khanpasha said that they would soon have to go out again, but that this time Nurpashi and Islam would have to come with them. A short time later, the four of them crowded into the back of the white car.

They were driven to the Colonel's base camp near the Ingushetian border with North Ossetia. The first thing Nurpashi noticed was that everyone was carrying weapons. He and Islam were told to sit apart from the rest of the group and prepare something to eat. They watched as the others began to argue fiercely between themselves. Nurpashi recalled that the dispute seemed to revolve around his brother's recent behaviour: was he in the pay of the security services? Why had he sold the car that the Colonel had given him? After a while, four members of the group drove Nurpashi and Islam away from the camp in the white car. 'They started asking us who we were working for. They were certain my brother was working for someone. They said, "It'd be better to tell us everything, because we're going to kill you anyway. You'll find it easier to account for yourself before Allah if you tell us the truth now." I told them that I didn't know anything. Then they read some verse from the Koran and repeated that they were going to kill us anyway and we should tell them the truth.' When this didn't produce results, Nurpashi says that the men forced him and Islam to dig holes in the ground: 'They gave us shovels and said, "Start digging your own graves."'

When the pair still refused to 'confess', they were put in the car and taken back to the camp in the forest. At this point, the group apparently gave up trying to prove that Khanpasha and his friends were spies and, satisfied that he was for them rather than against them, accepted the former rebel as a part of their band. If this testing had been the rationale for bringing Nurpashi and Islam, they were not now released. When the pair had been back at the camp for a while, Khanpasha came over to them and said, 'You do know that they won't let you go back home now, don't you? They're too frightened to because you've seen everything that they've got here: the base and everything.' When the entire group moved to a new camp in the middle of the night, Nurpashi and Islam were taken too. Now, as dawn broke, they were expected to obey the Colonel's command and climb into the green lorry along with everyone else. Most, if not all, of those in the group were now carrying large quantities of weapons and ammunition.

Those of the group who were sitting in the back of the lorry could not see where they were going, but the jolts and bumps they felt told them that they were travelling on very poor roads. The leaders had chosen a route to Beslan that avoided main roads and stuck to country lanes and even dirt tracks wherever possible, in the hope that the lorry would not be stopped or spotted by traffic police. Nonetheless, that was exactly what happened not long after they set off. Those sitting in the back, like Nurpashi Kulaev, who may or may not have known their destination, caught muffled fragments of a conversation between the driver and a traffic policeman, Inspector Gurazhev: 'Can I see your documents?. . . You are aware that this is not officially a road, aren't you?'

Soon the policeman's pistol had been taken from him and he found himself held at gunpoint. Turning the unwanted interruption to the group's advantage, the Colonel took charge of the policeman's patrol car and used it to provide an escort for the lorry. The policeman was forced to sit in the back seat as the two vehicles drove in convoy to Beslan. Pulling onto the main road, just a couple of miles from Beslan, they now drove more quickly towards the town. They arrived early and parked a few hundred metres from their destination. A few minutes later, the police patrol car drove up to the school behind the lorry. The terrorists in the car abandoned Gurazhev. Those in the back of the lorry, like Nurpashi Kulaev, were already piling out and running the short distance into the schoolyard. As soon as they hit the ground most of them started firing machine guns in the air. After a few minutes, Gurazhev – who was lucky to be alive – left the car and made his way to the local police station.

'NO CHANCE TO RUN AWAY'

'School Years'

On that bright first September day
I stepped shyly through those brilliant gates,
To read my first textbook and have my first class –
That's how all our school years begin.

Those wonderful school years
Of friendship and learning and song,
How quickly they disappear!
Never to return!
But surely they won't disappear without trace,
For no one can ever forget their school days.

Original words by E. Dolmatovskii
Music by D. Kabalevskii

A few minutes after nine o'clock, the new first-years, who had been waiting in the entrance hall of the school, started to descend the steps into the schoolyard. As they emerged into the bright sunlight, the children could see the assembled crowd –

well over a thousand of them – looking eagerly at them. Once out in the yard, every child, except one, was to parade in front of all their teachers, relatives and new fellow pupils before lining up in front of the platform for the headmistress's speech. The exception was one of the new first-year girls who was chosen in advance to perform the Ceremony of the First Bell. She was to be carried on the shoulders of one of the final-year boys to a place in the yard where she could ring the symbolic first bell of her and her peers' school lives. For many of the seven-year-olds this was the first public event they had ever taken part in and, walking through the doors, some of them looked anxious. Their new teachers were on hand to give them a pat on the shoulder and a final smile of reassurance.

Walking backwards down the steps just ahead of the children, one of whom was her own daughter Dana, Svetlana Dzherieva was trying to get as many pictures of them as possible. She recalls, 'I was walking in front of them, photographing them as I went. When about half of the year had come down the steps into the schoolyard, men in camouflage started running in from the direction of the railway lines. They had machine guns in their hands and they were shooting. At first I had no idea what was happening. I though that some criminals must have escaped from the prison and run into the school-yard. They took off their masks and shouted, "You are under siege." Then they started shooting even more.'

Svetlana had just walked past Kazbek Dzarasov, who had also taken up a position right next to the steps to watch the first-years filing out. Thirty-five-year-old Kazbek worked for one of the largest employers in Beslan, the drinks manufacturer Salute. He had studied at School No. 1 twenty years earlier. On 1 September 2004 he came with his mother, mainly to see his two sons start the new school year, but also to catch up with his own old schoolfriends. After seeing one son to his classroom, he had had his photograph taken along with some former schoolmates, before heading out to the yard for a cigarette before the ceremony. He was still smoking when the first-years began to emerge and an older pupil, arriving late for the ceremony, ran past him screaming that there were bearded, masked terrorists outside. Kazbek said, 'Naturally, I didn't believe the lad. Terrorists? What terrorists? But just as soon as I turned around, I saw these men running into the school grounds. I had no chance to run away before one of them turned on us and started shooting into the air from his machine gun.'

Amongst the amateur photographers and cinematographers in the schoolyard that morning, there was a small number who were professionally trained. One such was Karen Dinoradze, who had been asked by a local family to make a film about their daughter's first day at school. Proud parents with a little more disposable income than average had hired him in the past to film their children in the Ceremony of the First Bell. As the pupils started to emerge from the school, Karen spotted the subject of his film. 'One of the senior pupils picked up the girl and put her on his shoulders. I began to record and, when I first heard the gunfire, I remember noticing on the little display screen that only three minutes had passed. Then people armed with machine guns and dressed in military clothes ran in and started to take over the yard.'

Elsewhere in the yard, people's initial reactions to the raid were similar. With their attention focused on the little children, most did not spot the attackers until they were already in their midst. Many of the people at the celebration were standing with their back to the alleyway that formed the school's main entrance, along which the attackers approached. Though the shooting could be clearly heard above the loud music, it was so out of context that people misinterpreted it. The attack appeared to have been perfectly planned; the attackers appear to have been aware of the last-minute change of timing. Even when it became obvious that they were under siege, events were unfolding so quickly that many could not absorb the information.

Alik Tsagolov, the P.E. teacher, was standing on the side of the schoolyard next to the boiler house as the first-years emerged from the school. He suddenly heard some bangs. 'I thought to myself, "Who's managed to get such noisy balloons?" Then in a very short space of time, everyone started moving and people were screaming. Very quickly there was general panic. And it was only then that I understood what was going on. It would never have entered my head that such a thing could happen. They ran in from the entrance by the railway tracks. I wasn't facing them, so I didn't see them approach. It took me a while to realize that the noises were automatic rounds being fired. They surrounded us in a semi-circle, cutting off the other exit along School Alley and started forcing us all back into the schoolyard.'

Larisa Mamitova, the doctor, and her son Tamerlan had taken up a position closer to the main door, through which the first-years were emerging. Larisa wanted to get a good view of her neighbour's daughter walking down the steps. 'There were an awful lot of people there that day. An awful lot. I went and stood where the teachers usually stand. That's where they bring the first-years out and I wanted to get a good view of my little neighbour. All of the equipment was just beside us and the music was really blasting out. My son took himself off. He told me he was going over to say hello to his friends from his year. I said that was all right.' While they waited, Larisa chatted to some of her neighbours.

She saw some balloons flying up into the air just as the shooting started. Firing guns into the air at times of celebration is normal throughout the Caucasus, particularly at weddings and after the birth of children. Larisa assumed that someone had decided to do the same for their child's first day at school. 'I smiled to myself and thought, "Did you ever hear of such a thing? A gun salute for the children on their first day?" Then I looked up and saw soldiers running in wearing camouflage gear. The first one had no mask on: I wondered whether this was some kind of lesson or something. I would just never have thought that they were actually terrorists. Here we were in the centre of the town, with the police station just next door. There was just no way it could have been terrorists.' As she stood watching, people started to run, shouting for their children as they went. Unsure of what was going on, Larisa joined them, searching for her son and crying 'Tamik! Tamik!'

After the rush to get to the ceremony on time, Elvira Tuaeva had joined the other parents in the schoolyard. She was standing with her back to Comintern Street from where the attackers struck. 'We didn't even get time to turn around,' she says. 'There were some screams and then – suddenly – the terrorists. All but one were wearing masks. I can remember the one who wasn't so clearly. He was really well-built and he ran in front of everyone else, firing shots into the air.' This was the Colonel, leading his troops into battle and marked out from the ranks by his willingness – perhaps even his need – to be noticed and recognized by his victims. The next thing Elvira knew, she was being ordered towards the school building and had to try to withstand the force of the moving crowd as she looked around for her son and daughter.

Vera Salkazanova, a seventy-year-old grandmother, was sitting on a bench near the headmistress. Her four-year-old granddaughter Rada was by her side. They were watching out for Rada's brother Ruslan; it was his first day of school. Ruslan's mother had stayed with him inside the building as his new class prepared to make its entrance into the schoolyard. She had been placed beside the former headmaster and guest of honour, eighty-nine-year-old Tatarkan Sabanov. 'I noticed

that some of the balloons had flown up into the air and I
thought to myself that today's celebrations seemed particularly well thought out. Then I saw a man running in dressed
in black, firing a gun and shouting "Allahu Akbar!" I thought
it had to be some kind of practical joke or something. Then
another one came at us from the other side. I realized that I
was surrounded and I didn't know where to go.'

Alla Khanaeva, a thirty-three-year-old mother of three, had
brought her two daughters, Diana and Marianna, and her
son, Irbek, to school and had decided to stay to see the ceremony. She ended up standing beside the speakers which were
amplifying the music across the yard, camcorder in hand. The
noise was so great that it was difficult to concentrate on the
events unfolding in front of her. 'The music was unbearably
loud. It was at a crazy volume. I couldn't even hear what my
friend was saying to me, and she was standing right next to
me. As I recall, they were playing "School Years" and other
songs about school life. Then suddenly, the shots rang out.
They were shooting as they ran and they shouted at us, "Get
into the building! Get inside!"'

Alla could not understand what was happening. 'I certainly
didn't think for a moment at first that this was a terrorist
attack or that these were real fighters. It was only when they
started shouting at us to get into the building and the whole
crowd started pouring towards the school and they started
shooting at people's legs that I actually realized what was
going on.' Unlike many of the people around her, Alla didn't
head for the school doors immediately. She stood her ground
for what felt like quite a long time, watching the crowd move.
She said, 'I didn't know which of my three children I should
go looking for. I didn't know how I could hope to find anyone
in that mass of people.'

EDUCATING RUSSIA

Russians respect education. The importance that they place on the Day of Knowledge and the Ceremony of the First Bell is entirely in keeping with their attitudes towards schooling more generally. The crisply ironed suits and neatly pressed dresses of the new first-years, the complex choreography of the parade and, most of all, the pride on parents' faces signify Russians' attachment to education.

You may say that many in the UK place considerable emphasis on the education of their offspring too. They choose their child's school carefully, often years in advance of the child reaching school age. Many of them pay to send their children to private, and even public, schools; others purchase private tuition to supplement – or undo – the teaching of the state system. They drag themselves to sports matches, open evenings, concerts and nativities, and offer financial sweeteners for getting top grades in exams. But Russian parents go further. They have internalized the mantra about the benefits of learning to such an extent that many will actually impoverish themselves for the sake of their children's education.

Today's Russians have inherited their faith in the power of education from their parents and grandparents who, in turn, were taught it by the Soviet regime. In a country where commercial trading and the entrepreneurial spirit were vilified, the only legitimate route to betterment was through good performance at school. It was a route that Marxist doctrine could endorse: self-improvement through hard work, even if the work was being carried out over textbooks and not factory floors. More practically, schools were also places where the adults of tomorrow could be indoctrinated with the official ideologies of socialism, atheism and patriotism. It was Lenin, not Tony Blair, who first said, 'Education. Education. Education.'

The Bolsheviks assumed control of a country where the general level of education had been improving only slowly: illiteracy in 1917 was much more widespread in Russia than in any other great European power. Over the decades that followed, a centralized education system was put in place to ensure that all citizens of the state received a minimum level of schooling. By the time the USSR collapsed, nursery care was available to all. Specialist schools existed for many disciplines and subjects. A multitude of further and higher education institutions had been created to supplement the small number of universities and institutes inherited from the Tsarist regime. Busy workers were encouraged to attend night school to improve their career prospects. A disproportionate number of Soviet films were set in educational institutions; almost all of them advertised the merits of the system and the people it produced. Although the reality of education often failed to live up to the regime's hype, ordinary Russians came to believe that their system was one of the best in the world. They were grateful to the state for providing such an enviable start to their sons and daughters.

The celebrations that still accompany the first day of each new academic year in Russia show how these attitudes persist. In the UK the occasion passes largely unmarked. There might be a special assembly with an address by the headmaster but parents are not invited and new pupils are not especially to the fore. British school celebrations tend to focus on individuals' achievements. In Russia, the Day of Knowledge and the Ceremony of the First Bell concentrate on the experience of education itself. A piece of Soviet propaganda from the mid-80s calls the day 'the first important celebration of our childhood'.

The celebration itself was a relatively late addition to the long list of Soviet high days and holidays. The Day of Knowledge only received the state's formal endorsement in August 1969, though variations on the theme had been observed in various places for many years previously. In that month the All-Union Leninist Communist Union of Youth, more commonly known as the Komsomol, decreed that the event should be celebrated in every school in the country. It seems to have expressed so neatly people's feelings towards education that it became extremely popular and has outlived the demise of the Soviet system as a whole. When other, more venerable Soviet holidays are now recalled with nostalgia or, even worse, irony, the Day of Knowledge is still alive and well. Annually, 1.3 million seven-year-olds are feted as they go to school for the first time.

Of course, the content of the day has changed over time, though less than might be expected. It is still possible to hear old songs with Communist lyrics – like 'School Years' – though these are now played more for the parents and teachers. The ideologies and sartorial codes have been relaxed since the festival's adoption under General Secretary Brezhnev. The Marxist-Leninist slogans that were formerly hung from the windows and nailed to the walls have disappeared too. Schools are now less fastidious about the colour coordination of pupils' uniforms with the ribbons in their hair and the bunches of flowers they carry. However, uniform-wearing itself has been making a comeback in those schools which are keen to present a certain kind of image, Beslan's School No. 1 included.

The headmaster's speech, stripped of the references to Lenin and five-year plans, is much the same as it always was. In many schools, students (and teachers and parents) are still told to be thankful that they live in a country which places such importance on educating its young. It is once again the norm under Putin to show respect to the President. Mother Russia and her army might also feature in a Day of Knowledge speech. Other ideological holes have been plugged with a resurgent localism, which takes pride in sub-national identities like Ossetian – the equivalent of Scottish or Geordie in the UK – and the heritage of individual schools. At Beslan's School No. 1, for instance, the headmistress always allowed herself a few words on the school's reputation: it was easily the most popular and prestigious school in the town.

Underpinning the celebration and the ritual of the ringing of the first bell there is the same faith in education's wonder-working power as ever. Though Russians are no longer banned from engaging in commerce, opportunities are limited and unemployment is high. By giving their children as wide a range of educational chances as possible, parents hope to secure for them a decent future, even as the general populace's standard of living continues to drop. (Ironically the drop is partly caused by parents' financial investment in their children's education, whether in private tuition, university fees or bribes.)

To the few for whom money is no object all doors are open. English nannies, who were all the rage in aristocratic house-holds in the early nineteenth century, are once again in vogue, though you wouldn't find any in Beslan. Gated housing complexes have swings and climbing frames made of brightly painted Scandinavian wood. There are luxury private nurs-eries on the outskirts of Moscow where three-year-olds are taught foreign languages by native speakers, sometimes watched over by armed bodyguards. Those children can then attend fee-paying prep and boarding schools in Russia or abroad, before applying to study at Harvard or Oxford.

Rather than make do with whatever comes their way, parents with more modest means are also often willing to spend significant amounts of money on their child's education. Even before they reach university, which is no longer free for most in Russia, all but the poorest children can expect to have had private classes of some kind, either to help them in their school subjects or to introduce them to sports, music or chess. In the North Caucasus, in places like Beslan, boys are often taught martial arts: the connection between play-fighting and the warriors of the past, once almost lost, has been rediscovered.

Walking through the centre of a busy Caucasian town one afternoon, I turned off into a leafy square to escape the hot sun and noxious exhaust fumes. The shrubs and hedges had been allowed to grow high and it wasn't easy to see across the small park. Immediately, however, I heard the screams and shouts of young children. I rounded a corner to find a small band of six- or seven-year-olds who were beating each other up. Some had boxing gloves; others were using their bare fists and their feet. One, wearing a Liverpool football strip, was applying himself to his task with particular gusto. He was running between the others, who were mostly fighting in pairs, and seemed to be landing punches on them left, right and centre. Being quite a lot bigger than the rest, he had an unfair advantage. All of them were smiling, and the scene would have been normal enough – if slightly distasteful – but for the presence of a female teacher offering instruction and encouragement from the sidelines. Given my reasons for being in the Caucasus, I couldn't help feeling sad that parents were paying this woman to teach their sons how to hurt each other.

However, even when they are being instructed in the ways

of violence, Russian children are usually more charming than British ones. They are at once more gregarious and more polite; more likely to come over and talk to you, but less likely to stamp on your foot. Parents and grandparents – economic and social pressures mean grandparents often do most of the child-rearing – must be doing something right.

It is quite rare to meet a real brat, but that was what Milan was. Only ten years old, he was already a veteran bully, speaking to his grandmother, Oksana, like a tyrannical husband. Oksana was a French teacher in a school near Beslan. I met her during my visit to the region to discuss her experiences of working in the North Caucasus. In the short time that I spent in their flat, Milan never failed to go against her wishes. Looking back on that time, I now see that their dysfunctional relationship was caused by fundamental differences in their attitude towards education and their definition of success.

When Oksana asked him to do his homework, Milan told her to piss off. When she served us dinner, he said that it smelt disgusting. He insisted on drinking his milk cold, even though it clearly distressed Oksana, who, like all Russian grannies, was frightened he would get a chill. Picking up on this fear, Milan announced that he was going outside to play in the rain without an anorak. Oksana grabbed him by the arm but he made her release her grip by pummelling her hand with his free fist. Humiliated in front of her guest, she yelped in pain and he ran out the door.

Oksana wiped away a tear. The absent link between Milan and his grandmother was her daughter, Natasha. Unlike Oksana's son, who, like herself, was a talented (though unemployed) linguist, Natasha worked in a fur factory. She had left school at the earliest opportunity and refused all her mother's subsequent offers to pay for a university course. The fur factory was a bad job. When there were orders to fill, Natasha was required to work long shifts; when there were none she was laid off. The night that I stayed with Oksana, her daughter was on a midday-to-midnight shift, adding fur trim to a consignment of ladies' gloves. The work was only to last for a fortnight. For all its obvious drawbacks, Natasha liked her job because it demanded little of her attention. Her workmates were good fun and they often went on nights out together. While Oksana and I were talking, Natasha phoned to say that she would be going out clubbing when her shift ended; her mum shouldn't wait up and shouldn't bolt the door.

Oksana was cross with her daughter and did little to conceal it. If she went out, she would get drunk. When she came in, she would make no effort to be quiet: we would all – most importantly *I* would – be woken up. Natasha had been told that I was coming to visit, but had shown no interest (I can't say I blame her). 'She has no interest in anything that interests me,' Oksana said with resignation. 'She is like a cuckoo in my nest.' With her son, who now lived far away, Oksana had talked about literature and watched foreign films at the local cinema. With her daughter all she seemed able to do was argue.

Oksana wanted Milan to be like her own son, but he wanted to be like Natasha. School for him was like the fur factory for his mother: a place to spend time with his friends. He got by on as little work as possible and always resented going back to class after the holidays. His favourite pastime was computer games – 'His mother buys them for him, not me,' Oksana hastily explained. She told me that the boy had recently learnt the word 'snob' and was using it against her; she thought he'd been taught it by Natasha. Soon enough Milan came back inside – playing in the rain is not much fun – and Oksana tried to behave towards him as if nothing had happened. When I left their house the next morning, she was sitting in the kitchen leafing through a first edition of the poems of Byron that she had shown me the night before. Milan was lying in the living room playing *Tomb Raider*, and his mother was still in bed, having come in noisily at about four in the morning. The gulf between them seemed unbridgeable.

It must be said that Natasha is unusual in modern Russia for turning down her mother's offer to pay for some form of higher education. Almost every young adult I met was enrolled in a course at some university or other. Factories have shut all over Russia since the collapse of the Soviet Union. The children of working-class parents can have great difficulty in maintaining their class status. The likelihood that their children will move straight from school into unemployment causes many relatively poor parents to find the money to pay for a period of further or higher education.

Eighteen-year-old Rim had just completed his school career and started a university degree when I met him in the resort town of Pyatigorsk, about a hundred miles from Beslan. I was having a coffee on the newly renovated boulevard when Rim spotted me and came over. We had been introduced the previous evening but no more than a couple of words had passed between us. As he took his seat beside me, the two friends he had been promenading with waved over at me and then nodded at Rim. He had just been telling them about how he had met an Irishman the night before, and they were showing him how impressed they were that his story had now been corroborated.

As we sat – me drinking coffee, Rim chain-smoking – dozens of young students wandered past. Every so often a group I had seen before would wander back past us. Many of the women were extremely thin and wearing highly fashionable clothes; most were balancing on stilettos. Some of the men had gone for an 'Italian' look with tight jeans, close-fitting fine woollen tops and pointed leather slip-ons. Others wore sportswear, mostly from well-known labels. Only the occasional young man or woman was dressed badly in the poorly made short-sleeved shirts or synthetic blouses of Soviet tailoring. The general impression was of a rather brash group of people who took immense care about their appearance. Promenading along the middle of the boulevard, they contrasted starkly with the older people who were relegated to walking on the pavements along the edge: a much dowdier lot, and poorer looking too.

I told Rim that I found it difficult to believe that the fashionable students were related to the dreary-looking adults. 'They are related,' he says. 'The parents spoil their children here. They will do anything for them; pay any money. While they are studying, the children live like little princes and princesses and their parents have to work every hour God sends to pay for them.' Rim's own background is not unusual. His parents worked for years on the collective farms as little more than state-employed peasants, before buying a little plot of land of their own a few miles from Pyatigorsk. They sell the vegetables they grow at market and have recently started acting as middlemen for other smallholders. From what Rim said, it doesn't sound like they have much disposable income.

'They have to work very hard to pay my fees at the institute. This is only my first year of four and I have younger siblings. Life is not easy for them and I try to go home and help them at the weekends.' Rim told me that many of his friends take their parents' financial support for granted. Like most, Rim lives with a relative, but some students have even demanded money to rent their own flats in town. Others insist on taking annual holidays, sometimes abroad. A great number, who continue studying mainly because there would be nothing for them to do otherwise (no real jobs, that is), don't bother attending lectures at all and spend all of their time on the boulevard.

If this behaviour seems broadly similar to that of many British students, then it should not be forgotten that Russian students' future prospects are sadly different. A good education may be a necessary condition for social and professional advancement in Russia today, but it is not a sufficient one. The number of blue-collar jobs has plummeted, but this has not led to a rise in the number of white-collar ones. The call-centre or service-sector revolution in Britain, India and elsewhere has no equivalent in Russia.

Most jobs that require any education whatsoever are still in the public sector: in hospitals, the police, schools, universities, customs, the civil service, the armed forces. They have appalling salaries: for instance, policemen are paid £50 a month. Worst of all, people who want to do these jobs often have to pay bribes to get in because demand is so great. Having bought their positions, the successful employees have to recoup their costs and augment their meagre salaries by demanding bribes from their customers, patients, clients or students. Even when the merit of the applicants is the sole arbiter of who gets a job, the situation is often no less unfair. Candidates that look identical on paper are often of wildly differing abilities, for it is now common for parents to bribe teachers to give their children the top marks – the temptation to mark up for money is too great for some poorly paid lecturers. As one of Rim's friends later put it to me, 'Why would you sit in the library studying for exams all summer, when your parents can buy your grades for you, while you can sit in the sun?' In such circumstances, many Russian students' lives can be little more than a jolly binge, a hiatus before the drudgery of real life begins.

These problems are not entirely the fruits of post-Soviet economic decline and free market capitalism. In Communist times, the beneficial effects of education were frequently neutered by shortages and corruption. The centrally planned economy was paradoxically bad at planning for reality and a shortage of vacant posts in one year would often be followed by a shortage of trained people in the next. More invidiously, places at good nurseries, schools and universities, whilst technically available to all, were secretly reserved for Communist Party members. The results of entrance examinations were frequently ignored or doctored to produce the 'right' outcome. Children were given places at a specialist school, only to have them withdrawn at the last minute because a more deserving (for which read better-connected) pupil had appeared.

The worst thing awaiting the Russian man who is finally forced to leave full-time education is also a hangover from Soviet times: conscription into the armed forces. Without doubt, the conscript's experience has deteriorated since the fall of the Soviet Union. Although they have not been sent to fight in Chechnya for the last few years, conscripts' quality of life is still vile. Murdered journalist Anna Politkovskaya and others have written damning analyses of the institutionalized bullying that is endemic in some regiments of the army. New conscripts are frequently obliged to act as slaves of more senior ones, subjected to regular acts of sadism and humiliation and often forced to surrender all their possessions and most of their food. Deaths from bullying and suicide are not uncommon, while psychological scarring would seem to be guaranteed for those who survive.

Russians in higher education can postpone their military service until the end of their studies. At that point they serve for only one year, rather than the usual two. These are further compelling reasons for parents to pay for their sons to stay in education. Currently, only a tiny fraction of the eligible population completes its military service. Families with sufficient means pay bribes to the authorities to 'buy out' the remaining year that young male graduates should serve. Others go on the run; for a small number the threat of service is enough to make them leave the country altogether. Russians once felt pride in their armed forces not just because of their supposedly superior might but also because of their inherent respectability and integrity. Those days are a distant memory.

At the very start of my visit to Russia, I met Sait, a taxi driver who took me from Moscow airport to the centre of the capital. I had hurried from the baggage carousel to catch a train into the city centre. I was keen to avoid a taxi ride if I could because Russian airport drivers are experts at extortion, but I missed my train. The next one was not due to depart for over an hour and would have left me late for meeting my host. As I turned away from the ticket window Sait was upon me. He kept telling me what I knew already – that there would be no more trains for an hour – and rattled off a litany of different prices in Russian and English and German. At first I quickened my step – if I was going to take a taxi, it should be with anyone but him – but he kept pace. Then I came to a halt and said that we would have to agree a price before we set off. Another stream of numbers flew from his mouth, not linked to any currency and sometimes followed by phrases like 'per kilometre' and 'if the traffic isn't too bad'. Eventually, we made what I thought was a deal and I followed him to his car.

Once we were on the road, flying past billboards advertising a stylish middle-class existence, Sait introduced himself properly. He was a forty-five-year-old Muslim, originally from the southern Russian city of Nizhnii Novgorod. He had had six children with his first wife, before, in his words, 'trading her in for a newer model'. He told me that his new wife, Elvira, was fifteen years his junior and much less boring in bed than the old one. When he asked me what kind of women I liked, I changed the subject and asked him about his children.

The proud expression he had been wearing suddenly changed as he started talking about his eldest son, Ramzan. With only Sait working, there had been insufficient money to keep the boy in education when he turned eighteen. Two years of compulsory military service awaited Ramzan, but Sait had had no means of paying a bribe. Instead, he had turned to his only contact in the Russian military. Thanks to this friend, Ramzan was posted to a comparatively cushy place at a naval academy. (As in the UK, the navy is generally thought to be a more cultured place than the army.)

'Thankless' Ramzan had lasted only a few weeks of the gruelling regime before slitting his wrists. He had to spend ages in a military hospital and ultimately he was discharged from the armed forces on the grounds of mental illness. Sait was convinced that his son had faked the suicide attempt and was annoyed with him. He seemed to be annoyed for many reasons. It must have been embarrassing in front of the friend who had wangled Ramzan his posting. It was humiliating also to have a son who was officially categorized as mentally ill, whether or not the symptoms were real. In his eyes, Ramzan should not have taken the easy way out. Sait had done his military service as a teenager in the 70s, when it was almost impossible to avoid. Why should his son get an easier ride?

Whilst Ramzan's actions seemed entirely rational to me, I could understand Sait's main source of irritation with his hapless son. Since dropping out of the military, Ramzan had done nothing with himself. Moping around the house, he could find no work ('There are no jobs. And anyway, who would have him?') and was consequently just another mouth for the taxi driver to feed. That's why he had decided to get Ramzan to apply for a place on an engineering course at a state-owned polytechnic. On account of his mental illness, Sait felt certain he would qualify for discounted fees.

When we pulled up outside the train station in central Moscow where I was to meet my host, I proffered the fare that we had agreed – far more than the going rate. Sait immediately demanded more. Didn't I know how expensive petrol had become? Hadn't we agreed an extra five hundred roubles at the start? Sait and I both knew that I couldn't just get out of the car and walk away, as my luggage was locked in the boot of his Lada. Where he had been aggressive in his sales pitch at the airport, Sait, assured of his supremacy, was now happy to wait until I cracked. Eventually, I paid him an extra three hundred roubles and he gave me my luggage. Full of smiles, he shook my hand and told me what a privilege it had been to meet me. I nodded meaninglessly, comforted only by the thought that the extra money might well go towards Ramzan's education.

'YOU HAVE DONE NOTHING WRONG'

At 9.15 a.m. the crowd of parents, teachers and pupils was being forced to move closer and closer to the school building. With so many desperate people in the yard, the stampede quickly turned into a crush. The schoolyard was surrounded by buildings on three sides and partially enclosed on the fourth. The terrorists approached at such speed that they had effectively blocked this fourth side off by the time most people realized they were under attack. Very few people succeeded in escaping through the terrorists' cordon. Some who thought they had succeeded in getting away safely were shot in the legs as they ran. A number hid in the school's boiler house. Faced with no choice, most others began to pile into the school building, hoping that there they would find an escape or a hiding place. Minutes earlier a meticulously organized parade had been taking place; now there was chaos. It is almost impossible for survivors to find words to describe the shock that gripped them during these minutes.

Vera Salkazanova was not able to get out, but with her four-year-old granddaughter in her arms, she managed to make it to the boiler house, a long low building that ran along one side of the yard. She was joined by many others in search of a hiding place. Frantic, she crouched in the dark room, wondering what had become of her daughter-in-law Larisa and her other grandchild Ruslan, a seven-year-old who was just starting his school life. Fifteen-year-old Marianna Simonyan was hiding in the boiler room too. She recalls that, after a few minutes, 'the terrorists came up to the boiler house and said to our history teacher, Miss Gurieva, who was standing next to the boiler house door, that we would all have to come out. Miss Gurieva told us to come out and the terrorists forced us to go into the gym.'

As others had run past her away from the terrorists, the history teacher had remained next to the boiler house door, transfixed by fear. When many people had gone in, she noticed the door open and one of the school's odd-job men step through it. 'It was our workman, Karlov. He clearly wanted to help more people to hide there, but I motioned to him to go back in and stay hidden. One of the terrorists must have seen him though, because he came over to the boiler house immediately. He cocked his gun, ready to shoot. I told him not to and that there would be lots of children in there. I said that I'd go in and lead people out if he promised not to shoot anyone.' With all the urgency she could muster, Nadezhda started telling her colleagues, pupils and their parents to come out of their hiding place. As they did so they came face to face with the terrorists, and realized that they now had no choice but to follow the others into the school.

Vera Salkazanova started running across the schoolyard with her granddaughter Rada in her arms. When she had almost made it across the small patch of grass, she lost her grip on the child. 'I dropped Rada and I couldn't get down to pick her up. The crowd was pressing on me so much. She was being stamped on. Then that lad, the one they killed first – Betrozov was his name, I think – he told me not to worry, that he would get her for me. And he did. He passed her through the broken window. She started crying almost immediately – looking for me – so he lifted me up and helped me through as well.'

Nadezhda Gurieva can't remember any of the people she found in the boiler house that day except for one, the son of a colleague who was right at the back. She only recalls that, when he had gone, she was sure that the room was empty. 'Timur was definitely the last one in there. After that, one of the terrorists took a step inside, fired some shots at the ceiling and slammed the door shut behind him. He then walked behind us as we went into the school building.' But Nadezhda and the terrorist had been wrong when they thought that the boiler house had been emptied. At the very start of the attack, a small number of pupils and parents had made their way through the main room and into the pumping station at the back of the boiler house, closing the door tightly behind them. They were quiet enough not to give themselves away and sat cramped and silent for hours after the attack began. After lunch, they managed to attract the attention of some members of the security forces and, unbeknownst to the terrorists, the fifteen of them were rescued through the back of the building.

Everyone else who had hidden in the boiler house was forced into the school. With no other options, they were determined to try to escape that way. However, unnoticed by most of the crowd, some terrorists had gained entry to the school only a few seconds after the initial attack. They patrolled the corridors, searching out hiding places and threatening anyone they found with guns. Both inside and outside the building, the terrorists' order was the same: go to the gymnasium. It was still not half past nine.

Though Alla Khanaeva did not know it at the time, one of her daughters, thirteen-year-old Diana, succeeded in escaping from the schoolyard. When one of the women terrorists grabbed hold of her, Diana was able to pull herself free. Now behind the majority of the attackers, she ran down School Alley to freedom. But as soon as she had escaped, Diana was aware that most of her friends and the rest of her family had not; her mother, sister and brother had been swept into the school.

Svetlana Dzherieva had been right by the main entrance to the school when the terrorists first struck, photographing the first-years coming down the steps. However, in the few seconds that it took for her to run back into the building, some of the terrorists had already entered it. 'They were running along the corridors ahead of us, firing their guns as they went. There were little first-years clinging to the walls of the corridor and I tried to take them with me as I ran. I knew that there were toilets near the canteen and for some reason I thought that they had windows that let out onto the street. You had to go through two doors to get into the toilets. I took the children with me and closed first one door and then another behind us. We just stood there for two or three minutes. The children were crying and I comforted them.'

It quickly dawned on Svetlana that the toilet had no windows whatsoever. (Elsewhere, people were unable to escape through the windows because they had been barred to prevent vandals from breaking in.) The lack of air in the small toilet and the number of panicked, hyperventilating children quickly made it hard to breathe. 'It started to feel like we were suffocating. My throat felt constricted. It was as if something was taking my breath away. I turned the taps on and started pouring water over the children. Just then, the terrorists started breaking the doors down, first one, then the other. A terrorist ran in and grabbed me by my breasts. He swore at me and asked me what I thought I was doing in there. Then he hit me with the butt of his machine gun and I fell out of the toilets onto the floor in the corridor.' The terrorist who had hit her asked them for directions to the gym and her small group was led back along the corridor.

Larisa Mamitova found her fourteen-year-old son Tamerlan standing by the broken windows, crying his eyes out. 'He was shouting at me, "Mum, what's happening? What's happening?" I told him to calm down. I held him to me.' Just as she was trying to work out how she could lift both her son and herself through the broken windows, the gym's emergency exit burst open. The crowd turned and ran across the schoolyard towards it. Larisa and Tamerlan went too. They ran through the gym, into the school corridor and, without having any clear memory of how, they ended up in a classroom. Inside, people improvised hiding places and tried to be as quiet as possible, which was extremely hard. 'You could hear the shooting going on outside all the time. We started pushing children under desks and tables. I even opened a box to see if I could get a child in it. I couldn't because the boxes were too small.' A woman who was beside her was trying to call home on her mobile phone. Larisa told her to call the police instead but the woman couldn't get through. Just at that moment, a terrorist came in.

Elvira Tuaeva found her son and daughter, Khetag and Karina, relatively quickly. Grabbing hold of them, she forced herself through the school's main entrance door and ran along the corridor past the people who were climbing through the broken windows. Like the rest, she was looking for an escape route or at least a decent hiding place. When she reached the end of the long corridor, Elvira realized that Karina was no longer with her. 'I was with my friend, Albina Dudaeva – she died in the end – and I told her I'd lost Karina and had to go and find her. I asked if I could leave Khetag with her, if she would keep hold of him for me. I remember she even let go of her own children's hands to take hold of Khetag's. I don't know what I was doing. I mean, I was sane enough in a way, but trying to move against the flow of people along the corridor was impossible and, of course, there was no way out at the other end.'

As Elvira struggled unsuccessfully to find Karina, she overheard a conversation between one of the terrorists and a young boy, who could have been no older than ten: 'The boy was standing beside the terrorist, pulling at his trouser leg and saying to him, "I'm scared." He might even have used the terrorist's name, I don't remember. The terrorist said back, "Calm down. I'll make sure you get out." I'm sure the boy was a pupil of School No. 1. Maybe he had come from Chechnya originally. Why else would he have gone over to the terrorist and spoken to him when the rest of us couldn't get away from them quick enough?' Realizing that it was impossible to search for Karina, Elvira gave up and moved into the gym. She had had no time to hide in the end.

When the attackers stormed the schoolyard, Larisa Tomaeva, who was running late, hadn't even managed to take her daughter to join her class. The pair were picking their way through the crowds when she heard the sound of gunfire and saw the masked men. 'Everything suddenly went completely frantic. You honestly cannot describe what it was like then. Children everywhere were screaming, some for their mums, some for their dads, some for grannies. People were walking over the top of each other and anyone who ended up on the ground just got trampled on. Even the worst of nightmares couldn't begin to convey what it was like there during those first few minutes. Those poor little children never had a clue that this was what was going to happen to them. It was so unexpected, so out of the blue.'

Like everyone else, Larisa felt the terrorists trying to drive her into the school building, but was powerless to resist. When she found her son, who she had just left with his classmates, they started running towards the school. When they got to one of the sets of broken windows, they were able to get through without much difficulty because of piles of bricks and sand which had been left lying on the ground. In retrospect, Larisa found it suspicious that these building materials had been left in a position so convenient for getting into and out of the school. She decided this was evidence that the terrorists had been in Beslan before; perhaps that they had been aided and abetted by locals. 'The smashed windows were quite high and it wouldn't normally have been easy for me to get through them, especially when I had two children with me and I was wearing high heels. But I was able to run up one of the piles of sand with the children and get straight through the window, no problem. I'm sure they normally tidy the schoolyard up for the 1st of September celebrations, just like they do in every other school. The fact that they hadn't – that these piles had been left there – is proof to me that the whole operation was being planned a long time in advance.'

Larisa Tomaeva and her children hid in the first classroom they came to. Fifteen other people were already in there. One man, whose daughter was in the same class as Larisa's son, had already been shot and was losing a significant amount of blood. The P.E. teacher, Alik Tsagolov, had taken off his shirt and was using it to staunch the blood flow from the wound. Soon one of the gunmen came into the room. He told them to stay where they were for a few minutes – perhaps to allow time for the busy corridors to clear – and then ordered them all to the gym. Larisa recalls, 'I used the few minutes we had to tell my children that they were not to try to resist the attackers. We were to do everything they said, I told them. Other parents did the same, and we also said the same thing to the children in the room whose parents weren't there.' As they moved slowly towards the gym, one of the terrorists said to them, 'You have done nothing wrong. We aren't going to kill you.'

'THIS IS WAR!'

'He's forced to let the piping drop,
And we shall see our children stop!'
When, lo, as they reached the mountain-side,
A wondrous portal opened wide,
As if a cavern was suddenly hollowed;
And the Piper advanced and the children followed,
And when all were in to the very last,
The door in the mountain side shut fast.

Robert Browning, *The Pied Piper of Hamelin*, 1849

There were many people who had not accompanied their children and grandchildren to School No. 1 in Beslan on 1 September. Some parents who had wanted to attend the celebrations had been unable to get leave from work; others, especially those with older children, did not think it was necessary to go. As they started their own working day, they assumed that their children were safely in school. When the attack began, even those who were near enough to hear the gunfire and screams initially found it hard to believe that they were in any way sinister. The shock of the news as it spread was devastating.

Forty-nine-year-old Ruslan Bokoev was at work right beside School No. 1 when the attack started. A council gardener, Ruslan was tidying and planting out one of the small green spaces in the centre of Beslan when he heard the shots ring out. Shortly before, he had said goodbye to his son Stanislav, who was going into Year 9 at the school. 'I saw balloons flying up in the air and I heard what sounded like automatic rounds being fired. I thought it had to be some kind of gun salute or something, but I did think it was a bit odd if they were using machine guns. Then screaming women started running across the patch of grass where I was working. They were shouting that the school was under siege. That was at 9.17 a.m. exactly, because I remember looking at my watch.'

Ruslan followed the women out onto the street, where the situation was growing more panicked and confused by the minute. The relatively small number of escapees was quickly joined by many other people from nearby houses, offices and shops. The chaos all around made it hard for people to understand what was actually taking place. Ruslan says, 'There was nothing we could have done. At that point, we didn't have much of a clue about what was actually happening.' The words that he and others could make out from the screams of the people who were running towards them – words like 'terrorists', 'siege' and 'hostages' – made no sense in their small, unremarkable town.

The mother and father of twelve-year-old Agunda Gatsalova had also gone to work on the first morning of the new school year. Agunda had gone to school on her own. Her mother Rita was chatting to a colleague when she heard the loud bangs. At first she thought it might be the sound of fireworks, but even when she realized that it was gunfire she was not unduly perturbed. She remarked easily that times had changed since the days – before the collapse of the Soviet Union – when the sound of even a single stray shot was taken very seriously by the authorities. 'I remember when one shot was enough to bring the whole police force out onto the streets,' she had said to her colleague. Then a woman had come running into the office and asked the pair if they had heard what was going on. Rita recalls, 'The woman knew that my daughter went to School No. 1 and she said that it was under siege. I tried to phone someone but it was impossible to get through. I felt like my head had been chopped off.'

Rita ran outside and flagged down a car. She asked the driver to take her to School No. 1. As they drove, she saw her husband, Totraz, who had also left work when he heard the news. Across the town, even as events seemed to be unfolding very quickly, time also seemed to grind to a halt. He got into the car with her. Before they had even got close to the building the streets had become impassable. Traffic had ground to a halt on the usually empty roads and people were abandoning their vehicles to walk the rest of the way to the school. Amongst the crowds were hundreds of children, who had fled from other schools in the town as news of the attack spread. A few yards further along the street, Rita and Totraz reached a makeshift cordon. 'We got past the roadblock somehow and then Totraz just disappeared on me. I learned later that he had managed to get closer to the school by a roundabout route. In the end, I ran home and started waiting; I was in such a state.'

Fifty-two-year-old Kazbek Rubaev found out about the school siege from one of his colleagues. A driver for a local business, he had left his flat right beside the school at 7.45 to get to work on time. Fifteen minutes later his youngest son Khasan – the only one of his children who was still of school age – left too. He was eleven. Kazbek recalls, 'We were standing outside the factory, when one of the other drivers came in and said, as calm as you like, "Apparently, School No. 1 is under siege." I remember saying, "But the boy's there now. It's his first day back." I jumped in my car and drove to the school.' The area around the school was already packed with people when he got there.

Kazbek says that he knew it would end badly from the very beginning. His thoughts turned immediately to previous terrorist attacks in the region and he understood that they had not chosen their target at random. 'They came to kill,' he said. Gunfire was coming from the school building and Kazbek saw what he thought were the bodies of dead and injured people on the road. It seemed that some local men had been hit while returning the terrorists' fire with their own weapons. (It has become normal in Russia for men to keep a gun.) Like many other people who were nearby, Kazbek set off down an alleyway to take cover from the shooting. To his disgust he found the local police hiding there too. 'They were lying there as if nothing had happened. I asked them what they were going to do but they didn't have a clue.' When the shooting had died down, Kazbek came out of his hiding place and began the wait for news.

One of the local men who decided to shoot at the terrorists inside the school was Taimuraz Gasiev. On the morning of the attack the twenty-nine-year-old had been about to set off with his father and a friend to collect a consignment of meat for a local butcher. As their car waited at a crossroads on Comintern Street, Taimuraz noticed balloons flying up into the air above School No. 1. Seconds later he heard shots. Although one of his friends thought that the shooting was probably just a salute, Taimuraz drove as fast as he could towards the school. He was parking outside the leisure centre across the street when the first bullets hit the car. He was about to drive away but didn't get the chance before the car's engine caught fire. 'I leapt out and ran. My dad's legs aren't what they used to be and I had to shout at him to make him get away. We ran for it but my friend Kostya was still at the front wing of the car when the whole thing exploded.'

As Taimuraz ran, leaving Kostya to deal with his injuries, he was met by other young men from the nearby housing estates. One of them, Rusik Gappoev, was carrying two guns. He handed one to Taimuraz and they ran back towards the school across the allotments. Taimuraz says, 'I grew up in that school. I spent eleven years at it and I know it like the back of my hand. I probably don't even know my own house as well as I know the school. I told Rusik to keep behind me; that I would show him the best way to get in.' When they got reasonably close to the school, Rusik – a professional hunter – and Taimuraz lay down behind a pile of wood left out in the open. All the time there was shooting coming from the school. Suddenly, Rusik jumped up and said, 'I can't just lie here. My children are in there.' Taimuraz told him to stand his ground until a larger group of locals were in a position to march on the building. As Rusik ran off towards the school, Taimuraz grabbed his leg and one of his trainers came off in his hand. Rusik ran on regardless, taking up a position behind one of the school's gateposts.

Unable to decide what to do, Rusik ran back to his friend and asked for his missing shoe. Taimuraz was reluctant to return it but Rusik said, 'Come on, mate. You never know how long we'll have to lie here for. My foot will get cold.' Taimuraz released Rusik's trainer and both men now started to return the terrorists' fire. Rusik, the more experienced of the two, ordered Taimuraz to try to create a distraction that would cause the terrorists to reveal their locations. Rusik would stand by ready to pick them off. Taimuraz fired at the roof of the school, hoping that this might confuse the attackers.

Finally, an armed policeman lay down beside the two young men. He must have been trained because Taimuraz remembers that he fired only one shot, which was followed by screams of pain from inside the school building. But suddenly Rusik was up and running towards the school again: he was on his way back to the gatepost. As he went, he shouted to Taimuraz, like action heroes in the movies, 'Cover me while I run.' The terrorists, sensing perhaps the first real resistance, escalated their defence of the building. They started to fire indiscriminately from their machine guns. Taimuraz watched as bits of concrete flew from the gatepost where Rusik was crouching. 'I shouted at him not to move but I could see he was already injured. It was clear that he wasn't going to get out of that position alive.'

Some police reinforcements and more parents arrived, but it was a hopeless situation. Taimuraz says that the police shooters were too frightened to do much and stood behind a wall with their weapons trembling in their hands. The terrorists' position was too strong. The school was like a fortress providing them with security and, from the upstairs classrooms, an elevated position from which they could pick off would-be assailants. As another local man fell down injured, Taimuraz tried to cover his entire body with the wood he had been hiding behind. The shooting was so intense and the bullets were landing so close that he realized he was still in grave danger. He threw off the wood and decided to make a run for it.

When he reached the safety of a nearby building, Taimuraz found himself in the company of many more local police officers. Though armed, they were still not firing. He was enraged and demanded that they do something. 'They told me that they hadn't received an order to fire. They said it would be wrong to fire because it might make the terrorists angry. I was in no state to listen to crap like that and I remember that I tried to grab one of the policemen's guns off them. I got hold of the magazine in my hands and when I looked down I saw that it was full of blanks. The tips were plastic. I remember asking them, "What did you think you were coming to? A fairground shooting gallery? This is war!"' In answer to

Taimuraz's growing fury, the police said that their armourer had gone to the city and had taken the key to their arsenal with him.

Throughout the town, people were frantically trying to work out who was trapped inside the school. For the closest relatives it was impossible to get beyond the fact that their sons, daughters, mothers and fathers were hostages. Some thought about nieces and nephews and in-laws and cousins who were likely to have been attending the celebrations. Others remembered their neighbours and friends who had children at School No. 1. They tried to telephone and knocked on doors, and when they got no answer they feared the worst. Everyone in Beslan knew someone who was inside the school. They all hoped against hope that their loved ones might have got away, but in a morning of rumours there were few hints to suggest that many people had managed to escape.

And who were the attackers? Where had they come from? What did they want? Many had strong suspicions about their identity. In general, their suspicions were right. They assumed they were under attack because they were Ossetians; because they were Christians and because their regional republic had remained loyal to the Russian government. They thought that the terrorists had probably come from one of the neighbouring Russian provinces, either Chechnya or Ingushetia. With fear and trembling, they called to mind the details of other atrocities that had happened in the region. Though they were now the victims, the story in which they had become characters was an old, familiar one.

'YOU KILLED ALL SIX OF MY BROTHERS AND NOW I MUST KILL YOU'

The Caucasus is the strip of land that runs between the Black Sea and the Caspian. It is a region of mountains, valleys and fast-flowing rivers which is home to some of the oldest and most distinctive civilizations in the world. In some places its climate is subtropical; in others snow and ice never melt from one year to the next. It is a confused borderland, a liminal place between Europe and Asia made up of elements of both continents, but belonging fully to neither. Though the outside world now thinks of its people as poor and unsophisticated, they have been in the vanguard of developments in civilization on many occasions in the past. It was a vital staging post in the spread of Christianity beyond Asia Minor and in the movement of silk from East to West. It was probably the first place in the world where grapes were grown to make wine.

The region is divided by two enormous mountain ranges. To the north is the Great Caucasus, which separates Russia from Georgia and Azerbaijan. To the south the Lesser Caucasus runs north-west to south-east through Armenia and Georgia to Azerbaijan and Iran. Beslan is situated in the foothills of the

Great Caucasus, only forty miles from the highest of all the Caucasian peaks, Mount Kazbek, which rises for three miles above sea level. Its summit is almost always in the clouds, but nearer peaks, like Mount Stolovaya – a mere one-and-a-half miles above sea level – are clearly visible from Beslan, especially on cool, crisp mornings. At only twenty-eight-million years old, the mountains are young in geological terms, but the people who inhabit them, the languages they speak and the stories they tell are truly ancient by comparison with most human societies.

Though the connections between today's Caucasians and the tribes that came before them are unclear and hotly disputed, they are often real enough and a source of fierce pride and contention. The oldest peoples about whom stories still circulate exist in the half-light between myth, archaeology and prehistory. Sophisticated burial mounds have been found in the North Caucasus dating back more than four thousand years. They were built for important chieftains whose resting place was to be a carpet of rich and intricate gold and silver ornaments. About three thousand years ago, some of the inhabitants of the region tamed horses. They used the natural edge this gave them to take control of greater areas of land, extracting tributes as they went. With their increased wealth, they developed more complex societies. They became more reliant on trade and war to preserve and enhance their way of life.

As the centuries passed, one group of warrior nomads supplanted another, many of them from Central Asia and the Far East. The Scythians, Sarmatians, Huns and, eventually, the Mongols held sway over the other tribes who lived in the region. The knowledge we have of these peoples is patchy: in many cases even their names come from the modern-day places where archaeologists have dug up their remains. For the Greeks the area was a place of fascination and fear, lying at the edge of their empire. Though some Greeks traded with and lived alongside these nomadic peoples, they usually considered them to be little more than barbarians. (There are similarities in modern-day Russians' attitudes towards the indigenous population of the Caucasus.) The myths and stories that the Greeks entertained themselves with also ended at the Caucasus, a place that symbolized dangers and potential rewards in equal measure. It was here that the gods chained Prometheus to a rock for giving fire to men; here too that Jason sailed with his Argonauts in search of the Golden Fleece.

Two thousand years ago, a Greek scholar called Strabo, who had been born just to the south of the Caucasus in what is now northern Turkey, wrote a book which attempted to bring together everything that was known about the world, its landscape and peoples. In its descriptions of the people who lived in and around the Caucasus, his *Geographika* was alive to all of the legends of the place. Though the Greeks and the Romans now knew about the existence of India and beyond, they clearly still viewed the mountain range as a place beyond civilization.

Strabo wrote mainly of the people on the Caucasian coastline of the Black Sea – the part that was best known and the most easily reached by the Greeks and the Romans. 'These peoples live by robberies at sea,' he wrote. 'They sail against merchant-vessels and sometimes against a country or even a city. They hold the mastery of the sea. When they return to their own land, they have no anchors and they put their boats on their shoulders and carry them into the forests where they live. And they do the same in the countries of others, for they know how to live in forests. They start by hiding their boats and then set out to wander through the country, kidnapping people. They are usually happy to release these people for a ransom.'

We ought now to know better than to dismiss nomadic tribes as barbarians, as the Ancient Greeks and Romans did. Their evaluation of what constituted barbaric behaviour often overlooked their own propensity to cut stripes out of enemies, commit atrocities and enslave entire towns and cities. Likewise, culture only seemed cultured if it were the Greeks and Romans who were writing, painting, buying or selling it. In many respects, civilization was, and is, a matter of perspective.

Nonetheless, one of the things that struck Strabo and the geographers who went before him was the sheer number of different groups, languages and cultures that cohabited in the Caucasus. Describing the main Caucasian trading port of the time – where people came from far and wide to make their livings – Strabo wrote that there were representatives from seventy tribes. Other more sensational and less scholarly commentators, he added, had made out that there were three hundred ethnic groups in the city. 'All speak different languages, because they are so fierce and obstinate that they all live in their own groupings and refuse to have any intercourse with each other.'

This much remains true today. The Caucasus is a patchwork of different national and tribal groups, speaking different languages and weaving different myths about their ancestors out of the threads of the past. To the south of the Great Caucasus are the Georgians, Armenians and Azerbaijanis, now with their own wholly independent countries since the break-up of the Soviet Union. There are also Abkhazians, Adjarians and Svanetians with proud cultures but no or limited self-determination. The peoples who live to the north of the Great Caucasus are all ruled from Moscow, though they have varying degrees of autonomy in deciding their own affairs. They include the Karachai, the Circassians, the Kabardinians, the Balkars, the Ingushetians, the Chechens, the Daghestanis, the Lezghins – and the Ossetians.

Each of these groups has its own language. When they speak to each other, they do so in Russian, the language given to them by the colonizing power. Though many aspects of their recent history have been shared, they have their own distinct outlooks on the past. Where there is overlap in their histories and cultures, it tends to create arguments rather than cohesion and only an external threat can occasionally cause them to unite. Caucasians feel a more intimate connection to their ancient history than most modern people in the West. In their mythmaking, they are linked to the mighty warrior cultures of the distant past. Though they would not agree with Strabo's imputation that their ancient forebears were savages, they do view them as fierce and obstinate.

One of the most important connections modern Caucasians feel with the distant past is the Nartian Epic, a cycle of stories featuring characters from a mythical race of Caucasians known as the Narts. Versions of these legends are important to many Caucasian peoples, including Abkhazians, Balkars, Ingushetians and Chechens, but they have always been most closely associated with the Ossetians, the people who live in Beslan. Though little is known about the actual origins of the Narts or about which, if any, historical peoples they should be identified with, each ethnic group sees itself as the rightful heir to the Nartian inheritance. Caucasian children today still learn about the myths of the Narts. The stories have a playful, romantic quality that puts in relief their frequent descent into violence.

A central Nartian hero – known to all versions of the myths – is Soslan. In his stories, honourable and deceitful behaviour combine to ensure that the warrior has the upper hand over his opponents. Like other heroes in the tales, he does not just fight his own battles. The customs of the Narts – like those of many Caucasians today – oblige him to avenge the wrongs done to his relatives and ancestors, and to answer for the evils they perpetrated in their day. Even a chance encounter can force Soslan to pursue again an age-old vendetta.

In one tale, Soslan on horseback is found high on a Caucasian ridge, looking out over the plain below. From his vantage point, he sees what looks like a black spot moving across the land. Behind it, as it goes, a long dark line is forming. Eventually, Soslan is able to make out another man on horseback; the horse moves of its own volition because the rider is fast asleep. The dark line behind him is made by his lance, which is trailing on the ground. Once he can see that the man is a potential rival, Soslan sets upon him with his own lance and his bow and arrow. Obviously the sleeping man is roused by this, but – as might happen in a Spaghetti Western – only rubs his head and complains that the midges are bothering him. After some more sparring, the pair finally engage in conversation. The sleeping man is Totraz, son of Alibeg, and when he learns that his attacker is Soslan he says, 'You killed all six of my brothers and now I must kill you.'

Soslan agrees to a duel but begs Totraz first to let him go home to put his affairs in order. When Soslan swears an oath that he will return, Totraz agrees to a meeting in one week's time. Clearly worried about the impending battle, Soslan asks his sorceress mother for her help. She says that he will not be harmed if that is the will of the gods. However, unhappy to leave matters to the gods alone, she plots with Soslan to trick Totraz. She sends him out to hunt enough wolves for her to make him a coat from their skins. (The parallels with Jacob's treacherous impersonation of Esau in front of their mother Rebecca are clear.)

When the day of battle arrives, Soslan is sent to meet Totraz dressed in his new coat. His horse is garlanded with hundreds of small bells. His mother goes with him and, just before Totraz arrives, transforms herself into a cloud to hide

Soslan from his assailant. Totraz calls Soslan's name three times, but three times Soslan remains silent. Totraz is convinced that the other man has broken his oath and turns on his horse, ready to leave. At that point, the cloud dissipates and Soslan moves closer, demanding that Totraz stand and fight. But his opponent's horse has smelt the scent of wolves on Soslan's cloak and, terrified, begins to flee. Soslan seizes the opportunity to kill Totraz by shooting him repeatedly in the back with arrows. The trick goes undetected. Totraz's injuries lead his family to assume that he died a coward's death, fleeing from the enemy. Consequently, he is not fit to be buried with the other Narts.

The Nartian myths have a grim relevance in today's Caucasus: more than thirty of the men and boys held captive in School No. 1 were named Soslan. Caucasian men have always been quick to tell me about the importance they place on honour. They would lecture me about the imperative to defend relatives and the family name against attack and insult. When I have said that I place a high importance on my own personal safety, they have told me that I – like the Western decadence that has nurtured me – am weak and dissolute. Perhaps they are right; there is certainly something appealing about the moral clarity of the Caucasian defence of honour. However, many see this end as so worthwhile that all means necessary to achieve it may be justified. Like Soslan, they still resort to violence too quickly, and trickery and deception are often second nature.

'I WILL REMEMBER YOU'

By a quarter to ten on 1 September 2004, almost all the parents, teachers and pupils of School No. 1 had been forced into the gym. The room had never held so many people. It was no bigger than a municipal swimming pool – roughly 25 yards long and 10 yards wide – yet more than 1,200 people were now crammed inside. Escape no longer an option, their thoughts turned to locating relatives, classmates, favourite teachers. As each wave of new arrivals flooded in, panic and noise levels increased. Names were shouted out as people pushed past one another, desperate to find someone or to get as far from the terrorists as possible.

In these circumstances, it was imperative for the attackers to establish some kind of order amongst their terrified captives. There was little chance now that their plans could be frustrated by any organized resistance from the hostages. But utter chaos, if left unchecked, could swiftly create the circumstances in which an escape might be possible. As the noise and confusion increased, the terrorists' shouting became louder and more hysterical, and their shooting more frequent and sustained.

Seeing this change, some of the hostages feared that the

terrorists might turn their guns away from the ceiling and onto them. They tried to communicate this to those around them, but it had little effect. One man, forty-six-year-old Ruslan Betrozov, was so worried about what the terrorists might do next that he resolved to try to defuse the situation. Unlike many of the captors, Betrozov had remained reasonably rational and composed throughout the initial stages of the attack. It was he who had helped Vera Salkazanova and her granddaughter Rada – and many others besides – to climb through the broken windows and into the school. Now, he walked up to the terrorists and started trying to calm them down. He told them that if they stopped shooting and behaved less aggressively the hostages would quieten down by themselves. He said that their behaviour was only making the situation worse. The terrorists carried on regardless and the chaos in the hall continued, but Betrozov did not retreat. He continued to plead with the gunmen to hold their fire.

Suddenly, the terrorists' patience snapped. Larisa Tomaeva, the intensive-care nurse, had only just entered the gym from the classroom where she had briefly hidden. She was standing near Betrozov as he attempted to reason with the terrorists. She says, 'They forced him to the ground and shouted that if we weren't all as silent as the grave immediately, they would shoot him. But there was no way of getting everybody to be quiet. Betrozov was crouched down and he just kept calmly asking us all to quieten down. He was begging us to be silent. But, since nobody could get everybody quiet, the terrorists took him and dragged him a bit more into the centre of the gym and shot him through the back of the head.'

That shot, fired through a man's body at point-blank range, sounded different from those that had preceded it. It attracted the attention of many in the crowded gym, including Felisa Batagova. She had almost escaped the siege when she left her grandchildren alone in the school to return home and fetch their old textbooks. The trip had taken her longer than expected – she had stopped to get some chocolates for her granddaughter's teacher on the way – and she made it back to the school just as the celebrations began. She remembers hearing the first shots as she handed the box of chocolates to Alana's teacher. Now imprisoned inside the gym, she was anxiously searching for her grandchildren, calling out their names as she went, when she heard Betrozov being killed.

She recalled, 'He fell on the floor on his back. There was a tall terrorist in a mask standing over him and two others beside him. My sister grabbed her daughter and covered her eyes. I remember her asking, "Mummy, why has that man fallen over?" and I heard my sister saying that he had been taken sick with heart trouble.' Felisa claimed that, after he was shot, Betrozov looked at the terrorists above him and was heard to say 'I will remember you'; but this promise of vengeance from beyond the grave, so in keeping with Caucasian values, seems impossible.

Felisa remembered that then the terrorists forced a couple of the grown-up male hostages to carry Betrozov's corpse out of the room. As his body was dragged by its arms across the floor of the gym, people recoiled in horror. A corridor opened up through the middle of the packed room. The death cut through the hostages' panic and a kind of silence – full of stifled crying and screams – descended throughout the hall. As it moved through the gym, Betrozov's body left a long, dark line of blood in its wake. For some reason, the people carrying the dead man dragged him through the gym twice, first to one side and then back again, leaving the same bloody track as it went. Felisa is sure that the terrorists had ordered Betrozov's body to be paraded in this way as a warning. It had the desired effect: most people fell silent and found a place to sit down. While some had managed to locate their loved ones, many others, Felisa included, were obliged to sit uneasily beside people they only half knew, worrying about whether their loved ones were safe.

The terrorists were probably aware that the relative order they had imposed in the gym would not last for long. They moved quickly to secure their position. Using bombs, grenades and rockets, they booby-trapped the building. The nets of the basketball hoops at either end of the gym were tied shut and bombs were placed inside. Wires were stretched between the hoops across the entire length of the gym and more explosive devices were suspended from them. For Felisa Batagova, the bombs hanging from the wire across the room were the most frightening. 'They were all wrapped in Scotch tape, and the one that hung over the middle of the room was really, really low. I was constantly terrified that it was going to be knocked by someone's head, one of the tall lads. Every time someone was about to walk under it, we would shout at them to get their head down.'

The floorboards were pulled up in the centre of the room and explosives placed underneath. The largest devices were positioned on chairs. In some cases, school pupils were pressed into service and forced to handle deadly weapons. At one end of the hall, a bomb was attached to an improvised switch made out of two pieces of plywood. One of the terrorists had to keep his foot on the switch at all times to prevent the bomb from exploding.

Those hostages who were sitting closest to the bombs could see that they had been designed to cause maximum injury and damage. Nadezhda Gurieva, the history teacher, recalled, 'I was sitting beside two of the devices for the first two days of the siege. Both were slightly bigger than a briefcase. They were wrapped up in sellotape and you could see what was inside them. One of my pupils said to me, "Look, Miss, there're loads of bits of glass inside there." Some of the other bombs had completely see-through containers and you could see that they had been filled with ball bearings and shards of glass.'

While many of the male terrorists were busy filling the gym with explosives – an operation that took more than an hour – the two women were given the job of forcing hostages to surrender their mobile phones, cameras, camcorders, watches and handbags. Dressed in black, holding pistols and with their suicide-bomb belts primed, they moved through the room threatening people. According to Svetlana Dzherieva, they would frisk people if they suspected that objects were being concealed. Every so often, they would shout, 'If we find that you have a mobile phone that you have not given up, we will shoot twenty people.' Svetlana says that they also told children to remove crucifixes and crosses from around their necks. Her seven-year-old daughter, Dana, gave her cross to Svetlana, who could not bear to surrender it to the terrorists.

The pile of handbags and electronic equipment quickly grew at the front of the room. One of the terrorists started looking for a camcorder he could use in the gym. He chose

carefully, searching for the model with the longest battery life. When he found it, he started to record. Shots of the terrorists looking ready for battle are followed by a few frames which appear to show the school being fired on from outside. Pictures of frightened adults and children follow, their hands held above their heads. He zoomed in on the faces of those who were looking at him before panning away to survey the explosives that had been hung across the middle of the room. A proud terrorist points down to where his foot is holding down the detonator switch.

Months after the siege, Russian investigators contacted Alla Khanaeva to tell her that the camcorder the terrorists had used belonged to her. Alla recalled, 'They definitely used our camcorder to film, because the first few frames had been taken by my daughter. You could see us all in the film because she had started recording when we were still at home getting ready to go to the school.' The shots of Alla and her children, Diana, Marianna and Irbek, change abruptly into footage of the interior of the gym, crammed full of terrified hostages, masked gunmen and bombs. Later, when the gym had been thoroughly booby-trapped, the terrorists brought a television

in from one of the classrooms and hooked it up to the camcorder. They turned the screen round so that as many of the hostages as possible could see it and played the tape. The hostages got a preview of how their predicament would later be reported to hundreds of millions across the world.

'AS IF LIFE WASN'T DIFFICULT ENOUGH'

In Moscow, once I had paid Sait the taxi driver in full, I hurried into Paveletskii Station. I had got there just as the train I had missed at the airport was due to arrive. Travellers loaded down with luggage were pouring past me onto the station concourse and out into the warm Moscow night. After a few minutes, the flow of people dried up and I was left with just the station attendants for company. My hosts were nowhere to be seen; they had worked out that I was unlikely to have made the earlier train and had decided to meet me off the next one. I resigned myself to an hour of waiting. My expensive taxi ride had been a waste of money.

Paveletskii Station had been partially modernized: new signage alongside the old; rows of ultra-clean metal and glass kiosks in the middle of the pitted floor, attached to their surroundings by a dense network of dusty wires and plugs. Like most of Russia's railway stations late at night, it was an unpleasant place. The few passengers moved quickly through the station, unwilling to linger. Only drunks and the homeless tarried there, unable to move or determined to defend their claim to an indoor bed for the night.

The station attendants were bored. At ten o'clock they

probably had another two hours of their shifts to work and little to do. The ticket machines they were standing beside were automatic. Aged between forty and sixty, they looked bedraggled and careworn. For all that they had uniforms, they were not very far removed from the drunks and the tramps. They shouted and swore at each other. 'Fuck your mother!' one said to another who asked him to close a door that was banging in the wind. They goaded one another: three ganging up on a fourth to pull her hair as they laughed uncontrollably.

After about forty-five minutes, a young boy hobbled awkwardly across the concourse to where these station attendants were gathered. He was no more than fifteen years old; he might have been much younger. Wearing dirty jeans and a ripped bomber jacket, he had clearly been living on the streets for some time. When he turned briefly to face me, I could see that he had two black eyes and scars across his face. Somehow his ear had been ripped. It was clear from his inane smile and vacant gaze that he was not in his right mind. The station attendants were instantly interested in the newcomer. For the first time they became genuinely animated. Light-heartedly the boy pulled at their sleeves, grinning and laughing as they swatted his hands away. I overheard the attendants asking him when he had last eaten or washed. They shook their heads seemingly in pity when he answered them with insane giggles. Then he hugged them and kissed their hands.

Suddenly, one of the attendants flew into a rage with the boy because he wouldn't let go of her sleeve. Only seconds before, she had been playing along with his game. She lifted her hand and hit him as hard as she could across the head. The boy fell heavily onto the tiled floor and covered his head with his hands. He sobbed loudly. The woman laughed – nervously at first, but then with more confidence as her co-workers joined in. The attendants moved away from the boy while he picked himself up and hobbled away. As they congregated around another automatic turnstile, I wondered how many of them were parents themselves. They paid no attention to me.

Russia is a hard place to live in. Even if most people are not mistreated like the poor boy in Paveletskii Station, they are, in one way or another, more battered and bruised by life than people in the West. It has been like this for as long as anyone can remember. It is why the newly rich – in Moscow and, to a lesser extent, St Petersburg – try their hardest to avoid the realities of the cities they live in. In most cases, nothing about their lives is made in Russia. By paying outsized backhanders they are able to bypass entire bureaucratic procedures that must be endured by ordinary citizens, even when smaller bribes are forthcoming. Their foreign cars whiz down the middle of main streets at such speed that other Russians and their homemade cars fade to a blur. For the rest, the daily grind goes on, often interrupted only by aspirational soap operas and increasingly terminated by a premature death.

I expected that most people in Russia would have something to say about the siege at School No. 1 in Beslan. Much has been written in the Western press about how the attack was Russia's 9/11; an unprecedented act of violence that had altered fundamentally Russians' sense of the world they inhabit. But this was not what I found. As I travelled between Moscow and Beslan, most of those I met had no opinions about the event at all, as if they had hardly thought about it either at the time or since. It was strange to them that I was asking; some even seemed to resent it.

A few days after I watched the homeless boy knocked to the ground, I passed through another of Moscow's train stations, Kazanskaya. It was very early in the morning and I was about to board the train that, in twenty-eight hours, would take me to the Caucasus. As I approached my compartment,

I wondered who my companions for the journey would be. There was only one other person sitting there. He looked about fifty and was dishevelled and unshaven. His clothes were crumpled and stained. I greeted him nervously as I entered and then proceeded to apologize profusely for the disturbance I was causing by stowing my luggage and food supplies. But Russians do not say sorry readily and the man's response was an irritated, 'Why do you keep apologizing? Everybody has to put their bags away when they get on a train.' That said, I noticed that my travelling companion did not appear to have any luggage of his own. When I eventually sat down opposite him, our faces only a couple of feet apart, I introduced myself properly. He said only that his name was Volodya and that he was on his way home. It was another four hours before we spoke to one another.

The train moved through the outskirts of Moscow and beyond; I immersed myself in the Russian magazines and newspapers I had bought for the journey. The landscape passing by outside and the articles I was reading told the same story of a rundown country where only a tiny number of people live well. Many prefabricated tower blocks looked ready to collapse. The dirty factories appeared closed, though they were not. Station platforms had subsided; level-crossings were broken, their barriers stolen for scrap metal. And every

so often there would be an enormous, newly built detached house, standing on an uncultivated plot and looking utterly incongruous. Occasionally, I saw twenty or thirty of this kind of house built together, mimicking the English housing development. Outside almost every one was a black Audi, BMW or Mercedes.

In the Russian press a similar split is evident, although disproportionate attention is paid to the wealthy and their lifestyles. (Ordinary Russians don't buy newspapers any more.) Every one of the country's major cities seemed to have its own serial killers. In every region, some local officials had been caught with their hands in the till, while others had been murdered or beaten up when they wouldn't play along with organized criminals. A news journalist who exposed a match-fixing scam at a football club had been hospitalized after being 'mugged' by attackers who mysteriously knew her name. While some pensioners protested about the loss of their traditional right to free travel and other benefits, the months-old corpses of others emerged from underneath the melting snow and ice. Police investigators were doing everything possible to identify the bodies, the story said, and people who had missed loved ones were asked to come forward. And yet there was an almost total absence of any criticism or scrutiny of President Putin or the federal government.

In fact, the dictators and elected autocrats of the former Soviet Union were generally much more visible on the society pages of the press. Alongside actors, singers and fashion designers, they visited exhibition openings and cocktail parties. In one magazine, the recently ousted president of an autonomous region of Georgia was pictured making his debut in Moscow high society. The writer joked that the former potentate had had more free time since being deposed. Wearing a suit that made him look like a character from *The Sopranos*, the ex-president had been a guest at the launch of

Italian fashion designer Stefano Ricci's latest collection. Apparently, he wouldn't have missed it for the world.

The lifestyle sections of these publications and the pages of the glossy magazines seemed to discuss a parallel reality to the one inhabited by most Russians. There were articles comparing the top ten gas and electric barbecues and advising on the best French wines to lay down in one's cellar. Most Russians live in high-rise blocks of flats and do not have any outdoor space beyond a small balcony; many who are lucky enough to own a suburban allotment or a dacha use the land for subsistence farming and are not connected to the mains. The cellars of the tower blocks are filled with rusted-up Soviet heating systems and play host to rats and mosquitoes during the cold winters. Meanwhile, readers were advised about whether investments in property or shares would bring bigger returns. A double-page spread extolled the benefits of home insurance, even though, since the economic crash of 1998, most people in Russia won't even open a bank account.

As I read all this, Volodya sat unmoving, his hands resting on either side of his head, his eyes fixedly looking out the window. I decided that he probably wasn't even looking at the view: his eyes never followed any of the objects as they moved past. They seemed to be jammed open. I decided to give Volodya the newspapers I had finished with. I felt guilty for not having offered sooner. 'Help yourself to any of these,' I said, indicating the pile of publications. He snapped back, 'Why would I want to read those? They'll hardly tell me that life's got any better!' I laughed awkwardly and prepared to retreat into silence, when he asked me if he could have some of my water. I said yes and watched him as he wrapped his lips around the bottle neck, took two swigs of water and then wiped the spout with his dirty hand.

Volodya was now ready to talk and for the next four hours we chatted almost without stopping. I quickly understood that he had good reason to be surly. For the last two weeks, the forty-three-year-old had been on a training course in the city of Ulyanovsk, six hundred miles east of Moscow and thousands of miles from his home. Normally he worked for the railway and his job, laying and flattening the gravel that lies in between the railway sleepers on the tracks of the North Caucasian Railroad, was about to become mechanized for the first time since the railways were laid in the late nineteenth century. In Ulyanovsk, he and his colleagues had been learning how to operate and maintain the new machines. This was the third and final fortnight of training they had received and each time he had had to make an eighty-eight-hour round trip from his home. 'So do they put you up in a hotel in Ulyanovsk?' I asked. 'In a hotel?' he laughed. 'We sleep in an old railway carriage that has been decommissioned. There's no running water or washing facilities and it's infested with cockroaches.'

I asked him where his luggage was. He told me that he should have been on the train home from Moscow the day before. He had travelled from Ulyanovsk to the capital with a colleague. They had arrived the previous morning and had hurried across the city to make their connection to the Caucasus. With twenty minutes to spare, Volodya had given his luggage to the colleague and sent him ahead to board the train. He had then gone to buy some food for their journey. When he returned to the platform, the train had already departed. He was left with the clothes he was wearing, a bottle of vodka, a jar of pickles and eight roubles (about fourteen pence). After a night sleeping rough, during which he consumed both vodka and pickles, he had boarded this train to continue his journey. Despite his gruff exterior, he seemed to me increasingly weary and vulnerable as our conversation continued.

I smiled and said that the worst must surely be over now. Volodya looked unsure and told me about what awaited him when he left the train in the middle of the night. He would get off at the city of Rostov-on-Don and would then have to convince a taxi driver to take him home, twenty-five miles away, without any money. He hoped that his wife would have enough money to pay his fare. 'What if she doesn't?' I asked. 'I'll go round to my daughter's flat and see if she's got the money. We'll get it together somehow.' The next day he would have to drive a hundred miles to collect his luggage from his colleague, and the day after that he would be back at work, levelling gravel on the railroads.

I asked Volodya if he had ever levelled gravel on the railroad near Beslan. He said that he had worked there many times and had even been on the tracks just a few miles from the town on the day the siege began. Within a few hours of the siege starting his team had been joined by an armed policeman. He told me that the local security forces were initially concerned that the school siege might only be the beginning of an all-out attack on the region. They feared that terrorists might board trains in Chechnya and Ingushetia and hijack them once they had travelled further into Russia. Volodya was still unsure whether his team was being protected by the police or if they were suspects themselves. 'Nothing happened anyway,' he shrugged.

Volodya had very few thoughts on the school siege itself. 'The people get crazier the closer you go to the mountains,' was all he would say. 'They spend their lives fighting between themselves. You just wish they would leave the rest of us alone. As if life wasn't difficult enough.' It was just like the refugees from Chechnya who had come to live in his own town. Though they were all ethnically Russian, Volodya felt little sympathy for them. If they weren't getting involved in criminal activities, they were trying to get their hands on the few municipal flats and jobs that were available. People had had sympathy for them ten years ago when things first started to go wrong in the beleaguered region, but enough was enough: now even those who had relatives elsewhere in Russia had difficulty finding people to take them in.

For Volodya the siege in Beslan and the troubles of the North Caucasus more generally were dead-end topics. Soon we were back discussing his own concerns. He was certain that he or many of his colleagues would be made redundant once the new Czech-made machines came into service. Though he had respect for the equipment's capabilities ('You can't just hit them hard with a hammer when something goes wrong with them, like we used to do'), he was sure they were his enemies. 'It just won't take as many of us to do the job once the machines come. That's obvious.' According to Volodya, this was only the first step in a plan to privatize the railways and try to run them for profit. Thinking back to the phrases he learned at school, he said, 'Everything was supposed to belong to the people here. That's what they told us. But then you look and you see who "the people" really are. It turns out that the bosses were "the people" all along.'

I thought about how much the ability to appreciate another's suffering was predicated on having enough and to spare. Even stuck on a railway carriage that was moving slowly through European Russia, Volodya could find no time to contemplate the problems of Beslan. His own life was complicated enough without having to come to terms with other people's worries. His scant regard for the tragedy of Beslan or anything else that wasn't strictly connected with himself was not just selfishness: Volodya's life was already full of difficulties. And he seemed to face each day already exhausted from the days and weeks and months of work and worry that had gone before. In the middle of the night, I awoke just in time to see the door to the compartment slam shut. It was Volodya leaving the train to begin the next leg of his journey. Pride or inertia had led him to refuse all my offers of food and he must not, therefore, have had a meal for at least a day and a half.

There are many more people like Volodya in Russia than there are in the West. The causes of their distress are various, but the resulting preoccupation is the same. A disintegrated healthcare system, poor diet, endemic alcoholism, smoking and epidemics of AIDS and other sexually transmitted diseases mean that a much greater proportion of the population are forced to live with illness than in the West. Death, which is feared everywhere, is more preoccupying in Russia than in the rest of Europe because it comes so much sooner. A baby boy born in Russia today can expect to be dead before his fifty-ninth birthday. Psychologists I got to know in Beslan told me that there were plenty in the town who thought that the survivors of the siege had received more than their fair share of assistance: too many trips abroad; too many new toys; too much compensation; too much attention.

'THEY'RE AS GOOD AS DEAD ALREADY'

Almost as soon as they got their captives into the gym, the terrorists began to separate the men from the women and children. One of the terrorists went around ordering all the adult men out of the room. Very quickly, only a handful of men in their fifties and older remained, along with a small number of younger men who had escaped the terrorists' gaze in the crowded gym. The rest waited in the corridor outside.

At first glance, it might seem that the hostage-takers were acting purely pragmatically by removing all of the men of fighting age. But the terrorists were so obviously in control of the school that there was little real threat from any of the hostages, the men included. Eventually, it was the adult men who would have been the most likely to mount some kind of resistance. The strict rules of Caucasian masculinity required them, even more than men elsewhere, to defend their wives, mothers and children, however desperate their chances. But the likelihood of such opposition succeeding – given the fact that they were under armed guard and had no weapons of their own – would have been very small. As had long been the case, very few fathers and grandfathers had come to watch the celebrations and most of the schoolteachers were women as well.

The terrorists had probably taken the decision to isolate and neutralize the male hostages when they were planning the attack, long before they reached the school. It was a symbolic act. Though at this stage they clearly saw the women and children as collateral which could be used to achieve political aims, they felt differently about the male hostages. The women and children might yet be spared; the men could not be. Whether or not they had personally committed any acts of violence against the Chechens and the Ingush, these men were legitimate targets.

Perhaps the fact that they should all have served as conscripts in the Soviet or Russian army was enough. Certainly, the terrorists showed no interest in removing the seventeen- and eighteen-year-old school pupils from the hall, even though they might well have made better fighters than their fathers and grandfathers. The adult men were representatives of an enemy clan and an enemy army. The terrorists' reasoning would not have been lost on many of the parents and teachers in the school. They were Caucasians too. Once Ruslan Betrozov had been murdered, most of the men, and many of their wives and mothers, probably realized the gravity of their situation.

Kazbek Dzarasov was one of around thirty men ordered into the corridor. Thirty-four-year-old Sergei Urmanov, an electrical engineer in a local factory, was another. He had taken the day off work to accompany his daughter on her first day at school. 'I was very nervous. I practically didn't sleep the night before the ceremony. I was worried for my daughter's big day. There was only one child in the family and we really loved her.' Like many of the men standing waiting, he had studied in the same school twenty years before. Almost all of them knew each other by name. They looked at each other now and didn't dare to speak. The Colonel personally gave the orders that sealed their fate.

Though not overwhelming, the shooting at the school from outside was intensifying and one of the terrorists had been hit. Some of the men were made to stand on the window sills in those parts of the building where the firing was most sustained. Their neighbours outside would either see them and stop shooting or kill them.

The rest of the men were made to collect furniture from the school's classrooms to build into barricades against the windows and doors. They dragged tables, chairs and blackboards through the school on the orders of the gunmen. Some caught a last glimpse of their families as they carried furniture through the gym to fortify the fire escape at its far end. Kazbek Dzarasov was made to help. If they stumbled or seemed to hesitate at all, they were hit with the butts of the terrorists' guns.

Once the job was done, they were marched back to a small room near the gym and told to sit facing the wall with their hands above their heads. The terrorists then seemed to be waiting for the return of the Colonel to find out what to do next. One of the hostages asked if he could sit on his cap; the gunmen threw him a pillow instead. When the Colonel appeared, according to Kazbek, some of the hostages tried to quiz him about why he had chosen Beslan. They received no answer. Instead, as they faced the wall, they heard what sounded like the Colonel having an argument with the women suicide bombers. No one remembers exactly what time it was.

Suddenly, all the male terrorists withdrew from the small room, leaving the women alone with the hostages. The women's bomb belts were detonated, killing them and causing an enormous explosion. Many of the men were killed instantly. Others were left with terrible injuries. Body parts were scattered across the room. One man had lost his legs and buttocks but was still alive; another had lost his eyes. Blood was spurting from open wounds in all directions. A very small number had escaped with only minor injuries. Madina Khuzmieva's husband, forty-seven-year-old Murat Badoev, was one of the men blown to pieces. She suspected as much when he didn't return to the gym but one of the men who survived the bomb lied to protect her feelings, telling her that Murat was negotiating with the terrorists upstairs.

Had the Colonel planned all along to have the men killed by the women terrorists? Had they killed themselves willingly? As a Caucasian man, he would certainly have appreciated that for these men of fighting age to be wiped out by women was a humiliation. But he may also have been taking the opportunity to silence criticism in the ranks. Since the siege, people have speculated that the women terrorists were having second thoughts about what they were doing. Some survivors remember looks of horror in the women's faces. They say that the women did not know that they were going to attack a school. Alla Khanaeva heard one of the women as she argued with the Colonel. 'She spoke good Russian with no accent. She was shouting, "No. No. I won't do it. You said that we were going to attack a police station."' Alla kept on walking back into the gym but, a few seconds later, she knew that the woman was dead when she heard the explosion. Whatever they had planned for, it is hard to see how the Chechen market traders' deaths were dignified or glorious.

Sergei and Kazbek both survived the bomb blast in the morning. Sergei says, 'They told us that we would have to die and then the women suicide bombers blew themselves up. I came to because of the loud moaning beside me. I remember that I was having trouble hearing, but the screams and the moaning were still noisy enough to make out. I got to my feet and saw all around me the bodies of mutilated men. Kazbek was lying beside me and he had survived as well. Batraz and Murat were sitting up near me too. We all just sat leaning against the wall for a while.'

The terrorists entered the room again and forced the men to rip the door from its hinges and use it as a stretcher to carry the dead and injured up the stairs to another room. According to Kazbek, 'They made us take the bodies to Room 16 on the first floor. Why do I remember the number? Because when I was a student at the school, that was my classroom for a year. We asked them, "What are you going to do with the wounded?" and they said, "What difference does it make? They're as good as dead already." It was Khodov who said this.' Kazbek is convinced that the terrorists beat the rest of the injured men to death, 'finishing them off' as he puts it. When they had moved all the bodies upstairs, the surviving men were allowed to go back into the gym, where the other hostages gasped in shock at their bodies covered in cuts and blood. Later that day, the dead men's corpses were thrown out of the window of Room 16 onto the ground outside.

One of the men ordered to throw the bodies out of the window was Albert Sidakov, an employee of the North Ossetian Customs Office. The thirty-three-year-old had taken leave to see his son entering the first year. He had dressed up in a white suit and white shoes to mark the occasion. Midway through disposing of the bodies, Albert decided to jump out of the window himself. As he ran towards it, one of the terrorists killed him by shooting him repeatedly in the back. The position of Albert's wounds made him appear to be a coward, fleeing from his enemy, when really, as in the story of Soslan and Totraz, his killer was the coward.

The small number of men who remained in the gym when the rest were led away have had mixed feelings about their good fortune. Other hostages and some relatives of the dead men have implied that those who were not taken out must have been guilty of some kind of cowardice or collusion. One of these men was Alik Tsagolov, the P.E. teacher. When giving evidence at the trial of Nurpashi Kulaev (the terrorist who insists he was not really a terrorist) fifty-four-year-old Alik was confronted by another survivor of the siege. Like all witnesses in Russian criminal trials, Alik could be questioned not only by the defence and prosecution but also by the victims themselves. Alik's responses to the woman's thinly veiled accusations showed his own personal feelings of inadequacy.

'I have a question,' she shouted out. 'Were there other men who weren't forced to leave the gym?'

Alik snapped back, 'In case you didn't know, I wasn't the only man who survived.'

'It's just interesting to me because I remember that you weren't made to leave the gym like the rest. But you're a man too, aren't you? And you were sitting right beside the path through the middle of the gym, weren't you?'

'There was no way that they could have avoided seeing me, if that's what you mean. I was on my feet in the gym on several occasions.'

'Which is what makes it so interesting that you weren't made to go out with the rest.'

'You'd need to ask the terrorists about why that was, wouldn't you? According to you, I should have filled out a form requesting them to shoot me.'

'SEE WHAT A BAD BOY I AM'

The school siege had a devastating effect on the families of Beslan. In some instances, more family members were killed than survived. In the wake of the trauma, the families I met in Beslan tended to eulogize their dead. In such a macho society, the death of men is felt particularly acutely. They are presented as warrior martyrs, their deaths as the tragic and heroic end of lives devoted to wife and family. Life is lived in the name of the dead: the spirits of dead fathers still seem to hover over their families demanding remembrance and influence over family affairs. Mothers invoke the memory of absent fathers to make their unruly children behave; grandmothers tell their daughters-in-law that to start new relationships would be disrespectful.

But very often the memories of happy family life are sadly fictitious. The obligation to invent them is just one more hardship for individuals with much greater traumas to overcome; yet another act of denial which makes it harder to move on. I have never met so many unhappy families as I did in the North Caucasus – many of them in Beslan. At the same time, I have never been obliged to drink so many toasts to the family as an idea. Somewhere, deep in the foundations of these societies, there lies a massive and destabilizing contradiction.

One woman I met in Beslan felt it was very important that I understood more about this. We will call her Margarita. Though she had not been in the school herself, three of her close friends had died in the siege and she had stood on the street outside for most of the three days. She was in her early forties but looked younger. Her hair was jet black; her dress and make-up were more understated than usual in the Caucasus. In fact, she was very beautiful, but in a way that relied on sadness. The shortest silences would plunge her deep into thought and sometimes she lost the thread of our conversation entirely.

This was not the first time in the last few months that Margarita had told her story of the siege to a journalist or writer. Like many I met, she moved from scene to scene without enthusiasm. We had got as far as the death of the men before I interrupted her. 'What impact has that had on the town?' I asked. Margarita looked up at the ceiling and smiled. There followed a long pause. I sensed that she was wondering whether she could trust me with something. I promised her anonymity. 'Thanks. But that doesn't make it much easier,' she said.

Eventually she told me what was bothering her. 'Do you know what I can't stop thinking? I can't stop thinking about how few of our men were killed in the school. It's one of the few positives that we can take from the siege. And do you know how it's to be explained? Men in the Caucasus, and here in North Ossetia especially, take hardly any interest in bringing up their children. Most of the time they are absent from the home altogether. It's not that they have jobs to do – most of them are unemployed. They're just out hanging around with their mates, messing about with their cars or sleeping with their lovers. If you're a real man, it's embarrassing to be seen having too much to do with your children. You can lift them up and swing them round to show off that they're yours but that's about all. You lose interest in your wife as well when she's had a couple of children, and she's not supposed to say anything about it. If she does, you can give her a slap. When it came to taking the children to school for the first day of the year, in most families the job fell to mothers and grandmothers, even though many of them bring home more money than their husbands. So now we live in a town full of bad dads and hardly any mums.'

Margarita's words were shocking but I recognized the truth of them from my own experiences in the Caucasus. I was glad she had opened up. Without her honesty, I might not have dared to mention the problems that families in Russia, and in particular in the Caucasus, have to face. Many relationships are dysfunctional from the very start. It is far from rare for marriages in the North Caucasus to begin in violence and coercion. Men I met in Vladikavkaz, the state capital of North Ossetia, freely admitted that bride abduction still occurs. Most of them see something quaint – perhaps even amusing – in the custom. But it is hard to sustain this view when one focuses on what these abductions usually involve. Women are usually taken hostage by men they already know: sometimes current boyfriends or exes, sometimes just acquaintances. They are forced to have sex whether they want to or not and then taken back to their parents. The mother and father are informed of what has happened and encouraged to accept the kidnapper's offer of marriage. Many do, aware that their daughter's chances of making a successful match with anyone else have been severely compromised. Even in middle-class, metropolitan circles, it is still thought essential for Caucasian brides to be virgins. By contrast, men are expected to be sexually experienced.

This situation endures because most women still accept it. Young women from the Caucasus who have been my friends over the years have, almost without exception, referred to others who have sex before marriage as sluts and whores. Caucasian men in search of their first sexual experiences either visit prostitutes or sleep with ethnic Russians, who, like young people in much of the rest of Europe, tend to view their virginity as something to be lost sooner rather than later. Of course, many Ossetian or Chechen men are only too glad to have casual sex with an Ossetian or Chechen woman, but they may well start a whispering campaign against her afterwards and would be very unlikely to marry her.

Russia is a country of extramarital affairs and casual sexual encounters. In Soviet times, it was relatively normal for husbands and wives to holiday separately on trips organized by workplaces or trades unions. Men who simultaneously carry on relationships with wives, lovers and prostitutes are not unusual. In the Caucasus, it is common to treat honoured visitors to a night of sex with prostitutes in a private sauna; to refuse can be deemed insulting. Though fundamentalist religion frowns on such behaviour, there is little evidence that its spread has done much to alter these time-honoured traditions. The connection between macho masculinity and sexual promiscuity remains strong.

Husbands in happy and monogamous relationships can be stereotyped as weak, their fidelity taken as evidence that they are henpecked. Wives who expect anything different are thought unreasonable, sometimes even by their own parents. They are told to be patient or to dress more sexily. Women who leave their husbands are often portrayed as desiccated. If men who are serially unfaithful feel any remorse at all, it is usually for the pain they have caused to their children. But even this is seldom enough to make them stop.

Over the course of one long night during my time in the North Caucasus, I heard about one man's 'battle' to be faithful to his wife. I met Murat in the enormous, almost deserted bar of the Hotel Intourist in Pyatigorsk. I had gone there late in the evening feeling lonely and flat, in the hope of finding someone to talk to. Murat was in the same sort of mood and started the conversation. At first we talked about his two children, principally his fourteen-year-old daughter: how beautiful she was, how intelligent, how much he hoped that she would have an easier life than him. Murat and his wife had paid for their daughter to go on a school trip to London the previous year. She had seen Buckingham Palace and Westminster Abbey. He confided in me that in time he would dearly love to send her to one of the great universities of Britain or America. It would be her passport to a prosperous life.

Abruptly Murat's topic of conversation changed. 'Are you not surprised that I have a fourteen-year-old daughter?' he asked. 'I don't look old enough, do I?' 'No,' I said honestly. He was well dressed and his features were dark and attractive. He could have passed for thirty. 'I'm forty-four,' he announced and touched the gold crucifix round his neck, perhaps thanking God for his good looks. 'I have to look my best because of my job. I run the only Armani shop in the whole of the North Caucasus.' I must have looked incredulous because the next minute he was showing me the label on the back of his jeans to prove it.

After more small talk, Murat leaned in towards me and said, 'Tim, I need to talk to you about something very private.' He looked serious, even upset. 'I am a bad man. A very bad man'. I asked him why. 'Because I am ruining my beautiful children's lives. The thing I want to do least in the world and I can't help myself.'

'But why?' I asked again.

'Because I was having a relationship with this woman called Marina and my wife Oksana found out. Why do you think I'm drinking here? Oksana threw me out of the house and I've been living in a room in the hotel for the last two months. I never get to see my baby son or my daughter, and I don't think Oksana will ever agree to have me back again. I have a split personality. I want to do one thing but I end up doing the opposite all the time.'

Murat's distress was genuine but his problems were all of his own making. Marina was exactly half his age. She had come into the Armani shop one day eight months earlier and the two had started flirting with each other. At first it had just been text messages but quickly they were meeting for sex three or four times a week. 'She's nowhere near as intelligent as Oksana, but she's very pretty and she's good with that.' (Murat pointed at his crotch.) He had started the affair when his wife was pregnant with their son and he had assumed it would just be a fling. It was proving much more difficult to end than he had thought. Sex with Oksana had been dull and he was beginning to worry that, at thirty-eight, his wife had lost her appeal. His infidelity was uncovered when one of his wife's friends saw him in a bar, drunk and alone with Marina.

He read a text message he had just received, presumably from Marina, and grimaced. He was full of self-pity. 'The whole thing is a complete mess. I can't sleep and I walk around with a splitting headache the whole time from thinking about it. I don't want Marina. She is nothing. I don't love her at all. I want Oksana and my children. I want my newborn son and my daughter. It kills me not to be with them.' His daughter was old enough to come to the shop after school but he had only seen his baby son two or three times. 'He is my own flesh and blood, the continuation of my line,' he said. The boy was much more important to him than the girl.

Oksana would only consider having Murat back if he could show her three months of itemized mobile phone bills without the other woman's number on them. Clearly he could not do this while he was still seeing Marina. He looked at the phone, turning it over and over in his hand, as if blaming it for his predicament. He saw one reason for hope in the near future: in the autumn, Marina was going to start a course at hairdressing college in Moscow. She would be removed from his life.

A few minutes later, a young woman walked unsteadily up to the bar wearing a bikini top and denim hot-pants. It was long past midnight and the bar was deserted. A crimson rose hung by her side, with the bloom dangling just below her knee. I was almost certain she was a prostitute. The bar's manageress must have known her and asked her to leave. The woman showed no sign of leaving. She fell off one of her high heels and shrieked as her ankle twisted beneath her. Murat now got up. He asked her if she was all right and held her steady. They both seemed to realize simultaneously that they knew each other. He brought her back to his stool, though she continued to stand while he sat down. He held her close to him with his hand around her waist, lasciviously rubbing the edges of her skimpy outfit between his forefinger and thumb.

He smirked at me. 'See what a bad boy I am,' he said. But he was acting up now for the benefit of the prostitute. The

manageress still wanted rid of the girl and had come to stand beside us on the other side of the bar. Murat must have wanted her to go away because he started to describe in graphic detail his sexual fantasies. 'Can you guess what my greatest ambition is?' he asked me.

'To visit London with your son and daughter?' I suggested.

He laughed. 'I want to go to New York and hire the cheapest prostitute I can find. Not a Russian one, mind you. And I want to fuck her senseless in the cheapest, dirtiest motel room there is.'

The manageress had had enough. She told Murat to leave and take the prostitute with him. He moved with her to a table some distance from the bar and asked me to join him. I said that I was going to bed. The manageress apologized to me for Murat's behaviour and introduced herself as Maria. 'I can't stand those parasites,' she says. 'They give real working women a bad name. If it was up to me they wouldn't be allowed in at all, but the hotel management says we have to. Renting out rooms to the likes of Murat is one of the only ways they make money out of season. All the rooms on the seventh floor are kept free just in case.' I went to bed. I waved goodbye to Murat as I went, but he didn't notice.

In another hotel, in the centre of Vladikavkaz, I was woken in the middle of the night by shouting from the room across the corridor. The noise was a mixture of an angry man's shouts and a woman's screams and sobs. When I opened my door, I could hear the man screaming. 'I told you to shut your fucking mouth. Look at me, Yuliya. LOOK. AT. ME.' His own voice sounded strangulated, as if he were about to break down. He started to pound the walls. I imagined him slamming his fists against a wall just inches from her head. Every time he hit the wall, Yuliya shrieked. Suddenly there was a dull, thudding sound which grew quickly louder. It seemed that Yuliya was trying to escape. When she was nearly at the door, the man grabbed her and dragged her back into the room. She screamed very loudly.

Earlier that evening I had been phoned from reception by a prostitute who had been told which rooms had single men in them. She asked if I wanted to have some fun without leaving the hotel. Had this been Yuliya? Or perhaps the arguing couple were married? I was trying to work out what, if anything, I could do, when another hotel guest came out of his room, banged on their door and shouted 'Be quiet.' I phoned reception but there was no answer. I wasn't prepared to call the police, so I just sat and listened until it went quiet.

Violence against women is a major problem in Russia, if a hidden one. Wife-beating and rape within marriage are much more common than in the West, and violence against prostitutes is hardly remarked on at all. In 2003, according to the Moscow Helsinki Group, 9,000 Russian women died at the hands of their present or former partner; in the UK, the figure is about one hundred a year. The problems are gravest in traditional parts of the country, like the North Caucasus, where modern, secular lifestyles clash most obviously with traditional values. Many women in places like Beslan do not even view violence by a husband against his wife (much less forced sexual intercourse) as a crime.

Once in an abusive relationship most women would never dream of reporting it to the police. They risk being isolated by their families if they even discuss domestic violence in private. Margarita was especially brave to raise these issues in Beslan where the holy status of the family, and of fathers in particular, has gained such importance as a result of the siege. Even women with university degrees and professional careers often accept that in the home they will conform to stereotypes of the submissive wife. Fathers often show little interest in the home or the raising of children until they think that a mistake has been made. Then they exercise their patriarchal right to be heard and obeyed. The discovery of a wife's infidelity often brings immediate physical retribution.

So many families in modern Russia are being destroyed from within: by drink; by grinding poverty; by the personality-altering experience of military service; by double standards. In Beslan, the idea of the family came under attack in a new and perverse way. The shared experience of the school siege has brought the remnants of families closer together; without mutual respect and equality it will not keep them together.

'LET ME TAKE THEM YOUR DEMANDS'

Just after 11 a.m. on the first morning of the siege, a hesitant but composed figure emerged into the schoolyard of School No. 1, waving a piece of yellow material. It was Larisa Mamitova, the forty-five-year-old doctor who had gone straight to the celebrations from a night shift in casualty. From her deliberate stride it was clear that she was not an escapee. She had been sent out with a note outlining the terrorists' demands. A terrorist sniper followed her every move, ready to shoot her if she acted suspiciously. Larisa remembers every detail of how the events unfolded.

'The school doors had been barricaded with tables and some of the terrorists had to move them away. Then, as soon as the doors were opened, they ran away and hid. I walked slowly out of the building and started to wave the piece of material I'd brought with me. I'd ripped a yellow curtain in the library. As I went out, I saw a woman who'd been injured in the first attack collapsed beside the steps. The terrorists had instructed me only to go as far as the gates on Comintern Street. They had told me not to say a word, just to hand over the note, and turn around and come back. I walked past the injured woman, up to the gates and started shouting. "Come here! Somebody. Please! Come here and get this note!"

'Somebody came running over almost immediately. To start with, in the confusion, I thought that he couldn't understand me; that he didn't speak Ossetian, or something. I remember asking him, "Are you Ossetian?" He said he was and I told him that there were loads of us trapped inside; that the whole place was booby-trapped. "For the love of God," I said, "just don't shoot at the school, whatever you do." Then I handed over the note.

'Before I went back inside, I specifically remember telling him that there were at least a thousand of us in the gym. I made a point of saying this because, even at that stage, I'd heard a lower figure given out on the radio. One of the terrorists in the gym, the one who had to sit with his foot on the detonator switch, had a little pocket radio, which he kept fiddling with and trying to tune in to different stations. On one bulletin, I had heard them say that there were reports that 120 people had been taken hostage. That's why I was worried about it. "Don't believe what they're saying on the radio," I said. "There're more than a thousand of us."' Then she turned round and walked slowly back into the school.

The note that Larisa handed over gave away very little about what the terrorists wanted. It simply stated, 'We demand to negotiate with the President of the Republic of North Ossetia, Dzasokhov, with Zyazikov, the President of Ingushetia and with Rashailo the paediatrician. If any one of us is killed, we will shoot fifty people. If any one of us is wounded, we will kill twenty people. If five of us are killed, we will blow the whole school up. If you switch off the electricity for more than a minute we will shoot ten people.' A mobile telephone number was written across the top of the page.

The terrorists had decided not to make their demands

public at this stage apart from the names of the people they would negotiate with. The reasons for that decision were unclear. They may have been biding their time, allowing the tension in Russia to build. Perhaps they wanted the negotiations to produce results and understood that any public statement of their demands would constrain the Russian authorities' ability to do a deal.

If they were surprised by its content, everyone who saw the note thought that it must be part of the terrorists' carefully planned strategy. But the testimony of Larisa Mamitova, the woman who carried the note, paints a different picture of the group. Only their leader, the Colonel, seemed to have a clear idea about how they were to proceed. And even he had to rifle through his pockets in front of the doctor to find the right piece of paper. Most importantly, it was Larisa and not the terrorists who suggested that she could take their demands to the outside world. They were either unsure of what they wanted or uninterested in a negotiated political solution.

Larisa first came face to face with the terrorists very early on in the siege. She was called out of the gym to treat one of them who had been hit by a bullet from outside the school. (Perhaps this was the single shot fired by the police marksman which Taimuraz Gasiev remembered causing such screams when it hit its target.) In shock and terrified by the bombs that were being hung up all around her, Larisa had not heard the terrorist shouting for a doctor and only realized when someone alongside nudged her and said, 'You're a doctor, aren't you?'

She says, 'They led me out into the corridor and told me, "One of our men has been hit. Bandage him up. Examine him and bandage him up." Then they started getting medicine out of their rucksacks. I couldn't believe that. When I first went into the corridor, I had noticed how many weapons they had and how many rucksacks there were. It seemed that there were three or four rucksacks for each terrorist, and each one was packed full of stuff. They seemed to have everything from mineral water to toothbrushes and toothpaste. They handed me bandages, antiseptic wipe and iodine. Two of their men had been wounded as it turned out. One had been injured in the arm: the bullet had entered through his palm and come out at his elbow. The other had been hit in the stomach; the bullet was still lodged inside. It was clear that I wasn't going to be able to do much for him. He had turned pale and was drifting in and out of consciousness. I said he needed to lie down, but they told me there was no room for him to do this and made him sit up on a chair instead.'

As Larisa dressed the other terrorist's wounded arm, she started to ask him questions, almost as though she were treating him in casualty. 'What made you decide to take *children* hostage?' she asked. 'What are your demands? You must have some demands, otherwise you wouldn't have come here. "We demand only one thing, the removal of Russian troops from Chechnya. That's all we want."'

Something told Larisa that the terrorists had not yet made this demand known. She said to the injured man, 'Let me go out and tell them your demands. I will come back again. I won't try to run away. I'll just take them your demands, plain and simple. I mean, you're going to have to make contact with the government somehow, aren't you?'

'At first all he said to me was that they didn't need any help at all and that I should get on with what I was doing, but I kept insisting. "I beg you. Please let me take your demands out. There are children here who shouldn't be here at all, who haven't even reached school age yet. For their sake, if for nothing else, let me take your demands out." But then he said that it wasn't his decision to make, that it was up to the Colonel to decide. So I asked him to go to the Colonel and find out if I could be the one to go outside with their demands.' To her surprise, he complied.

'When he came back, he wanted to know who I had come to school with. I told him about Tamerlan and he sent me into the hall to fetch him. Back in the corridor, they made us sit on a chair and wait for the Colonel. They already started to warn me that if I tried to take a single step outside the school gates they would shoot my son. They said that I would be shot as well. I told them that I wouldn't be going anywhere: I said that I had no intention of leaving my son in the school all by himself.'

Even at this early stage, the heat in the gym was almost unbearable. The weather was unusually hot for September and Tamerlan, like many others, had already stripped down to his vest. It was soaking wet with sweat and became cold once he was out in the corridor. He started to shiver. When Larisa removed the boy's vest, the terrorist with the serious stomach wound offered him his camouflage jacket. Larisa wrapped it around her son's shoulders as they continued to wait. 'We waited for what felt like a very long time,' she says.

While they waited, Larisa was aware of the adult male hostages moving about around her, carrying tables and chairs and being ordered about by their captors. She saw the men led into a classroom and forced to squat on the floor and saw the door close just before the explosion that was intended to kill them. The terrorists standing by her were as surprised by the noise as she was and assumed they were under attack from outside. They started to shoot in all directions and, for a few moments, it seemed to Larisa that they might well kill each other as well as herself and her son.

One of the terrorists was seriously hurt in this burst of fire and, while the Colonel was making up his mind whether to see her or not, she tended to his wounds as she had those of the others: 'The fighters took me to this man who looked like an Arab. His face was not Russian or Caucasian. He had been mortally wounded. There was foam coming out of his mouth and he was already unconscious. They told me to do something for him, and handed me these phials and syringes. I told them that he was about to die and that there was nothing more I could do. I got a phial of Panadol and filled the syringe with it. I told one of the fighters to hold the wounded man's arm to help me find a vein, and then I injected the medicine.'

When she had done this, Larisa tried to go to the help of the male hostages she had seen being blown up. She got as far as the classroom they were in and saw that those who were still alive were literally crawling up the walls. 'I went up to one and pressed the remains of his trouser leg to one of his wounds. "Hold this here, or else you'll bleed to death," I told him. I was just going over to another when one of the terrorists told me that it was time to meet the Colonel.'

Larisa said goodbye to her son and was led to the school library. Inside, books and papers had been strewn across the floor by hostages desperate to barricade themselves in as the terrorists ran towards them at the beginning of the siege. The Colonel did not introduce himself but cleared space at a table with a sweep of his arm and motioned to the doctor to sit down. He seemed very on edge, barely in control of himself. 'He hunted through his pockets and found a piece of paper. He wrote down a telephone number and handed it to me. Then he started rifling through his pockets again. He kept pulling out bits of paper but not the one he wanted. At one point, I saw him unfold a piece of paper with a hand-drawn map of our school on it. He quickly shoved it back into his pocket.' Finally, he found what he was looking for. 'Write this down!' he barked at Larisa.

He spoke in Russian and Larisa wrote his words down in Russian. 'My hand was shaking so much and I was trying to write too quickly: I was terrified of missing something.' When they got to the bit where the Colonel mentioned the paediatrician Doctor Rashailo, Larisa corrected him and asked if he meant Doctor Roshal. In an instant, he became enraged: 'I told you to write Rashailo, didn't I? So write Rashailo!' As she prepared to go outside, the Colonel handed her a piece of red material and told her to wave it in the air. She knew that you were supposed to wave white material to show that you were unarmed and wondered what was behind the Colonel's offer of red. She ripped a yellow curtain off the wall instead and a terrorist accompanied her from the room.

After delivering her note, Larisa walked slowly back into the school. As soon as she was back inside, the terrorists rebuilt the barricade of tables against the doors. In vain she asked them if she could go out and rescue the injured woman who was still lying beside the steps. It was many months before she realized how fortunate it was that the terrorists had refused her request. The woman eventually summoned enough energy to drag herself to the gates and escape. Larisa was led back into the gym and reunited with Tamerlan on the way. She looked for the male hostages as she went past the classroom they had been in. It was empty. 'All of them had disappeared,' she says. 'I couldn't understand where they had gone. Not a single one of them was left. They'd all disappeared and their blood had even been wiped from the floor.'

THE LORD OF THE CAUCASUS

The disagreements and grievances at the heart of the Beslan siege are centuries old. It was only the most recent in a long line of atrocities that stretch back beyond living memory. Most of the adults and older children in the gym knew this and it added to their despair. The fate that awaited them seemed already to be set, had already come to pass in a thousand other places over hundreds of years. In the Caucasus compromise and conciliation are rare.

The Ossetians stand out in the North Caucasus. They are as native to the region as anyone else and their territory lies right in the centre of the land between the Black Sea and the Caspian, but they are viewed as strangers by most of their neighbours. By some, they are seen as traitors. While most Ossetians are pleased to be part of Russia, their neighbours' attitudes towards the country they live in range from wariness to out-and-out hatred. Most North Caucasians are Muslims or the descendants of Muslims, whereas most Ossetians are Christians. Through the years, these differences have often led to conflict but, even when they haven't, they have been perpetuated in the stories people tell their children and the maxims they live by. The rivalries never finish; the grievances are never avenged.

When the Russians first arrived in the North Caucasus in the eighteenth century, they wanted to pacify the local population and convert them to their religion, Orthodox Christianity. Because of the mountains and the ferocity of the local tribes, the area had never previously been conquered by an invading power. When the Russians began to take over, the region had been loosely under the influence of Persia for several hundred years and Islam was the main religion. The area, along with Georgia and Armenia on the other side of the mountains, acted as a buffer zone between the three great powers, Persia, Russia and the Ottoman Empire: when one power felt stronger it would try to force the others to retreat from their Caucasian territories. Fortifications were built and destroyed, and alliances and dynastic marriages were forged and broken. In the late sixteenth century, small bands of Russian Cossacks had managed to make a home in the valley of the River Terek, which flows through Beslan. Deeply religious, the Cossacks were famed for their skill in battle and had won a number of important privileges and freedoms from the Russian Tsar in return for their loyalty. Though they kept themselves at arm's length from the government in Moscow and later St Petersburg, their presence so deep in the Caucasus gave Russia a vital foothold in the area. By the mid-eighteenth century, Russia felt strong enough to attempt to take control of the region as a whole and, through a combination of diplomacy, evangelism and violence, began to advance southwards once more.

One of the first signs of Russia's intentions was an increase in the number of missionaries sent to the tribes. Their efforts were mostly fruitless; many were killed or chased away by unreceptive clans. But they had great success with the Ossetians, who felt particular enmity towards the Persians and may have retained some cultural vestiges of earlier contact with Christianity, hundreds of years before. In 1741, an

Ossetian army had achieved a stunning military victory over the Muslim Persians, capturing their leader, the Khan, in the process. Russia must have had this in mind when it despatched its first, top-secret mission to the tribe in 1745. Over the next couple of decades, the new faith took root with mass baptisms and the opening of new congregations.

Ossetians tell you that their forefathers found it easy to adapt to the new religion because it had been with them all along, since their ancestors – known as the Alans – had accepted Christianity from Byzantium in 910 AD. Like the forebears of all Caucasian peoples, the Alans are remembered as noble and belligerent nomads who, though small in number, punched above their weight, sometimes humbling the great powers around them. Though their attachment to Christianity was almost certainly terminated by the Mongol invasions, the Alans are cited by North Ossetians to show how long they have been connected with the true religion: not recent converts but old defenders of the faith. In nationalistic North Ossetia today, Alans are everywhere. Alan is one of the most common names for Ossetian men; over seventy of the hostages in the siege were called Alan or Alana. The main football club is called Alaniya and the official name of the autonomous republic is North Ossetia–Alaniya.

In the mid-eighteenth century, the conversion of the Ossetians to Christianity provoked the surrounding Muslim tribes. As Russia hoped, the Ossetian converts were quickly forced to ask for political and military protection. The Russians moved in and built a fortress at Mozdok, which still stands in North Ossetia today. When the first centre of Ossetian Christianity was destroyed by Muslim attackers in 1769, the Russians helped to build a new one. Only a few years later, in 1774, the Ossetians chose to join the Russian Empire voluntarily and Russia had achieved control over a strategically vital piece of land. In 1784, Russia laid the foundations of the city of Vladikavkaz, its most southerly settlement ever, hard against the Great Caucasus mountain range. The city is still the North Ossetian capital; its name means 'Lord of the Caucasus'.

From its strategic position at the heart of the territory, Russia fought for and achieved control of the whole of the area between the Black Sea and the Caspian, both north and south of the mountains. Some tribes and states capitulated very quickly; the nakedness of Russia's supremacy over them was veiled with protestations of mutual friendship and protection. Others offered stiffer resistance, none more so than the Chechens and the Ingush, whose lands bordered the Ossetians'. Their refusal to be mastered by outsiders became legendary. Against the might of one of Europe's greatest military forces – the army which had defeated Napoleon – they fought bravely and successfully for over fifty years. Their campaigns were motivated by fierce national pride and galvanized by religious zeal. Russia was only able to call the North Caucasus wholly its own after 1859, more than a century after it had started trying to convert the Ossetians.

Over five decades, Russian commanders gathered their armies each summer to launch attacks on the mountainous homeland of the rebel fighters in Chechnya and Ingushetia. Amongst the soldiers there were always many Ossetian Christians and local Russian Cossacks, the people who had most to lose from the triumph of their Islamic neighbours. Like the Americans in Vietnam, the Russians found it easy to move deep into rebel territory; the guerrillas did not try to hold a line and would not stand and fight. Instead, they would attack the Russians from behind, often ambushing the troops as they returned to base camps for provisions. Before winter, the Russians had usually been forced into retreat. This situation, repeated year after year, was extremely demoralizing for the Russian army. The troops became willing to contemplate anything that would give them an edge over their opponents, however cruel and depraved. Chechen and Ingush villages were as a matter of course presumed to be harbouring guerrillas and were burned to the ground; adult and adolescent males were assumed to be fighters and were killed.

The resistance finally collapsed when Russia, unable to bear the costly and humiliating situation any longer, committed unprecedented numbers of troops to the conflict in the late 1850s. With a quarter of a million men to carry out a scorched-earth policy, the Russians succeeded in driving the rebels out of all their strongholds simultaneously. In the process they captured Imam Shamil, the guerrillas' religious and military leader. Born in what is now Dagestan in 1797, Shamil was a charismatic leader who commanded the respect of the Russian officers he fought and attracted the attention of many people outside Russia. Unlike modern-day Caucasian rebel leaders, he was not killed by the Russians and instead went on to enjoy a kind of celebrity status amongst his former enemies; two of his sons even went on to serve in the Tsar's army and were ennobled.

One hundred and fifty years later the imam's namesake, Shamil Basaev, was the mastermind behind the siege of Beslan's School No. 1. The man who had given the Colonel his orders and weaponry came from a clan famous for resisting the Russians and had been named deliberately after the great nineteenth-century warlord.

Though Ossetians were overwhelmingly pro-Russian, those who lived in the mountains were sometimes taken for enemies by the ignorant and suspicious Tsarist forces. With no firm borders, Ossetian and the Ingush villages were mixed together, and only those who had lived in the mountains for a lifetime knew the precise lie of the land. The population was particularly mixed in the land immediately to the east of the River Terek. Some Ossetians had never been reached by the

Christian missionaries and remained Muslims. Ossetian villages could be cleared and razed to the ground simply on the suspicion that they were Ingush. Worse, soldiers driven to distraction by the unending conflict stopped caring which of the Caucasian tribes – friend or foe – they were dealing with. More than half a million people were forcibly evicted from the mountains by the Russian army between the 1840s and 1860s. If they were not killed, they were usually sent to live in the foothills, where, the Tsarist government hoped, they would learn more civilized ways.

The vast majority of the displaced people were Ingush and Chechens, but some were Ossetians. Among them was a fifty-four-year-old man called Beslan Tulatov who, along with a small number of other exiles, founded a new settlement about twelve miles north of Vladikavkaz. Like many others, he had come from a cleared village in the mountains east of the River Terek. For the first century of its existence the village was known as Tulatovo, but then changed its name to that of its founder's first name, Beslan. A grim Soviet statue commemorating him now stands near Beslan's railway station: Tulatov's outsized hand clutches a board with his name on it. The village had only sixty-two inhabitants in 1866; by 1917 there were 430. The increase was mainly due to the decision to make Beslan a junction on the railway line linking Moscow and St Petersburg to Vladikavkaz, Grozny and ultimately the oil wells around Baku. The railway attracted manufacturers, because it enabled them to sell their products to a greater number of customers. By the beginning of the twentieth century the town boasted a distillery, a desiccating plant and a starch and molasses factory.

Although they were only a tiny part of its vast empire, Russia had a very special relationship with its Caucasian territories. In part, this was because of the area's strategic significance, but there were less tangible reasons as well. The

fight to conquer the tribes made the land more precious to the Russians, enhancing the value of its landscape and history. By conquering the Caucasus, Russia had laid claim to the inheritance of the Ancient Greeks. Russia had finally found a contrast to the dreary monotony of the steppe, which stretched for thousands of miles from Ukraine in the west to Vladivostok in the east. It is no exaggeration to say that the Russians fell in love with the Caucasus.

I felt the same when I woke on the train from Moscow to a Caucasian landscape. The villages that I was passing now looked no wealthier than the ones further north, but the setting was much more beautiful and inspiring. Everywhere, hills and mountains broke through the horizon, which the day before had been an unchanging flat line. The dirty snow that had still clung to the April ground had melted everywhere in the Caucasus, except on the highest peaks, replaced by new grass and spring flowers. It is easy to romanticize the Caucasus.

Even when the war against the Chechens and the Ingush was at its fiercest in the nineteenth century, hundreds of Russian aristocrats made long and dangerous journeys to spend their summers in the shadow of the mountains. In 1835 one Russian traveller said that the mountains were 'to Russian nobles what Mecca is for Muslims'. They were drawn to the wild landscape, out of which bubbled precious mineral waters which were supposed to cure all kinds of diseases. They tended to stay at the purpose-built spa resorts which developed around the natural springs at Pyatigorsk and Zheleznovodsk. For the most part, they were out of harm's way and, by the 1820s, it was extremely rare for any rebel fighting to interrupt their holidays. Like visitors to Bath and Baden-Baden, they passed the time observing (or ignoring) their strict spa diets, attending balls and playing cards. Many hoped for a holiday fling.

Not that these visitors wanted to ignore the troubles of the region entirely. This was the age of Romanticism and many educated people thought it essential to have an 'authentic' experience of their surroundings, even if it was necessarily staged and simulated. Like aristocratic versions of modern-day backpackers, they dearly hoped to encounter something a bit out of the ordinary and unplanned. They listened jealously to the stories from the front line, told to them by injured army officers who had been sent to the spa for a cure at the Tsar's expense. They went on day-trips to visit the natives in peaceful tribal villages nearby, watching and applauding their dances and horsemanship. Like Rousseau in Paris, some even dressed up in native costumes for the weekly balls. And, of course, the constant, if slight, threat of attack gave additional bite to the whole experience.

In their dreams, they went even further into enemy territory. In 1837, the Russian author Elena Gan wrote a parody of these holidaymakers' fantasies, 'A Memoir of Zheleznovodsk'. Its female narrator, in search of an authentic Caucasian experience, rides too far from the spa and is taken hostage by mountain guerrillas. When she resists being raped by her captors, the woman is instead murdered by them. Finally, her experiences are exposed as a hoax: far from being victim to the wild Caucasian savages, she has only fallen asleep and dreamed the entire adventure, with the trashy novel which provided the inspiration still in her hand.

The region inspired a host of literary and artistic works which have remained central to Russia's sense of identity right up to the present. Two of Russia's greatest writers, Alexander Pushkin and Mikhail Lermontov, found inspiration there. Lermontov made the Caucasus his home when he was exiled there by the Tsar in the 1830s, first fighting at the front line and then taking up residence in Pyatigorsk. He died in the town, in a duel sparked by a petty insult, when he was only twenty-six years old. Thanks to Russia's centrally planned curriculum, these writers' Caucasian poems, novels and stories are still set texts in schools from St Petersburg to the Far East as well as in Grozny and Beslan. Though essentially patronizing and self-serving, the stories they wrote were often well-intentioned. They admired the hot-blooded bravery and integrity of the Caucasian rebels, contrasting it with the iciness and dishonesty they saw in their own, supposedly civilized, society. In a way, they loved the place and 'believed in' its people. But this was still a long way from believing in the rebels' cause. They understood that the primitive behaviour that was so alluring in stories and poems was not viable in everyday life. Whatever grievances the Russians had with their own corrupt and tyrannical government, most continued to believe in the essential greatness of their country, its faith and its empire.

'THERE ARE MORE THAN 1,300 OF US'

Even before the siege, it was already clear to Russia's press and television journalists that 1 September 2004 was going to be a major news day. Moscow was still reeling from its worst terrorist attacks since a terrible theatre siege two years earlier: on 24 August, two aeroplanes which had taken off from the Russian capital had been blown up in mid-flight by the former flatmates of the Beslan female terrorists, killing everyone on board; at 8.05 p.m. on 31 August, only thirteen hours before the siege began, a bomb had gone off outside a busy Moscow metro station, killing ten people instantly and injuring fifty-one. The morning news bulletins had speculated about which groups might be responsible for the spate of attacks and whether they had links to Al-Qaeda. More victims of the metro station bombing had been named, and the parents of one young man were pictured leaving flowers at the scene of his death. And, of course, all the news programmes mentioned the 1.3 million children who were going to school for the first time.

At 10.16 a.m., news that the school had been besieged was first carried on the wires. The two-line story stated incorrectly that negotiations were under way. The Russian press and the television channels rushed their top journalists to the town. They tried to get as close to the school as possible, becoming part of the chorus that had gathered to watch and comment on the tragedy that was developing inside. When the seriousness of what was happening became apparent, journalists from all over the world followed. Across Russia, Beslan was the only story; internationally, it was the first item on most news bulletins. The footage, which played incessantly on Russian television screens, showed groups of people standing near the school at varying stages of panic, exhaustion and chaos. Alongside them the concentrations of troops and military equipment grew heavier and heavier. Far away, President Putin, the Minister of the Interior and others were shown holding calm but resolute meetings and press conferences. In reality there was little information for the media to divulge. Much of what was going on inside the school was to remain a mystery until the siege was over. Other facts were concealed by the authorities, or had been deliberately distorted before being handed over to journalists. Much that was said was quickly contradicted, while the desperate citizens of Beslan became unreliable witnesses to what was going on in front of their eyes. Though the event took place under intense, perhaps unprecedented, media attention, the journalists frequently looked on with unseeing eyes.

In one critical way, the media's misreporting of the event played a part in the siege itself. Inside the school, the terrorists had access to radio and television. They, along with those hostages who were near enough to hear, listened with disbelief as reporters repeatedly gave out estimates of the number of hostages which were wildly understated. The news programmes were only reporting the figures they had received from the authorities and the terrorists understood this. They were enraged at what they took to be an attempt to belittle their 'achievement' and underplay the scale of the crisis.

Larisa Mamitova had heard the first estimate of 120 hostages and had tried to impress on the man she handed the terrorists' note to that it was totally wrong. Her insistence that more than a thousand people were trapped inside was not reported. That there were about 120 hostages continued to be repeated on bulletins until around 5.30 p.m. on 1 September. Then journalists were suddenly told that there were between three and four hundred hostages in the school, still less than a quarter of the real figure. By the time of the breakfast news programmes on 2 September, the estimate had become much more precise (though it remained completely wrong). The Russian authorities and, following them, every news organization in the world stated that there were 354 hostages.

With each hour that the figures were left uncorrected, the terrorists became more and more angry. As Svetlana Dzherieva, sitting under one of the basketball hoops in the gym with her seven-year-old daughter Dana, recalled, 'They were incensed by the numbers. On the second day near lunchtime they lost it completely. They started shouting at us. "Nobody wants you!" they said. "Everyone has abandoned you! They're saying on the television that there are only three hundred and something people in here." I remember they laughed at us about it. One of the terrorists said, "If they want there to be only 354 hostages in here, then we can do that for them."'

Undoubtedly, the main effect of these mistakes was to make the terrorists crueller. According to Felisa Batagova, grandmother of Alana and Khetag, 'Our attackers came and told us what the reports were saying. First that there were only 120 of us and then that there were only 354. "You're like lambs to the slaughter, aren't you?" they said. "You're just like a roomful of sluts and drug addicts as far as they're concerned. You're no good to anybody. Fifteen hundred of you sitting in here and they just keep on saying three hundred."' The terrorists' indignation was so great that periodically they ordered schoolteachers to count the hostages in the gym.

There has never been an adequate explanation of the disparity between the number of hostages in the gym and the much smaller figures given out by the authorities. Understandably, conspiracy theorists have had a field day interpreting this miscalculation. Very soon after the siege had begun, local people had started to compile lists of the family members and neighbours who were thought to be inside. Officials say that the number of names on the lists was 354. It would be startling if this were true. Even so, it was common knowledge that the school had over nine hundred pupils. Official statistics revealed that there had been 986 pupils at the school at the end of the previous academic year. The Minister of Education in North Ossetia at the time, Alina Levitskaya, has said that she clearly remembers asking one of her civil servants if this information had been passed to the crisis committee; they assured her that it had. It was not credible that only a third of the school's pupils – never mind their teachers and parents – would have turned out to mark one of the most important days in the school year.

The crowds of people standing around outside couldn't believe there were so few people trapped in the school. Twenty-nine-year-old Taimuraz Gasiev says, 'I spent eleven years at that school and I never heard of there being only 350 pupils at the celebration, even without counting parents and teachers. There would always have been more than that. The ones who were going to school for the first time would bring their entire families and lots of relatives. And on that day, the kindergarten was closed so people had brought their toddlers and babies along too. I was surprised by the figures they were giving out. I said to myself, how could there be only 350 people in there, if there are a thousand registered pupils at the school? There must be at least a thousand people in there.' Some local people vented their rage on the journalists in their midst, blaming the messenger for the faulty information. A number of journalists and members of the production crews of Russian and foreign television channels and newspapers were roughed up by local youths, some brandishing rifles.

The mother of Albert Sidakov, who was shot in the back by one of the terrorists as he tried to escape on the first day, can see no justification for the error. She is convinced that the number given out was not even an accurate reflection of the lists that had been compiled in front of her. 'How could they give out that number? Nobody can answer me that question,' she says. 'Basic arithmetic would tell you it was wrong: if there had only been twenty people to a class and at least three classes to a year, that would be sixty people per year, and there were far more than that because it was a very good school. Sixty times eleven is 660, not 350. So why did they give out false information? Why? Just looking at the lists that were circulating and counting up in your head, you could tell that the official figure was wrong. I counted five hundred names on the list that was being compiled near me. There were lists being made in three other places. So why did they give out those wrong numbers? The government must have known they were wrong from the very first day.'

The man who had the job of announcing official estimates of the number of hostages in School No. 1 was Lev Dzugaev, then head of the North Ossetian President's Information and Analysis Office. At the trial of Nurpashi Kulaev, Dzugaev was asked repeatedly to account for the wrong information he had given. He came across as officious and dislikeable. He got angry with the constant questioning on the same theme, but could give no adequate defence of his actions. In the end he said, 'Not one of the figures that we are discussing now was

right. On a recording of some television footage I saw someone in the crowds holding a placard aloft which said that
there were 800 hostages in the school. This turned out not to
be an accurate reflection of reality either, didn't it? So if I had
said there were 800 or 1,000 hostages, I would have been just
as inaccurate as when I said there were 354.'

Dzugaev's words reflect the authorities' handling of the
siege in general: mismanagement and incompetence that have
been followed by an arrogant resistance to criticism and
accountability; chaos inside the school matched by chaos outside. Before Larisa Mamitova emerged from the school with
the terrorists' first communication, a crisis committee had
been formed and large concentrations of army, police and
other emergency services had established a cordon around the
school, moving locals back to what was considered a safe distance. An assortment of different military and emergency
organizations had been scrambled to the town. Like the relatives of the hostages, the soldiers and emergency workers were
left waiting for any development, kicking the dust and smoking. For some reason, the cordon was not very secure: on
several occasions, local men, angered by the lack of developments, succeeded in breaking through.

Supposedly at the centre of the government's response to
the siege, the crisis committee was a shadowy and dysfunctional body. During its short life it had two heads: At some
point on the first day President Dzasokhov handed control
on to Vasilii Andreev, the head of the North Ossetian branch
of the Federal Security Service or FSB, the successor to the
KGB. Some of the people who were supposedly members of
the committee were not informed of the fact until after the
siege was over. Other groups vied with it for supremacy, and
more senior officials, especially those from Moscow, ignored
it altogether. It managed to do some obvious things:
Vladikavkaz Airport, which is on the outskirts of Beslan,

was closed, as was North Ossetia's border. A trained police negotiator was brought from Vladikavkaz, and food and medical supplies were requested. Beyond this, the committee's response was weak. Even though there were thousands of relatives thronging Beslan's streets, the authorities failed to compile accurate information about the identity of the hostages. They issued contradictory orders and, even worse, it seems likely that a number of them had conversations with the terrorists which were kept secret from the official negotiator and other members of the committee.

Quite rightly, the local Minister of Education, fifty-year-old Alina Levitskaya, was made a member of the crisis committee. But, though she hurried to Beslan after hearing of the attack and offered her services directly and in person to the North Ossetian President, her membership of the committee was kept secret from her. She had stood for some minutes in the room that was operating as a headquarters, watching her male colleagues who were clustered around a map spread out on a table. As well as President Dzasokhov, there was the Chairman of the North Ossetian parliament, Taimuraz Mamsurov, all of the local security chiefs and some federal officials as well. When the President spoke to her, he told her to return to Vladikavkaz and do her best to ensure that the Republic's other schools continued to operate as normally as possible. This was strange in itself, given that most North Ossetian schools had closed spontaneously on hearing of the siege. Alina obeyed the instructions, returning to Beslan each evening during the siege to stand in the crowds of relatives hoping to hear about what was going on. She wanted to show solidarity with the relatives of those inside and was anxious to find out if she knew anyone who was being held in the building. She did not return to the control room she had been in on the first day.

Alina was shocked to learn, several days after the end of the siege, that she had been a member of the crisis committee. She says, 'I found out that I was a member of the committee sitting in parliament on 10 September, when the leader of the government was called upon to make a speech. People started asking him questions and from his answers I found out for the first time that there had been a crisis committee, that it had been led by Major-General Andreev and that I had apparently been on it. Up to then I just assumed that the military and the Special Forces would have had control of everything. I neither attended a single meeting of the committee, nor was I invited to. No one asked my opinion about anything. In fact, I hardly spoke at all to any of the people on the committee throughout the entire siege.'

According to protocol, the official crisis committee should have had absolute control of all decisions and actions taken by the authorities. But there is reason to believe that it operated mainly as a facade for the real decision-makers behind the scenes. They were President Putin's close associates, the national heads of the FSB, Nikolai Patrushev, Vladimir Pronichev and Vladimir Anisimov. Many people are convinced that this kitchen cabinet, operating with the blessing, and possibly the presence, of Putin himself, took all the significant decisions, ignoring or pulling rank on the official committee as the situation required. The official crisis committee could not just be disbanded as its operation provided vital cover, and eventually a scapegoat, for those who really wielded power. When leadership of the committee was transferred from President Dzasokhov to Major-General Andreev its dependence on and subordination to the FSB in Moscow was complete. Patrushev was Andreev's boss; in hierarchical Russia, it was unthinkable that the general would go against his superior's orders. The decision to make an FSB man head of the crisis committee seems to have been taken by President Putin himself.

What is known of the rescue effort relates mostly to the activities of the official crisis committee. Even much of this is patchy and contradictory because of the failure to keep written records and the fact that those involved often have widely divergent memories of what took place. Suspicions are raised further by the fact that each official's story exonerates them absolutely.

When they received Larisa Mamitova's note from the terrorists the officials had mixed feelings. Though they were relieved to be able to make contact with the school, they remained worried by the approach of the terrorists. There were no demands for the release of Chechen or Ingush prisoners from North Ossetian jails, as some on the crisis committee had leaked to the media. There was a feeling that this would have been a price worth paying for the release of the hostages. They had not yet made explicit their demand for the removal of Russian troops from Chechnya, a demand so extreme that it could have been dismissed as unrealistic: at the time of the Beslan siege, there were still over 50,000 Russian troops stationed in the separatist republic, backed up by another 250,000 garrisoned in neighbouring regions, including North Ossetia. Instead, the terrorists had asked to speak to some high-ranking politicians, President Dzasokhov among them. This was at once reasonable and chilling. If they agreed to negotiate and then failed, the politicians would be personally implicated. If the negotiations were to be held face to face, the politicians might well be killed. Nonetheless, it was clear to the authorities that a refusal to negotiate with the terrorists would be indefensible to most of the general public, who felt little love for their elected representatives at the best of times.

The person waiting to begin negotiations on the government side was Vitalii Zangionov, a forty-three-year-old with professional training who belonged to the North Ossetian FSB. He had been dispatched to Beslan soon after the start of the siege and had been waiting all morning to make contact with the terrorists. Zangionov explains the responsibilities of the negotiator: 'I had to try to make psychological contact with the terrorists, not just to work out their demands, but also to build up psychological profiles of them. This way, we can eventually hope to appeal to them as human beings, as ordinary citizens. We can hope to convince them not to commit criminal acts and not to allow others around them to either. We can induce them to make demands and wait while they are met. This is what I tried to do in Beslan.'

Zangionov did not see the note but he was given the mobile phone number and told to start negotiations. 'We started trying to phone the number. The line was dead. The phone had been switched off.' Their hearts sank as they kept dialling without success. They were at a loss to understand what had happened; many decided that this was the terrorists' sick joke. As lunchtime approached, the crisis committee was becoming increasingly desperate. They now drafted in the leader of North Ossetia's small community of indigenous Muslims and asked him to talk with the terrorists via a megaphone. It was implausible that the terrorists would welcome such overtures: Ossetians, whether Muslim or Christian, are disliked by Ingushetians and Chechens. Zangionov drove the Mufti as close to the school as possible in a police car. Each time he addressed the school through the megaphone, apparently speaking in Chechen and Arabic, the car came under fire. No other contact was made.

Inside the school, Larisa Mamitova kept watch closely to see if the outside world had made contact with the terrorists. As time passed, she became more and more concerned that negotiations were not taking place. The terrorists on guard in the gym kept saying that the government's failure to phone meant that it couldn't care less about the hostages. Larisa overheard a report on the portable radio of one of the terrorists which stated that the telephone number she had given to the authorities didn't work. She bravely got to her feet and approached the terrorist. She insisted that he take her back to see the Colonel and he agreed.

Standing on the staircase, looking up, Larisa saw the Colonel emerging from the staffroom.

'"What are you doing here?" he said to me.

'"You do know, don't you, that the number you've given them doesn't work? They can't get in touch with you." I answered. "Let me take another note out."

'"What do you mean, they can't get in touch with us? They can any time they want to; they just don't want to. How do you know whether my phone is blocked or not?"

'When I told him that I'd heard it on the radio, he asked me who had allowed me to listen to a radio. I told him that I had overheard it by chance, while I was sitting in the gym. I went up the stairs to him and he started writing again. Then he took hold of what he had written, screwed it into a ball and threw it away.

'I picked it up. "Please! I beg you to let me take this out to them. I won't ask you for anything else again. Just let me take it out and that'll be it." He got me to write the rest of the note. He said none of them were able to because they were so on edge: "Our nerves are at breaking point."'

Taking her son's white T-shirt with her, Larisa set off to deliver this second note. Snipers were again placed in the first-floor windows to deter her from trying to escape. The terrorists who opened the doors for her quickly ran and hid. She walked up to the gates onto Comintern Street and started screaming and shouting to get the attention of someone in the crowds. 'Nobody came near me. They all stood looking and some told me to come over to them. "I'm not allowed to!" I shouted. "Someone will have to come over here and take the note!" But still nobody came.'

Suddenly a man ran up to the other gates, which led out into a housing estate. He told Larisa to come to him but she hesitated, reluctant to do anything that might irritate her captors. 'In the end I went. I screamed at him, "Don't believe what they are saying on the radio and the television. It's all lies. There are more than 1,300 of us." (I had counted all the hostages in one corner of the gym for myself and then multiplied the number up. That's how I got to 1,300.) "The whole place is booby-trapped. For God's sake, don't let anyone shoot at us. Get them to phone on the new number."'

Back in the gym once more, Larisa knew within minutes that contact had finally been made. All the terrorists suddenly looked elated. They were talking excitedly to each other in Chechen and Ingush. She could make out the names Dzasokhov, Zyazikov and Roshal: people they now felt confident they would get to see.

The new number was given to Zangionov. He dialled it and one of the terrorists answered. 'I introduced myself as a representative of the leadership of North Ossetia. Then I explained why we hadn't been able to make contact with them earlier; that the telephone number they had given was blocked. The terrorist on the other end answered with profuse swearing ... He was swearing so much it was difficult to understand him. But the gist of what he told me was that he had just shot twenty people and blown up another twenty in a classroom.' The demand to speak with Presidents Dzasokhov and Zyazikov and Dr Roshal was reiterated, and a new name was added to the list, Aslambek Aslakhanov, President Putin's special advisor on Chechen affairs.

'The terrorists' negotiator says, "If you don't get us them in the next three hours, I'll kill another twenty hostages. And so on, and so on, until they do arrive. I've got plenty of time and plenty of hostages as well." I told him that we hadn't been expecting something like this to happen and that the people they wanted to speak to weren't readily accessible; that we'd have to round them up. He just repeated that they had plenty of time to wait. I remember them saying they'd wait up to three days while we brought them the people they wanted to talk to.' Zangionov managed to get the terrorist to agree to receive calls from him every half hour or so. Before the call ended, the negotiator warned the terrorists not to harm any of the hostages and asked them what other demands they had. His response was, 'We have no other demands.'

In the conversations that followed, Zangionov was assisted by a psychologist who sat listening to every call. The negotiator's challenge was to elicit as much information as possible from the terrorists and, even more importantly, establish a relationship with them. Zangionov admits that on both fronts he had little success. 'Unfortunately over the course of the three days, I wasn't able to establish any kind of psychological relationship, no matter how hard I tried. Everything they were offered they refused. They swore at us and insulted us all the time. We offered them an escape corridor to safety. We offered them money. We offered them a human shield. But they turned everything down. They said that they hadn't come here for money and that they wouldn't be bought by us.' The negotiator tried to get them to talk to representatives of the media. 'We thought that they might be more willing to explain their demands to journalists. There were representatives of Al-Jazeera and the main Russian TV channels there, and we offered them anyone they wanted. But they only wanted to negotiate with the four politicians they had named – that was it. Even if we offered them the chance to talk to one or other of them alone, they refused and demanded to see four of them at once. They told me, "We need all four. If you send one in on his own, we will shoot him."'

Zangionov also tried to get the terrorists to allow supplies of food and water into the school. Every half hour, the voices on the other end of the line refused: according to them, there was no need because the children had announced their own hunger strike in sympathy with the terrorists' aims.

'THE REVOLUTION FUCKED EVERYTHING UP'

The antagonism between the peoples of the North Caucasus developed over millennia, passed on not just from generation to generation, but also between different tribes. However, the specific grudges and grievances that are the flesh on those rancorous bones today are much younger, and mostly date from the twentieth century. Though some people hark back to wrongs committed in previous centuries, most in the North Caucasus can find enough unfairness in their recent history to justify anger and revenge. For different ethnic groups the starting points and important episodes are different, but the narrative of dispossession and distrust is the same. Insofar as I understand the psychologies of these intensely local dynamics, I have Vadim to thank for it.

I first met Vadim on a street corner, our mutual acquaintance hastily withdrawing once the introductions were complete. We smiled at one another and Vadim shrugged. We were both uncertain about how to proceed. All I had been told was that he was a Cossack and could tell me about the history of the North Caucasus, in particular about Chechnya, where he had lived most of his life. This was important because the war-torn republic's turmoil and distress had direct links to the siege of School No. 1, but it wasn't safe for me to go there myself. I learned more about the Caucasus, past and present, from him than from anyone else I have ever met. Through his own sobering biography and those of the friends he described, Vadim showed me what the impact of the twentieth century has been on the North Caucasus.

Born in Grozny in 1931, at the time of our meeting he was seventy-three. Short and plump, though with the look of someone who had lost weight through illness or stress, Vadim was hardly ever without a cigarette. Having not smoked for thirty years, he had re-acquired the habit in his late sixties: 'In Grozny in the 90s, there didn't seem much point in trying to prolong your life.' Because he was a Cossack, I had been suspicious that Vadim's version of history would be noticeably anti-Chechen and Ingush, and pro-Russian and Ossetian; I had assumed that he would be just one more heavily biased voice to add to all the others. I was wrong. Although he held high office in the local Cossack assembly, Vadim could see the events he had lived through from the perspective of all the different ethnic and sectarian groups involved. He had a natural gift for empathy that not only made him relatively impartial but also breathed new life into the anecdotes and family stories he told me.

Vadim took me back to 1917, the year that saw the beginning of many of the problems still causing violence and unrest in the Caucasus today. Through the winter of 1916 and 1917, many people in Europe were enduring terrible privations; but the people of Russia were suffering more than most. As the Great War rumbled on, the Russians lived under the constant threat of hunger, disease and death. These miseries led them to take grave steps to change their situation, removing Tsar Nicholas II from his throne in February 1917 and thereby ending centuries of autocratic rule. Throughout the vast territory of the old empire, people reacted in different ways to this event. Without doubt, there were those who felt sorrow and foreboding at the momentous attack on the Divine Right of Kings; but there were few who would not have agreed that the Romanovs had done much to hasten their own demise. Vadim's grandfather was one of those who greeted the event with excitement. With hindsight, Vadim disagreed: 'The Revolution fucked everything up down here.'

Vadim's grandfather was delighted by Tsar Nicholas's passing because of his political beliefs. He was one of the leaders of the Menshevik faction of the Social Democratic Workers Party in Grozny and had long ago come to the conclusion that there could be no accommodation with the Tsar. This was the chance he and his political comrades had awaited for decades: a chance to argue their ideals and policies freely without threat of persecution and, surely, to play a part in moving Russia towards both socialism and democracy. Vadim's father, a teenager in the years immediately following the Revolution, was also enthralled by the exciting events he saw taking place around him. He had been born at the height of the Russian Empire's earlier, unsuccessful, revolution in 1905 and, after school, went on to graduate from Grozny's prestigious Pushkin Institute in the 1920s as an engineer, one of the professions most valued by Communists.

In the excitement of the first few months after the Revolution, Vadim's grandfather, like people with political convictions throughout the country, debated with his opponents, joined and abandoned short-lived alliances all the time, and tried to interest the masses in his message. In the power vacuum, impromptu councils and parliaments sprang up everywhere. Some groups were able to claim limited authority over the areas in which they operated. But more often these politicians could only speak reliably on behalf of their own narrow set of admirers. Even the biggest centres of power, the Provisional Government and the Petrograd Soviet, both based in the capital, had little clout outside the city and its hinterland.

The irrelevance of conventional politicians was most marked in the North Caucasus, where their ideological standpoints, whether Marxist, like Vadim's grandfather's, liberal or conservative, had least to say to ordinary people. Certainly, many people in the region, like most Russians, wanted an end to the war and more land to farm; they needed more food and desperately wanted to stop sending their able-bodied sons to the front line. But they also viewed their predicament through the prisms of ethnicity, religion and ancestral territories. As they emerged from Tsarist domination, the peoples of the North Caucasus were determined to become masters of their own destinies.

There were plenty who felt that the region must split from Russia, irrespective of whether Russia became democratic or not. There were others who feared such a bold move. Many with Western political ideologies favoured a settlement that would lead to a unified North Caucasian state, whether inside Russia or not. Vadim's grandfather was one of them; he hoped to create a kind of precursor to Yugoslavia, a North Caucasian 'rainbow nation'.

But, while these self-appointed representatives debated with one another and canvassed amongst their small constituencies, ordinary North Caucasians felt the old enmities begin to stir again. Disputes and grudges, some of them stretching back beyond living memory, came to the forefront of people's minds as the general chaos seemed to goad them into action. According to a British spy who was working for anti-Communist forces in the North Caucasus, 'the collapse of central authority and the absence of other appeals to their loyalties produced in people an unconscious reversion to dormant loyalties of a more local character'. Out of these age-old divisions, national identities had begun to form, and many tribal leaders in the North Caucasus learned to express their ambitions in the new jargon of nation states and self-determination. When politicians like Vadim's grandfather did have success with ordinary people in a particular town or village, it was often because of their ethnic identity or following a decision to hitch their wagon to some local dispute.

Before long the removal of strong central control led to the outbreak of fighting across the North Caucasus. At first, the violence was sporadic and isolated, not very different from the low-level riots and revolts that had become commonplace during the last years of the Tsar's rule. In late 1917 the fighting began to intensify. In Grozny, Vadim's father witnessed pitched battles between Cossacks and Chechens, which led to the city's oil wells, its main source of income, being set alight. The fires burned for eighteen months. Where Ossetians and Ingush lived near to one another there was fighting too. In December, five of Vladikavkaz's Ingush population were murdered, probably by Ossetians, leading to acts of retaliation by other Ingush in and around the city. The muted New Year celebrations for 1918 saw Ossetians from the villages around the city, including Beslan, forming themselves into paramilitary bands and marching in to 'rescue' the local population from Ingush aggression. They were assisted in this by the Cossacks.

Vadim's grandfather, like many of the politically active, looked on with growing dismay, convinced that, by fighting one another, ordinary people – the peasants and the workers – were acting against their own best interests. Another extremely significant event at the end of 1917 also caused him concern: the news that a rival faction of the Social Democratic Workers Party, the Bolsheviks led by Lenin, had seized control of the Petrograd Soviet and had removed the Provisional Government from power. The party had split acrimoniously in 1903 and now operated as two separate entities. The Bolsheviks, renamed the Communist Party, were to rule

Russia for the next seventy-three years. Though Vadim's grandfather had a certain amount of sympathy for any socialist group, he believed the Bolsheviks to be thuggish and underhand. In his eyes, they had deliberately misinterpreted Marx's theories to justify their own plans. Though he was prepared to offer them his support wherever they were the main socialist presence in the North Caucasus, he hoped that their brand of revolution would not be the one to win through.

Throughout late 1917 and the first half of 1918, socialists of all persuasions, the Bolsheviks included, continued to encourage warring ethnic groups to make common cause against their class enemies. Sergei Kirov, the local Bolshevik leader, like Vadim's Menshevik grandfather, was upset by the lack of cooperation between Caucasians of similar economic classes. Early in 1918, he described how a 'black hand' was stirring up ethnic hatred across the region in an attempt to frustrate the revolution. (Like many others with socialist convictions, he refused to accept that ethnic strife was more organic in the North Caucasus than any other form of protest.) There were patronizing attempts by North Caucasian socialists and liberals to arbitrate in disputes between different ethnic groups, but these were usually unsuccessful. The councils and other self-appointed groups had no authority to propose, much less enforce, changes to the status quo, so their advice usually amounted to 'wait and see': everything would be sorted out once a socialist state had been created.

By the middle of 1918, much of the rest of Russia was collapsing into civil war. Anti-socialist armies, known as the Whites, were being formed by Russians sympathetic to the deposed Tsar or the Provisional Government and were receiving some support from Western countries, including the United Kingdom. It was inevitable that the North Caucasus – as strategically vital as it had been in the eighteenth century – would be drawn into any wider conflict. The civil war was to be exceptionally vicious. For every Russian who benefited from the orgy of violence, there were dozens throughout the old empire who endured worse privations than they had ever known before, even at the height of the Great War. Crimes against humanity – rapes, torture and summary executions – were daily occurrences. Alliances of convenience were formed between groups with disparate aims. As in all civil wars, treachery and betrayal were everywhere. In the North Caucasus, where retribution and vendetta were ways of life, the situation was even worse than elsewhere. The British spy based in the region later said that Caucasian men 'still knew how to use knives and I saw bodies of women with their breasts cut off, pregnant women with their bellies split open, men with the penis cut off and stuck into the mouth to add insult to injury'.

Increasingly sensing the likelihood of an attack from outside, the socialist politicians in the region were keen to have as much support as possible amongst the local population, especially of the armed variety. Suddenly they ditched their former even-handed approach and took sides in ethnic disputes. Generally, they backed the Chechens and Ingush, and assumed that ordinary Ossetians and Cossacks would support the pro-Tsarist, pro-Orthodox Whites. In socialist terms, they justified this decision by saying that the Chechens and the Ingush, and other Muslim mountain tribes, had been more persecuted than the Ossetians and Cossacks under the Tsarist regime. Now, when the Chechens and the Ingush demanded that the Cossacks and Ossetians hand over significant amounts of land that had been stolen from them, the socialists backed them up, including some, like Vadim's grandfather, who were Cossacks and Ossetians by birth. That this move won them the support of some of the most tenacious and brutal fighters anywhere in the former Russian Empire cannot have been lost on the socialists.

With their new supporters the Chechens and Ingush felt relatively secure throughout the remainder of 1918. But, early in the next year, the socialists of the North Caucasus were forced to flee as the largely pro-Tsarist Whites took over the region. General Denikin's Volunteer Army marched into the resort town of Pyatigorsk on 20 January and continued westwards, taking the Chechen capital Grozny only sixteen days later and reaching Vladikavkaz five days after that. In taking Grozny, the Whites reputedly captured 50,000 Red prisoners of war, many of them Chechen and Ingush fighters. The pendulum had swung briefly in favour of the Ossetians and the Cossacks. Many of them joined Denikin's forces to help them hold on to the North Caucasus.

The Chechens and the Ingush fought against the Whites, hastening the return of the official Red Army towards the end of the year. For once, they were on the winning side; the Ossetians and the Cossacks had been forsaken by the new Russians. When the Communist forces flooded back into the region, finally reaching Vladikavkaz in March 1920, they returned for good, having destroyed the Whites elsewhere.

The victorious Communist Party set about organizing the North Caucasus as it saw fit. They rewarded the Chechens and Ingush with the long-awaited transfer of Cossack and Ossetian land. To indicate the permanency of the change, a year later, the Communist regime deported thousands of Cossacks to other parts of Russia. As late as 1926, as part of a package of administrative changes, the government awarded the newly created autonomous Ingush Republic a significant amount of land that many thought of as Ossetian. North Ossetians insist to this day that this territory contained only one Ingush inhabitant for every twenty Ossetians.

In all things, the Chechens and Ingush were initially

favoured above the Ossetians and the Cossacks. The Communists developed and promulgated theories about the innately revolutionary mindset of these peoples that were not very different from Romantic notions of noble savagery from a century earlier. With some exceptions, the Ossetians and Cossacks were backward and reactionary, and were variously described as feudal and bourgeois. Vadim's family was not amongst the Cossacks evicted from the North Caucasus by the Communists in the early 1920s. Living in Grozny, they were urbanized and modern, just the kind of people whose support the new regime wanted. The Mensheviks, Vadim's grandfather's political movement, were disbanded by the victorious Bolsheviks, who had established themselves at the helm of a one-party state. Nonetheless, having survived the initial purge, he and his children were accepted as 'fellow travellers' of the new regime and allowed to play a part in the building of socialism. In 1924, Vadim's father was invited to become a member of the Communist Party, the only way in to the new elite. He agreed. 'It was the normal thing to do back then,' Vadim told me.

Though not in a high position, Vadim's father, with his engineering qualifications, was an important cog in the young socialist state as it sought to modernize itself in the late 1920s and early 30s. Then as now oil was a vital Russian export. Vadim's father was put in charge of constructing a pipeline to carry it across the North Caucasus from the fields near Grozny to the tankers on the Black Sea. 'My father had several thousand men under him,' Vadim told me proudly as we stepped into the meeting room of the Cossack assembly, housed in a small, neat cottage. He bowed before the icon of the Virgin Mary and crossed himself three times. For Vadim, there was no contradiction between his father's achievements in the service of Communism and his own fervently held faith in God; nor did he feel that his

Orthodox beliefs automatically made him an enemy of Muslims and Jews. Sitting down only briefly, Vadim told me that we would have to go back outside. In the dim porch once more, he lit a cigarette and explained, 'I never smoke in front of the Mother of God'.

Despite the new state's bias towards the Chechens and Ingush, there were still some among the mountain peoples who were not prepared to accept it. A proportion of the Chechen population continued to fight after the end of the Civil War, turning their guns on the Communist forces who wanted to be seen as their champions. Throughout 1920 and 1921, as life regained some normality elsewhere, the Red Army was obliged to continue fighting a campaign against this small band of mountain guerrillas. As in the nineteenth century, soldiers who had gained control of an entire continent were made to look incompetent by a small band of poorly armed fighters. Living mainly in the most mountainous parts of the region, these warriors were not prepared to submit to any outside rule. Highly religious and self-consciously copying the nineteenth-century resistance fighters headed by Shamil, this group despised everyone, including fellow Chechens, who had accepted the deal offered by the godless socialists. Their leader promised 'to weave a rope to hang the students, the engineers, the intellectuals and more generally all those who write from left to right'. Communist government was no different to Tsarist government: both were Russian and, therefore, evil.

When the Soviet government turned against the Chechens and the Ingush in the 1940s, accusing them of collaborating with the Nazis, those who had kept up the fight against Communist and Russian rule felt vindicated. As one Chechen writer put it to me, 'normal service from the Russians was resumed'. Russians, whatever their political persuasion, could never accept the Chechen and Ingush way of life, with its emphasis on freedom and independence. More importantly, Russians could never be trusted to deal fairly with anyone. Amongst those who fought the Red Army the longest in the 1920s was the Basaev clan, one of whom was the grandfather of Shamil, the terrorist who, eighty years later, was the mastermind of the siege at School No. 1.

'THERE WASN'T EVEN ANY AIR TO BREATHE'

As darkness began to fall in Beslan on 1 September, it became obvious to all that they would be spending the night there. There was to be no quick escape, but in many ways nightfall came as a relief. All day the weather in Beslan had been sunny and hot. Inside the gym it had been stifling and only with evening did the unbearable temperature begin to drop a little. Even so the hostages continued to remove their clothing, leaving themselves with only enough to stay decent. Eventually, their thoughts turned to sleep. Mothers and grandmothers counselled the young to rest. They made promises they could not keep about how things would be different in the morning.

To help maintain quiet in the gym the terrorists sent mothers with babies to sit in one of the changing rooms along the corridor. Many children were so exhausted that they were ready to go to sleep and this also made the crowded hall less noisy. Consequently the terrorists on guard became calmer; the silence they had shouted and screamed for was ultimately achieved by a combination of darkness, hunger and exhaustion. Even some of the adult captives, anxious and scared though they were, closed their eyes for a time and forgot briefly their terrible surroundings, before their own thoughts or the sound of gunfire brought them sharply back to reality. For many, however, the night was a time to be alone with their fears. A stormy downpour in the middle of the night refreshed the air a little. Nevertheless, the night was only slightly less awful than the day. Mother of three, Larisa Tomaeva, said, 'How we got through that first night God alone knows.'

Early in the evening, Larisa Mamitova had been given permission to go to the toilet. Every so often on the first day the terrorists allowed hostages out of the gym in groups of ten. The numbers involved, the length of time it took and the frequency with which the privilege was withdrawn meant that only a tiny fraction of the hostages got the opportunity. Mostly they were the people sitting closest to the entrance, and, once outside, they were able to drink water from the taps as well as relieve themselves. Larisa was one of a lucky few.

As she came back into the hall, one of the terrorists handed her a plastic bag containing Snickers bars, dates and raisins; he told her to hand them out to the youngest hostages. This act went against the terrorists' policy, as stated to the official government negotiator Zangionov, of forcing the hostages to observe a hunger strike. It is almost certain that the food had been raided from the school canteen and it is probable that the terrorist who gave it to Larisa was acting without the Colonel's knowledge. Perhaps he hoped to silence the screaming children; perhaps the abject cruelty of refusing to feed them had pricked his conscience. Larisa moved through the room, handing food out to mothers and telling them to give the food to the youngest sitting around them.

Not for the last time, the many scenes of distress that she saw as she walked through the gym stuck in Larisa's mind. Many people, the children especially, were desperate for the toilet. Although it was more than twelve hours since they had last been, many were still holding on, trying to preserve their dignity in front of parents, teachers and friends. Most acute were the destructive effects of the heat. 'The babies were shrieking so much. It was unbearable in there; it was so stuffy. Even the terrorists started taking their masks and camouflage jackets off because of the heat. They started walking around in just their vests. It was hard to breath. People had undressed their children as well and were starting to undress themselves. It was intolerable.'

Once Larisa was back in her place beside Tamerlan, Khodov, the terrorists' second-in-command, began asking her questions.

'Where do you work?'

'Here, in the town hospital. And in the hospital in Elkhotovo.'

'In Elkhotovo?'

'"Yes," I said, and I thought to myself that he had probably never heard of the place.' Suddenly, Khodov turned on Larisa and started shouting at her incomprehensibly; something had made him very angry.

Weeks later someone told Larisa that Vladimir Khodov had spent much of his childhood in the small town of Elkhotovo, about twenty miles from Beslan. His Ukrainian Christian mother was a nurse there and had worked alongside Larisa. When the doctor thought about it, she remembered the woman. She had even known that there were two sons in the family. But she was not close to the woman and did not hear about her children's problems, neither Boris's conviction for murder, nor Vladimir's for rape. 'Maybe he got frightened that I would recognize him or something. Maybe that explains his sudden aggressiveness,' she said.

There was no question of sleep for Larisa. Traumatized by everything she had seen and heard and done during that first day, her mind was racing. She found herself unable to take her eyes off the terrorists sitting near her. In particular, she kept a

constant watch on the man who had his foot on the improvised detonator switch. Each time he was relieved by another
terrorist, she grew particularly anxious. The process they went
through was still etched in her memory. 'They were very careful changing over,' she recalled. 'When one was about to get
up, two others would hold the switch down with their hands,
while he lifted his foot off it. The new man would sit down
and move his foot onto it very slowly and the other two
would remove their hands.'

The P.E. teacher Alik Tsagolov was one of many hostages
who required regular medication. Alik was a diabetic and, by
the evening of the first day of the siege, he was beginning to
feel the adverse effects of the lack of food, water and insulin.
Like many older diabetics, he also suffered from poor circu-
lation and, without his pills, was getting pains in his limbs.
Hemmed in on the floor of the gym, Alik couldn't find the
space to rub life back into his numb legs. 'When I tried to lift
myself up, there wasn't even room to put the palm of my hand
on the floor,' he said. 'They had crammed us in there like sar-
dines in a can, so that there wasn't even any air to breathe.
Over the course of the siege, I was left terribly dehydrated.
Once before in my life I had been without water or food for
six days but that was nothing compared to how I felt even by
the evening of the first day in the school.'

Alik remembered seeing some buckets of water being carried in on the first day but he was sitting towards the back of
the gym and they had been emptied long before they got anywhere near him. 'People wanted their medications even more
than they wanted water. But nobody got any medication as far
as I saw. We just shared out the medicines hostages had in
their pockets between those of us who needed them. When
asked, the terrorists would lie and say, "This is no hospital,
you know. We have a man injured and we haven't asked for
any medication."' From the very outset, Larisa Mamitova had

been ordered to treat injured terrorists. Alik did not sleep while in the gym. Instead, he sat up listening for the shots which the terrorists periodically exchanged with the outside world. He waited expectantly for each fresh burst of fire until the shooting no longer even caused him to start.

Other people were deep in thought as well, their children dozing around them and on top of them, making pillows out of their stomachs and thighs. While her children slept, Elvira Tuaeva reflected on what she believed to be the terrorists' demands. The rumour had reached her – as it had many people in the gym – that they were asking for the complete withdrawal of Russian troops from Chechnya. The very idea seemed absurd to her. 'When I heard that, I just sighed. I remember thinking, "Oh my God! It can't be true. They couldn't really have thought that such a global issue could be solved by holding our children hostage." Naturally I was really frightened by that; not for myself but for the children. For all the children.' Elvira's own son and daughter were beside her. During the first moments of the siege she had been unable to find Karina, but the two had been reunited inside the gym.

In the rest of Beslan, very few people slept either. Just outside the school, many worried bystanders continued their vigil through the night. They hardly noticed the torrential rain as it soaked through the clothes they had put on hours before, at the beginning of a hot, sunny day. Though the air became fresher, the thunder and lightning heightened the sense of doom.

'SO YOU'VE NOTICED, THEN'

When I was tired or wanted to be alone in Beslan, there was a small bakery I would visit for coffee. It was dark inside and very basic. The only coffee was Nescafé; there was only one type of sweet pastry; and the single table and chair were both rickety. As I sat there reading the paper or writing up my notes, I seemed to be invisible. People came to buy loaves and went away again without giving me a second glance. Elsewhere in the town, they would give me hostile stares, guessing that I was another journalist in search of a story. At first the aged shop assistant Lena said nothing to me either as I ordered one coffee after another, gossiping instead with her friends and customers.

Some days had passed before Lena spoke to me. She asked me first what I was doing in the town. When I told her she looked at me for a long time, her hands positioned at her waist. I sensed that she was trying to decide what to tell me. Finally, 'You know it was the Ingush that did it, don't you?'

'The terrorists were a mixture of Ingush and Chechens, weren't they?' I corrected her.

Lena had come out from behind the counter to stand by the

wobbly table. 'It would never have happened if Stalin was still around. He was the friend of Ossetians. Nobody dared lay a finger on us then. I remember. There were no terrorists then.'

After all the silence, Lena's talkativeness took me by surprise. She told me that the local people felt such gratitude towards the dictator that they had erected a bust of him on a plinth in the main street. The money for the project had been raised by public subscription in the last five to ten years. Lena was adamant that I should go and see it. 'It's only when a great man dies that people realize what they've lost,' she said. 'Now people know how good he was to us, they want to honour him.' I thought to myself that it was amazing how potent and long-lasting a despot's personality cult can be.

Lena's attitude towards Stalin is not unusual in Russia today. After decades when the mention of his name caused loyal Communist Party members to wince and despite the endless stream of facts about his cruelty and sadism, the Great Leader is now more popular than at any time since 1956. In the last few years, official statues paid for with public money have been erected in a number of Russian cities. Pensioners like Lena in particular hanker after the certainties of that period: the society of obedience, which commanded respect internationally, where wealth was distributed fairly. But Stalin is held in the highest regard by many in North Ossetia. Despite the atrocities and harshness of his regime, he is viewed as the last Russian leader who truly had their interests at heart and appreciated their loyalty.

In reality, Stalin is a poor hero for any Russian, a madman who saw enemies everywhere and stopped at nothing to enforce his own will. In contrast to the Ossetians, the Chechens and Ingush and most others in the North Caucasus view Stalin as the man who persecuted them almost to extinction.

When Lenin died in 1924, a four-year power struggle ensued for the leadership of the Soviet Union. Eventually Josef Stalin

A portrait of Stalin on sale at a stall in Vladikavkaz

manoeuvred himself into a position of control. Born in the Georgian town of Gori as Josef Vissarionovich Dzhugashvili, he was a man with extensive personal knowledge of the Caucasus. He was raised by his mother Katerina. His father, probably a violent alcoholic, is a shadowy figure and was mostly absent. Some people have alleged that he was an Ossetian who went to Gori to find work. Some Ossetians thus claim the great dictator for themselves; their enemies use the fact to explain his supposed partiality towards the nation.

Under Stalin's rule the pace of change in the Soviet Union increased exponentially; so too did the amount of violence visited upon its citizens. For Stalin, violence and progress were inseparable. There was hardly anyone in the entire country who did not suffer because of Stalin's rule. Even those who were once his favourites fell from favour and were punished. One wave of repressions followed another, until almost no family was left untouched by the successive acts of state-sponsored terrorism. Even when the secret police were not involved, the fanatical manner in which Stalin went about his modernization programmes meant that many people's lives got worse instead of better.

In the early 1930s, the plan to amalgamate all of the country's farms into enormous state-run concerns and turn all farmers into workers of the state was a disaster. Collectivization caused enormous famines in which millions died. Farmers who resisted the destruction of age-old ways of life were branded as traitors and accused ridiculously of being members of the anti-revolutionary bourgeoisie. They were stripped of their land; many were deported to other parts of the country and a great number were killed. Resistance to collectivization was greatest in the most traditional areas of the country, particularly in the North Caucasus. Uprisings occurred in Chechnya and Ingushetia in the early 1930s. A number of Communist officials were murdered but the unrest was mercilessly and swiftly smothered by the Red Army. Ten years on from the Civil War, there was no longer any question of who was in the ascendancy.

Like everyone else in the Soviet Union, the Ossetians suffered under Stalin's crazy policies too, but their opposition was more muted than their neighbours'. In propaganda terms, the 1930s were boom years for North Ossetia, and for Beslan in particular. In 1927, a decision was taken to turn the small town's existing starch and molasses plant into an enormous maize-processing factory. The new concern, which opened in 1932, was apparently the second largest in the world. It is known locally as BMK and is still a major employer in the town. Beslan's population swelled, reaching almost 8,000 by 1939. A Workers' Club was built in 1936, complete with a hall for concerts and a small theatre. In the square outside, a statue was put up to the Ossetian national poet, Kosta Khetagurov. Reworking the old stereotype of loyal Ossetia, the impression was created that Ossetians were the most modern, hard-working and reliable ethnic group in the North

Caucasus. By contrast, it was increasingly clear that the Chechens and Ingush, though they had been very good at fighting the Whites in the Civil War, were not cut out for socialism.

Politically things improved for North Ossetia and worsened for Chechens, Ingush and others in the region, though these distinctions existed in an environment where the great mass of the population experienced hardship. Initially, after the Civil War, the various peoples of the North Caucasus had been lumped together in a single administrative unit, the Autonomous Mountain Republic. This had achieved little and was replaced in 1926 by a number of smaller territorial units created along ethnic lines. The North Ossetians had their own autonomous republic as did the Ingush and the Chechens. Uniquely, both the North Ossetians and the young Ingush republic had their administrative offices in Vladikavkaz, which existed as a kind of free city between the two. Apart from Vladikavkaz, a Russian creation with significant populations from both ethnicities, there was no city of sufficient size in either republic to act as an administrative centre.

Under Stalin in the 1930s this cohabitation ended. Vladikavkaz was given to North Ossetia, while the Ingush and Chechen republics were amalgamated into a single entity. Since that date, many Ingush have sought the 'return' of Vladikavkaz and many Ossetians have asserted that it always belonged to them. Not long ago, one notably rabid Ossetian commentator wrote that the Ingush had been allowed to keep their offices in the 'Ossetian capital' between 1924 and 1933 because they were too lazy and stupid to build themselves a single decent village, never mind a city.

Checking into my hotel in the centre of Vladikavkaz, I remarked casually to the woman at reception that the city looked beautifully bright and tidy in the spring sunshine. She smiled and repaid the praise by complimenting my shrewdness: 'So you've noticed, then ... Most people do notice how much cleaner and tidier things are in our little republic than in any of the others round about.' Many inferences flowed from this polite statement. Ossetians were not just cleaner than their neighbours, in this woman's opinion, they were better in many other ways as well; the people they had to live amongst were not just dirty, they were dangerous as well. She, and others like her, sounded more like colonials complaining about the natives – white settlers in Rhodesia or French Algerians – than representatives of an indigenous Caucasian people.

In the mid-1930s, the Soviet Union suddenly became an even more dangerous place to live in. The crimes committed by the state during the rest of the decade and throughout the next were to be colossal and horrific. Starting with its own supporters and sympathetic socialists, the Stalinist state moved through society arresting, convicting, torturing, jailing and killing millions of its own people. The misdemeanours people were accused of were conceived by minds that were paranoid and sadistic and fed by state-nurtured terror. Only Stalin, at the helm, acted with clarity and impunity. In theory, 'enemies of the people' had usually tried to destabilize Russian Communism in some way, often with the help of foreign powers, such as the United Kingdom and the United States.

To start with, in 1934, Stalin targeted those he thought might pose a threat to his leadership. Later, one had only to belong to the kinds of groups that might be resistant to Stalin's will. By the time Vadim's father was arrested in Grozny in 1938, the secret police had begun operating a quota system for arrests and executions: on 30 July 1937, the secret police had been told to arrest 259,450 people by the end of November; 28 per cent of detainees were to be killed. The following March, a new target for a further 57,200 arrests was imposed. They were to be even more threatening and consequently 84 per cent of them were to be murdered.

These quotas were only one element of the enormously successful death machine. Orders from the top were matched with hysterical enthusiasm from below. Networks of informers were ready to denounce colleagues and neighbours whose behaviour they found personally or politically distasteful or against whom they bore a grudge. Vadim's mother was always convinced that her husband was denounced by a jealous colleague. All across the North Caucasus, many Cossack, Ossetian, Chechen and Ingush families suffered in the same way because the regime had not yet begun to select its victims by their ethnicity.

'I remember it so well,' Vadim told me, though he was only seven at the time. The Secret Police came to their home with pistols and took his father away. At the time of his arrest, he had been in charge of constructing another oil pipeline in the Dagestani port of Izberbash on the Caspian Sea. Only a few weeks later, after a rubber-stamp trial, he was sawing wood in a prison mill in the frozen wastes of Siberia. 'They accused him of being an enemy of the people. They charged him under Section 58, but he didn't admit his guilt. If he had, they would have shot him for sure.' After losing her husband, Vadim's mother was evicted from her three-room flat and she and her two children were made to live in a single room.

For three years young Vadim heard nothing of his exiled father. Then, unannounced, he returned from imprisonment in 1941. Vadim has never been sure why he was released but thought that his father's brother might have had a hand in it. 'I heard once that he made a special plea on my father's behalf to a friend who worked high up in Gosplan, the Soviet State Planning Commission.' Vadim thought his father was probably freed because his skills as an engineer were desperately needed in the war against Nazi Germany which had just begun and had taken the entire Soviet nation by surprise.

Early on the morning of 22 June 1941, German troops had marched across the Soviet border and begun an amazingly swift advance through the country. Stalin was not prepared for an attack. His subjects had been lulled into a false sense of security by the Nazi–Soviet Pact which the dictator had signed with his opposite number in 1939. Even when faced with the attack itself, Stalin continued to search for alternative explanations, refusing to allow his generals to fight the advancing German forces for a full three hours. Within weeks, the Germans had gained control over almost half of the Soviet population and with them half of the country's infrastructure, including vital factories, raw materials and transport networks. Whatever the reasons for Vadim's father's release from prison, many more specialists with vital expertise were left in Siberia by the stubborn and fanatical regime.

The Second World War is viewed by many Russians as the Soviet Union's greatest achievement. At immense personal and national cost, the nation emerged victorious. Russians who are critical of every other aspect of Stalin's rule praise his management of the war. But while the sacrifices made by millions of Soviet citizens to rid Europe of Nazism cannot be honoured highly enough, the leader's own contribution was more questionable. As ordinary Soviet citizens did their best to fight the war, the leadership of the country continued to devote considerable energy to the hunt for internal enemies.

Now Stalin and his henchmen relied on ethnicity to determine who their enemies were. They built on a policy of mass deportation which had been trialled in the 1930s but, as with Hitler's Final Solution, they now perfected the process, dehumanizing it entirely and increasing the scale enormously. Back in the 1930s, indigenous Finnish, Polish, Iranian, Chinese and Kurdish populations had been forcibly resettled in the least hospitable parts of the Soviet Union. In 1937, 172,000 ethnic Koreans were evicted from their homeland in the Far East and made to live in the Kazakh desert. Soon after the start of the war, Stalin ordered the deportation of 900,000 ethnic Germans to Siberia and Kazakhstan. These deportees were never permitted to return.

Ostensibly, the purpose of the deportations was to prevent Germans from being able to collaborate with the Nazis. The same rationale was used to justify the deportations of other peoples that followed. In reality, ethnicity was not the main factor encouraging Soviet citizens to collaborate with the enemy. The desperate conditions of the preceding fifteen years of Stalinist rule were excuse enough. Russians and Ukrainians were defectors just as much, and – given the country's geography and demography – probably more, than other groups. Stalin was directly responsible for their treachery, for it was he who had created the world of fear, injustice and hunger in which they lived.

In the circumstances, it was surprising that so few people decided to sink their fortunes with the enemy. Wherever the Nazis had been, Stalin saw new enemies and took the opportunity to deport the ethnic minorities he found there. As the war wore on, the manner of their deportations grew more summary. The peoples of the North Caucasus were to suffer the most.

Early in 1942, the Germans began to enter the Caucasus from the north and the west. They occupied most of the west of the region, as far as Vladikavkaz in the south, and even pushed into parts of Chechen and Ingush territory to the north. Ultimately, they were halted and forced to turn back before they could reach Grozny, which as it had been for the Whites, was a key goal because of its oil wells. The Red Army defeated the Germans in Vladikavkaz in November 1942, and by January of the following year the occupiers had been removed from the entire mountain region. Key specialists and their families who had been evacuated from North Caucasian cities in advance of the German attack were allowed to return and the immediate threat of death at the hands of a foreign power was removed.

Just a few months after his father's return from his Siberian exile, Vadim's entire family was evacuated to the city of Orsk, hundreds of miles away near the border with Kazakhstan. His father worked in a factory there, while ten-year-old Vadim recovered from a serious bout of typhoid and eventually went to school. Though his father was engaged in important work, Vadim told me that their rations were insufficient. As in other wartime economies, the black market and informal barter were essential to survival. 'When we were on the way to Orsk, my father got off the train at one point and collected some enormous crystals of rock salt. In Orsk, my mother made ends meet by selling that salt and buying chickens with the money.' Early in 1943, after the Nazis' decisive defeat in Stalingrad to the north had made further intrusions less likely, Vadim's family were brought back to resume their life in Grozny.

Despite its victory in the region, the Stalinist regime was not happy with the behaviour of most of the indigenous North Caucasian tribes. Though the focus of the war had shifted away from the North Caucasus, Stalin remained obsessed with the place and began to hatch plans to deport hundreds of thousands of its inhabitants, apparently convinced that many had collaborated with the Nazis. First to go, in 1943, were 70,000 Karachais and 90,000 Kalmyks, evicted, like others before them, to the wastelands of Kazakhstan and Kirghizstan. Massive numbers of Security Service and military personnel were committed to the operations. According to some estimates, at times the 'deporters' outnumbered the 'deported' by two to one. On the freight trains that were commandeered to take 'enemy nations' to their new homes the death rate was very high. The Buddhist Kalmyks suffered disproportionately because they were transported at the height of winter. A yet more audacious deportation was in the making.

Early on the morning of 23 February 1944, twelve-year-old
Vadim was probably getting ready to attend a compulsory celebration for Red Army Day, one of thousands that were
taking place across the Soviet Union. He can't remember
because of what happened next. Suddenly his best friend's
father was standing at the door of their flat in Grozny. His
entire family, along with every other Chechen and Ingush in
the city and throughout the autonomous republic, had been
given two hours to pack enough clothes and food for a week
and told to present themselves at the central railway station.
They were to be deported to the desert. Vadim remembers
that Murat's father was quite calm. He asked Vadim's father
if he knew what was going on. He did not. Unbelieving, just
before lunchtime, Vadim walked his best friend to the train
station and said goodbye to him. They used to spend all their
time together. They loved wrestling. Only the day before they
had had their photograph taken together. Vadim takes out the
small black-and-white picture and shows it to me. Two smiling boys against a wall. They did not meet again for fourteen
years.

Vadim's immediate family was not affected by the deportations. Though his father had been imprisoned as a traitor only
a few years before, as an ethnic Cossack he was not 'eligible'
for banishment under the new criteria. But, elsewhere in the
city, his father's cousin Zhenya was preparing to leave. 'She
had married a Chechen man called Kazariev in 1923, just
after the Revolution. My father was the secretary of the local
branch of the Komsomol back then – he'd have been nineteen
or twenty – and it was he who introduced Zhenya to Said.' At
the time of the deportations, Said Kazariev had risen to be
Minister for Trade in the local government. Nonetheless, as a
Chechen, he was to be deported. His wife could have stayed
behind if she wanted to but she decided to travel with him to
Alma-Ata, then the capital of Kazakhstan. 'She wouldn't leave

her husband and so she went,' Vadim said with a wry smile. 'Wasn't she a great woman? Wasn't she devoted?' The two households worked hard throughout the day to transfer as much furniture and belongings as they could from Said and Zhenya's flat to Vadim's; the items remained there until 1957.

In the space of a week, 400,000 Chechens and 90,000 Ingush had been put on trains and sent to the east. The operation had been overseen by the highest authorities in the land, including Stalin himself and the psychotic leader of the secret police, Lavrentii Beria, who stayed in Grozny throughout. The choice of Red Army Day for the beginning of the manoeuvre was a sick twist almost certainly chosen by the leader himself. 120,000 secret police and internal security personnel were used in the operation, along with 13,000 railway goods wagons – all diverted to the North Caucasus during the most difficult war that Russia has ever fought. Long before the appointed day they had built up a presence in the large population centres and had penetrated deep into the mountains. Everything went according to plan. On 23 February, Beria sent a chillingly bureaucratic message to Stalin which read,

Today, at dawn, we began the operation to deport the Chechens and Ingush. The deportation is proceeding satisfactorily. There is nothing noteworthy to report. There have been six instances when people have offered resistance but they were all overcome either by arrest or the use of firepower. Of those identified for removal in connection with the operation 842 have been arrested. By 11 o'clock this morning, 94,741 people had been removed from their homes (i.e. more than 20 per cent of the total number requiring deportation) and 20,023 had been loaded onto railway wagons.

National Commissar for Internal Affairs of the USSR and General Commissar for State Security, L. Beria

In the mid-1950s, an American House of Representatives committee took evidence from a Soviet defector who had taken part in the deportations in a Chechen village. In this instance, the callous organizers had maintained the fiction of a day of celebration right up till the last moment:

On February 23, 1944, a festival was organized in every vil-lage to celebrate the anniversary of the foundation of the Soviet Army. There were bands, processions with slogans and banners, and speeches in praise of the Army and the regime. An officer of the M.V.D. brought the festival to an end by denouncing the entire people as collaborators and informing them of their collective sentence of transporta-tion. They were loaded into trains and dispatched to an unknown destination in Central Asia; local officials and Communist Party leaders were transported with the rest.

In many places, this ethnic cleansing was more brutal than any that had gone before. Many people – more than Beria hinted in his memo – were killed before they ever got to the trains. A heavy snowfall made it impossible for troops to march Chechens out of the remotest mountain villages and in many cases they chose to kill them instead, sometimes by burning them alive in their houses. Acknowledging the signif-icant Ingush population who lived in North Ossetia, the authorities sent troops to deport them too. By mid-March, 32,000 Ingush had been removed from their republic.

Whatever their other hardships, the North Ossetians undoubtedly benefited from these barbaric events, though they were utterly beyond their control. Their autonomous republic grew as districts of the old Chechen–Ingush republic were transferred to them. For the most part these had been Ingush lands, but all trace of their former owners was now erased. The districts were given Ossetian names: one became

Kosta Khetagurov district; others were Nartian and Alanian districts. Around 30,000 ethnic Ossetians, mostly from Georgia, moved into the vacated lands on a semi-voluntary, semi-compulsory basis. Once they had left, their home villages were barred to them. Unlike the deported Chechen and Ingush, however, they had ready-made homes and farms to move into. Of course, life continued to be hard for many, even most, Ossetians throughout the war and for the remainder of Stalin's reign. But it is hard to dispute the fact that the nation as a whole had once again become Moscow's favourite.

Eventually, the Second World War ended in victory for the Soviet Union. Since then, the victory and the sacrifices that made it possible have been commemorated annually on 9 May. The day remains much more important than other equivalent holidays in Western Europe, and is a central part of Russian national identity. In fact, hardly anything about the way that the war is remembered has changed since the collapse of Communism in the early 1990s. Saddest of all, the atrocities committed by Stalin against his own people are hardly ever mentioned; not only atrocities against ethnic minorities in the Caucasus and elsewhere, but also against returning Red Army heroes who were sent to prison camps for having become 'contaminated' by exposure to the West.

While in the North Caucasus, I was invited to attend one of these ceremonies in a school in Pyatigorsk. Parents and grandparents had crowded into the assembly hall along with a couple of rows of veterans to watch the children on the stage perform their act of remembrance. The scene had obvious and painful similarities to the Day of Knowledge celebrations in Beslan a few months before. These were not lost on the organizers, and a local police officer was checking passports at the school entrance. The ceremony was very accomplished; it felt as if the children were trying to prove to the veterans that they had understood the story of the war correctly. A banner across the proscenium arch announced, 'We Bow Down Before Those Great Years'. Many in the audience who were far too young to remember the war cried openly on several occasions as the programme of songs and readings and brief dramatic pieces was performed.

But the gaps in their narratives were as interesting to me as anything else. 'We must remember those who still wake up at night and hear the sound of bombs ringing in their ears,' the headmistress said in her address. But she meant only Nazi bombs. Most frighteningly, one young girl gave an oration which ended with the words, 'Though some now try to rewrite history, the truth remains the same.' Amongst the rousing sentiments, I had to fight to recall that some of the deportations had happened just down the road. All the talk was of brotherhood and unity. I heard the line, 'O Caucasus! We are all one another's brothers here. And we have one mother – Russia!'

The Ossetians were never targeted by Stalin for their ethnicity. The republic was given a special commendation for its

efforts in the war and, unlike the other embarrassing national minorities in the region, it became a place to which the Soviet government proudly brought foreign delegations. In the early 1950s, Indira Gandhi visited Vladikavkaz, as did a party from the pro-Stalinist British–Soviet Friendship Society. There had been a little coverage of the Chechen and Ingush deportations in the British media when news had trickled out after the war and, though their views were ideologically biased, the British visitors seemed to understand the lie of the land well enough. On his return, one of them, Brian Pearce, wrote, 'After the war, former Chechen–Ingush territories (the population of which was given the chance to develop elsewhere in the USSR) were assigned to North Ossetia.'

The British Stalinists were taken to see the BMK factory in Beslan. The place, which had been raised to the status of a town in 1950, continued to go from strength to strength. The visitors met shop stewards, many of whom were women, and saw the local shops stuffed with produce and consumer goods, evidence not only of cynical window-dressing, but also that the premises must have been models for their time. On their return from Beslan they wrote articles for a pamphlet, with titles like 'Making Maize More Useful' and 'From Poverty to Riches'.

As they toured around Beslan, the 1953 visitors probably saw many statues and portraits of Stalin prominently displayed. At that stage, just a few months after his death, the personality cult was still alive and well.

After I had finished my coffee in Lena's bakery, I went to see the Great Leader for myself. Though the location and the plinth were new, the bust was old. Throughout the Soviet Union, all monuments to Stalin were removed after Khrushchev's Secret Speech in 1956, in which he denounced some of his predecessor's worst excesses. His likeness survived only in a very small number of places. One of them, it seems,

was Beslan: an indication, if not proof positive, of an enduring and ardent affection. I walked towards the monument but
stopped several yards short of his bronzed face. I became
aware of locals staring at me, as they stood at the main bus-
stop and sat in their cars. Under the combined force of his and
their gaze, I was unsure about what it would be right to do. I
took a photograph of the statue and the large wreath that had
recently been placed underneath it (an offering from a grateful admirer) and walked quickly away.

'YOUR FATE IS ABOUT TO BE DECIDED'

As the second day in the gym dawned, the hostages wondered whether their prospects had got better or worse overnight. They were hungrier and thirstier than on the previous day. Though the night had brought rain, the day promised to be sultry again. Some still had faith that they would be rescued; others felt that a point in time had been crossed that made compromise and negotiation less rather than more likely. For hostages facing the windows, the monotonous view of other parts of the school building was depressing; the inability to see what the authorities were planning just out of sight increased the sense of powerlessness. Children woke up fractious and irritable; many had temporarily forgotten the events of the previous day. Enraged by the media's underestimation of the number of hostages, the terrorists now became crueller and less reasonable.

Elvira Tuaeva was one of many hostages who were concerned by the lack of any sign of negotiation. She was sitting with her two children, twelve-year-old Karina and ten-year-old Khetag. 'I was beside Irina, one of my colleagues from the gas board where I worked. She had come to school with her children and her mother-in-law. By lunchtime, I think, it became clear to us that no one from our side had started real negotiations with the terrorists yet. The terrorists themselves were telling us, "You are like a flock of innocent sheep that nobody gives a damn about."'

With desperation taking away her fear, Elvira decided to try convincing the terrorists to release some of the children. 'I asked them why they had decided to take so many children hostage and one of them said, "My children have been shot as well. Do you think your children are any better than mine? I have no interest whatsoever in what happens to your children."' She tried again, telling them that there would be nothing to be gained by holding on to the children. A terrorist replied to her, 'Dzasokhov is *your* president. *You* voted for him. He has stood idly by while the Russians have marched across your territory into Chechnya to kill our sisters and brothers, our mothers and children. Did you do anything to try to prevent that? Did you?'

Larisa Mamitova, the doctor who had twice delivered the terrorists' demands to the outside world, was given an even more difficult task to perform during the second day of the siege. She was put in charge of taking children to the toilets, a privilege which the terrorists offered and withdrew constantly. She had to be sensitive at all times to the fluctuating moods of those on duty to avoid exposing herself or the children to unnecessary danger. At around 10 a.m., the terrorists decided that even children would no longer be allowed to drink water. And they ordered Larisa to enforce the ban.

A terrorist turned off the tap that had been running constantly in one of the toilets since the beginning of the siege. He said to Larisa, 'If I see a single child going to the tap – even if it is your own child – I will shoot them dead.' After leading children to the toilet, Larisa then had to stand by the tap and explain to those who ran up to it that the water supply was poisoned. 'Then the children would ask if they could just wash their hands in it, and I had to explain to them that the water would hurt their hands as well. I couldn't bear to tell them that the terrorists had banned us from drinking.'

However, Larisa bravely did her best to flout the terrorists' instructions whenever she could. She devised a way of helping at least some of the most vulnerable children to take on water. She remembered that, in addition to the tap in the toilet, there was another in an adjacent shower room. When babies and toddlers were allowed out of the sports hall to go to the toilet an adult was also permitted to accompany them. Larisa whispered to these adults, mostly mothers, about the other tap. She told them to take their children into the shower room and let them drink from the tap, but to make sure that they dried their mouths afterwards and didn't get any water on their clothes. She dared not risk telling the older children who came out alone because she couldn't be certain that they would keep the secret.

Nevertheless, soon enough, one of the terrorists worked out what was going on. He screamed at Larisa, 'Didn't I tell you that they weren't allowed anything to drink!' Larisa's reply was unconvincing – 'I've never been in the school before. I didn't know that there was a tap in there' – but the man left her unharmed. Both the toilet and the shower room were now declared out of bounds, and some older school pupils were drafted in to pull up the floorboards and dig a pit in one of the classrooms using their bare hands. From now on this was to be the only toilet.

As the second morning of the siege wore on, conditions in the gym grew still worse. No more buckets of water and soaked rags were brought into the room. It became clear to Larisa that the hostages were getting more desperate. Her training and experience meant that she could spot the symptoms of stress and paranoia better than most. 'Some people were beginning to get hysterical. The terrorists never seemed to stop shooting at the ceiling. Some of the weakest hostages, especially very young children, were suffering from paralysis and in danger of losing consciousness. There was a girl in the gym who was a diabetic. She was lying beside her mother, but her breathing had become very laboured and she was going to die. They allowed me to take her out of the gym and lay her down in a changing room. I suppose I should have told the mother what would happen, but of course instead what I said was, "There's nothing to worry about. She's just sleeping. Calm down. It's all going to be okay." It was so difficult. I remember picking the girl up in my arms and almost running out of the gym with her.'

The passage of time hadn't made Larisa's memories of the gym any easier to bear. 'I find it hard to think about it at all now,' she said. 'I would announce that I could take people out to the toilet in groups of ten. Two or three hundred people would all start getting to their feet and start moving into the central pathway that there was through the middle of the hall, and then the terrorists would start shooting. The children would be scared stiff.'

Suddenly, early in the afternoon, just after what would normally have been lunchtime, the terrorists told Larisa that no more children were to go to the toilet. They couldn't put up with the commotion any longer. The passageway through the middle of the gym needed to be kept clear in readiness for the arrival of some VIPs. The terrorists' mood had improved; where they had been angry and on edge before, they now became more cocky. Grandmother Felisa Batagova heard them shouting, 'Quiet! For God's sake shut up. Your fate is about to be decided.' It suddenly seemed that there might be reason for hope.

'YOU COULD STAY OUT AS LATE AS YOU LIKED'

In March 1953, Stalin died and life in the Soviet Union began to develop some signs of normality. Change was slow and initially the differences amounted only to a slight slackening of the tension that for so long had gripped the nation. Within two months of his leader's death, Stalin's main henchman Lavrentii Beria had been arrested and, before the end of the year, had been shot. But it was only in 1956, with Khrushchev's limited denunciation of the Great Denouncer, that most ordinary people got a weak guarantee that there would be no return to the total and random brutality of the past. The gap created by the passing of the personality cult left many Soviet citizens with feelings of uncertainty. Some would never believe that Stalin had known about, much less sanctioned, the excesses of the 1930s and 40s. Though a kind of normality developed, it was never to be the same as normality in the West.

The restrictions on exiled nations like the Chechens and Ingush had been eased first in 1954, but the new rules allowed them only to travel further within the regions they had been deported to. It took until 1957, the year after Khrushchev's Secret Speech, for proper redress to come for at least some of the ethnic groups Stalin had deported. In that year, deported Ingush and Chechens were allowed – under certain conditions – to return to their homeland.

At the time that the legislation went through, Vadim was living amongst Ingush and Chechens in Kazakhstan. In 1953 he had been sent to the republic to do his military service in an enormous aerodrome. Spotted early on as a clever young man, he had been spared more menial tasks and given a job in the intelligence department. 'I could beat all of the intelligence officers at chess,' he told me smiling. 'When our shift ended, I would play them until two or three in the morning. The next morning, they would always allow me to lie in a bit longer than the rest to sleep off the effects of the chess.' He hadn't played properly for years and wanted to know if I could play. Not nearly well enough to get a lie-in, I said.

After he was discharged, instead of going home to Grozny, Vadim had got a job as a welder in an enormous factory in one of the towns where large numbers of Chechen deportees had been sent. I suspected there were emotional and psychological reasons why the twenty-two-year-old had decided to search out the deportees in Kazakhstan, but he was not willing to go into them. He told me, 'I didn't stay because there were people from the Caucasus around. I stayed because there was work to be done.' Vadim was able to live in the centre of the town, whereas the Chechens had to live in what were little more than shanty towns on the outskirts. Nevertheless, he visited them often: 'I practically lived in their houses and they took me in as if I was their own. They refused any money I ever offered them even though I was earning a good wage then and their life was hard. I took to bringing them presents instead, as is our way in the Caucasus.'

Life had indeed been hard for the Chechens and Ingush in exile. Those who had not died on the trains carrying them east were initially beset by hunger, disease and homelessness.

Because of the lightening speed with which the deportations had happened, many families had become separated. In Kazakhstan, these separations had been set in stone, as people on different trains were sent to different towns and villages. Because of severe restrictions on travel this meant that years went by when relatives, even brothers and sisters and husbands and wives, were not able to see one another.

Understandably, when the announcement was made thousands of Chechens and Ingush packed up their possessions and bought tickets for the long journey home. Vadim travelled with them as they went back to Grozny for the first time in many years. He was reunited with his old friend Mints, and discovered that his father had been officially rehabilitated in 1956. Life felt better than ever before. To Vadim it seemed that most people in the city agreed that it was right for the Chechens to be allowed home. 'There was no distinction made about whether you were Chechen or Ingush or Russian. People helped them to get set up again.' Returning deportees were even entitled to a grant from the Soviet government with which they could buy back their former home or rent and furnish a new one.

To start with, this money oiled the cogs in relations between residents and returning exiles, as everyone tried to get their hands on it. But on both sides resentment and recriminations simmered just under the surface. Because of the forced immigration that had taken place in the wake of the emigration in 1944, there was a shortage of land and dwellings to go round. The recreated Chechen and Ingush Autonomous Republic was given new districts to the north and the west. Naturally, many returnees were reluctant to go to a new place and wanted to return to their ancestral home.

In the west, there was a partial return of the land that had been made over to North Ossetia in 1944. Only some of the former Ingush territory was given back, however, and the land around Vladikavkaz and Beslan on the right bank of the River Terek still belongs to Ossetia today. Needless to say, this solution suited no one. Ossetians felt punished for having done nothing wrong; their loyalty and patriotism were once again being ignored. Middle-aged Ossetians I have spoken to remember the money that was paid to returning deportees and it still rankles. The Ingush, already the poor relations in their alliance with Chechnya, felt that part of their ancestral heartland was being withheld from them. In the Soviet world, where racism was institutionalized, North Ossetian administrative control over the right-bank lands made it very difficult for Ingush families to return there, further fuelling the traditional strains in Ingush–Ossetian relations.

On more than one occasion, the simmering tensions between Chechens and Ingush on one side and Ossetians and Russians on the other boiled over. The catalyst for these eruptions was often something relatively minor. Vadim got a job as a welder in the Grozny gasworks soon after he returned. One day in 1958 he was at work when he heard that a recently demobilized Russian soldier in town on leave had been stabbed to death by some Chechen lads in an argument. 'The whole city ground to a standstill,' he told me. 'There were walkouts across the town. The factories closed down; the gasworks too. All the Russians were incensed that a Russian had been murdered. There were all sorts of strikes and meetings and demonstrations. Many of them were organized by the local Communist Party, if I remember correctly.'

Vadim knew that the ex-serviceman had been killed by Chechens, but he also knew that the murder was not really an ethnic attack: 'They didn't kill him for being Russian. They'd all been at a dance in a suburb of Grozny one night. It had an enormous chemical plant in it. They were dancing and then they fell out about something, like young people do. But the

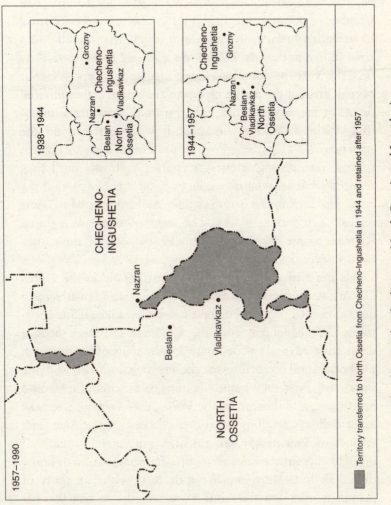

The changing border between North Ossetia and Ingushetia

Territory transferred to North Ossetia from Checheno-Ingushetia in 1944 and retained after 1957

1938–1944

Grozny
Nazran
Checheno-Ingushetia
Beslan
North Ossetia
Vladikavkaz

1944–1957

Checheno-Ingushetia
Grozny
Nazran
Beslan
Vladikavkaz
North Ossetia

1957–1990

CHECHENO-INGUSHETIA
Nazran
Beslan
Vladikavkaz
NORTH OSSETIA

Chechen lads had daggers on them and, in the heat of the moment, the sailor got stabbed.'

Though he could see this was the case, Vadim admitted that he, too, had been caught up in the groundswell of anti-Chechen opinion. 'It wasn't about the Chechens as Chechens,' he defended himself. 'It was about saying that we all had a right to live in the city. I didn't do anything bad anyway.' As was the case in countless other instances of spontaneous protest around the Soviet bloc, the government sent the Red Army in to restore order. 'They started arresting loads of Russians and locking them up. It was terrible. And the Chechens . . . They were nowhere to be seen. They just disappeared like melting snow. Of course, that was until they realized what was actually going on; once they saw that the army was locking up Russians the Chechens started to come out of their hiding places. The sight of Russians fighting Russians made them laugh. It was the kind of thing they would never do, under any circumstances.'

But most of the time and for most people in the North Caucasus, the period between 1957 and 1987 was one of unprecedented calm and modest prosperity. Like all Soviet citizens, they benefited from the Communist Party's fear of unleashing anymore wide-ranging campaigns of terror which might rebound on themselves. Slowly their standard of living improved. First they gained better access to education and healthcare, and then, from the 1970s, they were able to take more holidays and buy consumer goods such as fridges and televisions. Few people had any affection for the system that brought them these improvements, and many came to know that their lives were improving more slowly than those of people in other countries. But it was nonetheless true that life became easier: more predictable and more comfortable.

Officially the deportations were never mentioned. The family of nations with Russia as the big brother had been re-established. Artistic exchanges took place between North Ossetia and Checheno–Ingushetia. In 1967, a week-long festival of Chechen and Ingush cultural events was organized in Vladikavkaz. A reciprocal event was held ten years later in Grozny.

But even away from all this superficiality good relations were often formed between different groups. On my train journey from Beslan back to Moscow I shared my compartment with Leda and Sveta, a mother and daughter who were on their way from Vladikavkaz to Blagoveshchensk, a city on the Chinese border. These were the first two of their eight nights on the train. Leda, who was sixty-nine and in poor health, was moving to the city in the Far East to be with her forty-seven-year-old daughter. She had been born in North Ossetia and had lived there all her life. She was taking only two large canvas bags of belongings with her. Understandably, both women spent lots of time talking about the past as we travelled away from the Caucasus towards Moscow, a place which Leda had never seen.

Though both women were unlikely ever to see their homeland again, neither was particularly sentimental. Leda had had enough of her neighbours in the last few years and, while she looked back fondly on happier days, she knew that they had gone for ever. 'That's it. Over. Done,' she kept saying about her past life. 'Your health's the only thing that matters, and I'll live a bit longer in Blagoveshchensk.' And then, 'There was no friendship left there. All week, people were calling in to say goodbye to me, but the whole time they were looking to see what they could take from my flat. They'd smile at you, but the next second they'd make a fur coat out of your pelt.'

In the past, Leda remembered, people had looked out for one another. They had had fun as well. In the late 1960s, she had taken her children on holiday to the Black Sea coast once a year. There had been socials and dances every week, as well as all the normal weddings and birthdays. Sveta agreed. A

decade later, at the height of Brezhnev's uninspiring premier-
ship, life had been very enjoyable. Trips to the Aurora cinema
to see Soviet and dubbed French and Italian comedies and
thrillers were a weekly event. Occasionally, there were
rumours of black-market perfumes or records arriving in the
city. 'My favourite thing was always just walking up and
down the boulevard in Vladikavkaz with my girlfriends and
an ice cream, making eyes at the boys who walked past. The
city was totally safe then; you could stay out as late as you
liked.'

At the Institute of Transport Studies where she studied
Sveta had had a wide circle of friends: Chechens, Ingush,
Ossetians and Russians. 'Of course, we all knew about the
differences between us. The Chechens and the Ingush were
somehow separate. They didn't even get on that well with
each other, I seem to remember.' Once she saw a Chechen and
an Ingush student come to blows when the Chechen said that
his nation was more sophisticated than the Ingush. 'They have
always been quick to take offence,' Sveta added. In 1980,
when in hospital giving birth to her first son, Sveta was in a
bed beside a Chechen woman. 'She was a lovely person and
we stayed in touch over the years. We would meet up on our
lunch hours and walk up and down the boulevard. Both her
children died in infancy because they were rhesus babies. Her
husband was very good to her through it all. My children all
lived, but my husband left me for another woman.'

The stain of deportation continued to cling to the Chechens
and Ingush. Other Soviet citizens looked on them as people
who had been pardoned but not exonerated. It was taken for
granted that they had collaborated with the Nazis far more
than anyone else in the USSR. At home, parents passed such
views on to their children. However, the tensions between
different ethnic groups bubbled to the surface only intermit-
tently. In the winter of 1972–3 prominent members of the

Ingush intelligentsia sent a letter to the Central Committee of the Communist Party of the Soviet Union requesting the return to Ingush ownership of the land to the east of Vladikavkaz and Beslan. The letter led to street protests by Ingush in the centre of Grozny. Soldiers with water cannon were deployed to disperse them.

Perhaps as a result of these demonstrations, the racist residency policies in North Ossetia were relaxed somewhat in the late 1970s. Ingush families began to move back to the land on the east of the River Terek and the Ingush population of Vladikavkaz increased once more. This brought renewed tensions as the Ossetians thought that they were being sold out by the Soviet government. The murder of an Ossetian taxi driver near the Ingush town of Nazran in 1981 was the spark needed to ignite anti-Ingush violence in North Ossetia. The funeral in Vladikavkaz became a massive demonstration which quickly turned violent. The mob demanded the removal of Ingush residents from the city and the surrounding countryside. There was violence against the local Ingush population, who defended themselves as best they could. Once again, Moscow was forced to act as referee. As they had in Grozny in 1973, the Red Army and the KGB now deployed against the Ossetians. The demonstrations had the tacit support of the local North Ossetian Communist government which was then sacked and replaced with ethnic Russians.

News of the riots leaked out of the Soviet Union. On 12 November 1981, *The Times* wrote:

Troops and armoured vehicles were called out last week in Ordzhonikidze [the Communist-era name for Vladikavkaz], the capital of the North Ossetian autonomous republic, and a curfew was imposed following clashes between the city's Ossetian and Ingushi populations. The city is said now to be calm.

Some have seen this event as the beginning of the latest phase in North Caucasian ethnic strife, a vital link in the chain that leads to Beslan.

In recent years, the balance in the North Caucasus between normal life and extraordinary events has shifted decisively. It is much more difficult to maintain a decent standard of living; 'going without' has become the norm. Simultaneously, more people feel the grievances of their national or social grouping as personal injuries and are prepared to act to address them, even resorting to violence. The fate of the teachers, parents and children of Beslan's School No. 1 is the most striking, but by no means the only, example of how North Caucasians are once again being deprived of the right to pursue personal happiness and success.

'IT FELT LIKE THERE WAS SOMETHING TO HOPE FOR AGAIN'

Despite the terrorists' calls for silence, news that someone was about to be allowed into the school spread quickly through the gym. The hostages were excited. They assumed that the four men named in the terrorists' note were coming. But they were wrong. None of these men ever made it into the school, and the man who did, Ruslan Aushev, had once been the terrorists' sworn enemy.

Since the government negotiator Vitalii Zangionov had established communication with the terrorists late in the afternoon on the first day, the authorities' strategy for dealing with the siege had not progressed very much. Throughout the first and second days, they had failed to improve conditions for the hostages in any way. Nor had much been done to hasten their release. As far as most bystanders could tell, the crisis committee's main contribution was a continuing build-up of personnel and equipment. On the second day, tanks and armoured personnel carriers were ordered to be brought from Vladikavkaz. At the same time, an army field hospital arrived to add to the civilian medics and paramedics. Despite having been fired on by the terrorists the previous day, the Muftis of North Ossetia and Ingushetia were drafted in once more. This time they made a joint television address appealing for calm. It had no effect.

The lack of coordination between different government organizations, especially the Interior Ministry and the FSB, continued. After lunchtime on 2 September, police in the village of Farn, less than a mile outside Beslan, received calls from panicked members of the public who claimed they had just seen their local school taken over by terrorists. Knowing no better, the local police cautiously went to investigate. They found that the empty school had been attacked by Special Forces, who were practising for the storming of School No. 1. No one in the FSB had thought to warn either the terrified residents of the village or the rest of the government.

Beslan residents who heard of the storming exercise in Farn felt that their worst fears were being realized. They had worried from the outset that the Russians would try to storm School No. 1. On several occasions during the first two days, members of the crisis committee and other officials had given interviews promising that they did not intend to end the siege by storming the school. They had stated that their only aim was to save the lives of the children and adults inside and that they would go to any lengths to do this. Though friends and families understood the need for a military presence outside the school as a precaution, they were anxious that violence or shock tactics should not be part of the government's response. In effect, everyone kept pointing to the need for a healthy negotiating process. What they got – if the patchwork of rumours and half-truths that have emerged are to be believed – was a chaotic and disorganized mess.

The four men the terrorists had demanded to speak with all had connections to the unrest in the Caucasus, though none of them could be called the main players. For whatever reason, the Colonel had not demanded to see President Putin or any of his cabinet, or any of the leaders of the Moscow-friendly Chechen government. Consequently, their demands were considerably more realistic than they might have been. Nor had he used his note to detail the specific outcomes that he wanted the school siege to achieve. Many hostages in the school had heard terrorists say that they wanted the complete withdrawal of all Russian troops from Chechnya but this was not made public, a fact which arguably made it easier for the politicians to justify negotiations. Of course, none of this changed the fact that, for the four men themselves, to go into the school would have been to put their lives in grave danger. Moreover, if they had been murdered inside the school, an enormous propaganda victory would have been handed to the terrorists.

The first man on the terrorists' list, North Ossetian President Aleksandr Dzasokhov, was already in Beslan when the hostage-takers' demand first emerged. It seems that he was immediately willing to go into the school on his own to begin negotiations. Eyewitnesses corroborate his assertion that he had to be persuaded not to. Already seventy at the time of the siege, Dzasokhov had given much of his life to the service of young people, first as a local leader of the Communist youth movement, the Komsomol, and eventually as its deputy chairman nationwide. 'As far as I was concerned, I said out loud that I was going to go into the school. But literally only a few minutes later, I was told that if I tried to I would be arrested. It seems that was the decision of the head of the crisis committee. But I was prepared to go in. I'm not saying that Khuchbarov, the Colonel, would have allowed me in, because I know that every time our negotiator told him that one of the people he wanted was available to talk to, he said that they needed all four simultaneously.'

In fact, by the end of the first day of the siege, two of the four men were in Beslan. The eminent paediatrician, Dr

Leonid Roshal – whose name the Colonel had insistently mis-spelt as Rashailo – had arrived on a plane from Moscow at around 8 p.m. The seventy-one-year-old paediatrician had had a distinguished career, rising to be an adviser to the World Health Organization and the Russian President's Human Rights Commission. He was named the best children's doctor in the world by journalists in 1996. After taking part in the relief effort for the Armenian earthquake in 1988, Roshal had been instrumental in forming a group of children's doctors who would be willing to travel long distances at short notice to help with the aftermath of disasters.

It was therefore with good reason that he had been a nego-tiator in an earlier Chechen terrorist attack, the Moscow Theatre siege of 2002. During the earlier siege, Roshal had entered the theatre on several occasions, negotiating with the terrorists, providing medical help and securing the early release of a number of child hostages. Though rather self-important and pompous, Roshal was widely praised for his conspicuous heroism during that siege, which ended so tragi-cally thanks to governmental error. However, since that time, he had been accused on some rebel websites of being a col-laborator, who had fed key information back to the FSB.

When Roshal arrived in Beslan, he was put in telephone contact with the terrorists very quickly. Permission was given by Valerii Andreev, the FSB man at the head of the crisis com-mittee. First, Vitalii Zangionov asked the terrorist negotiator if he was prepared to talk to Roshal. 'The order came that the doctor was to be allowed to speak with the criminals. I phoned my contact in the school and told him that there was an opportunity to talk with Roshal and that, if he was not against it, I would pass the receiver over there and then.' Zangionov recalled that, earlier in the evening during the enormous rainstorm, the telephone line to the school had briefly gone down. This had annoyed the terrorists and so now, before agreeing to talk to Roshal, their negotiator said, 'We will speak with him, but if the connection breaks again we will shoot everyone in the gym. We will blow them to bits.'

Vitalii handed over the telephone to Roshal. Despite his undoubted skills as a doctor, Roshal made for an unlikely negotiator, his manner brusque and haughty. The terrorist started by threatening to shoot everyone in the gym.

Roshal answered, 'Now listen to me, young lad! Let us have no more talk about shooting people.' Like Zangionov, he received an earful of abusive language in response. He snapped back, 'I will not be spoken to in that manner either, young lad!"

He spoke to the terrorists' representative for almost two hours during the first night of the siege. He immediately and fearlessly offered to come into the school with a bag full of medicines to treat anyone who was sick or had been injured. He stressed that he was willing to treat terrorists as well as hostages. But time and again the terrorists refused. In the end, the doctor was told that if he came anywhere near the school alone he would be shot.

This conversation raises all kinds of difficult questions about the Russian government's handling of the siege. If the terrorists were prepared to talk to Roshal alone and on the telephone, would they not have been prepared to converse with President Dzasokhov under the same terms? Undoubtedly, the terrorists were cruel and irrational people, whose word could not be trusted. The content of Roshal's phone call shows how difficult it would have been to hold any meaningful negotiations with them. But the very fact of the conversation contradicts FSB officials' insistence that the terrorists would only speak with all of the people they had demanded to see at once and face to face. Even more than ordinary people, hostage-takers are known to be susceptible to flattery. The arrival of the famous paediatrician in Beslan was a sign of their power. Intoxicated by their success, the terrorists may well have decided that it was worth deviating from their plan and talking to the man alone and by phone, if only to taunt and insult him. Were they offered the chance to talk to President Dzasokhov on the same terms? Perhaps he, a more down-to-earth man than Roshal, would have had more success in a telephone conversation.

Roshal and Dzasokhov were at least present in Beslan, but the other two men mentioned in the note were not: the whereabouts of Aslambek Aslakhanov and Murat Zyazikov during the siege remain mysterious. It is hard to work out when they learned that the terrorists had demanded to speak to them, and even harder to see who, if anyone, advised them on how to react.

Aslambek Aslakhanov was President Putin's personal adviser on the south of Russia at the time of the school siege. A Chechen born just before the deportations, Aslakhanov had risen an impressive distance through the ranks of Soviet society, battling against its inbuilt anti-Chechen prejudice by proving his dedication to successive regimes in Moscow. In the sports arena, he became a master of sambo and judo, while developing a successful career in the security services, achievements similar to Putin's own. He had started, in the late 1960s, as a detective in the USSR's economic crime unit, and then rose to become deputy head of the entire criminal investigation department. Further promotion made him the country's senior chief inspector. In 1990, he was elected to the first democratic Russian assembly, representing a Chechen constituency and speaking out for the law and order lobby which had been his life's work.

Aslakhanov had been appointed as Putin's adviser only days after being told to withdraw his candidacy for the Chechen presidency in 2003. Putin, it seems, had wanted the former policeman to serve in one capacity but not another and, with his typical disdain for the untidiness of fully demo-cratic processes, had intervened to make his wishes reality. Whatever he thought of Putin's decision, Aslakhanov has reason to be grateful that he was forced to pull out of the elec-tion: the winner was blown to pieces in a terrorist attack in Grozny just a few months before the Beslan school siege.

Little is known about Aslakhanov's movements between 1 and 3 September. He eventually arrived in Beslan around lunchtime on the third day of the siege, when it was already too late to do anything. Visiting a local hospital a few days later, he insisted that it had been his intention to negotiate if required and that, arriving when he did on the third day was just a regrettable misfortune. With some irony, one of the patients he spoke to later recalled, 'Then he gave out his busi-ness cards. "In case I can be of any help," he said.'

The confusion about Aslakhanov's real role was increased by an interview he gave to a foreign television channel about six weeks after the siege. In it he said that he *had* actually been conducting negotiations with the terrorists by telephone since the first day of the siege; that he had informed the head of President Putin's administration about this; and that he had expressed a desire to travel to Beslan immediately. Even more bizarrely, he went on to state that he had been told by the ter-rorists about the real number of hostages on the first day and had passed this information to the media. Through these negotiations he said he had learned also of the terrorists' polit-ical demands: the withdrawal of all Russian troops from Chechnya and complete independence from Russia.

Murat Zyazikov, despite being the president of the neigh-bouring Republic of Ingushetia where many of the terrorists in School No. 1 came from, proved the most difficult of the four men to find during the three days of the siege. The forty-seven-year-old, who was born in Kyrgyzstan in the year that the Ingush deportees were pardoned, had studied history and law at university. On graduation, however, he had pursued a career in the domestic branches of the KGB. After the collapse of the Soviet Union, he took up senior posts in the Ingushetian government and the local FSB. He had been Putin's preferred choice for the local presidency when it became available in 2002 and he was duly elected. However, he never succeeded in winning the hearts and minds of his electorate, who continued to look at him as a place-man with little knowledge of Ingush problems. In a political system packed with loyal servants, Zyazikov manages to sound more toadying than most. Typical press releases read like this: 'It annoys the terrorists that our little republic is really getting on its feet and is beginning to attract a lot of inward investment. It truly is a multicultural part of the Russian Federation, where problems of social welfare and job creation are being actively solved.' For all the spin, he has been a beleaguered leader and has survived a number of assassination attempts. Of the four men the terrorists demanded to see, he was the one with most to fear.

But he never came to Beslan and senior members of the crisis committee agree that it was impossible to find him. It has been assumed that he went into hiding, an action for which he has since been ridiculed throughout the North Caucasus, where running away is not allowed. In answer to these allegations, Zyazikov has implied that he was obeying the orders of President Putin. 'I was ready to go to Beslan at a moment's notice,' he said. 'But the President of Russia told me in a telephone call that I shouldn't. Since the terrorists hadn't advanced any real demands, it seemed clear that there wasn't going to be anything to negotiate about. They wanted to achieve a propaganda coup. In addition to taking all of our children hostage, they wanted to get someone highly placed as well. If I could have given myself in exchange for the release of some of the children, that would have been different . . . But as it was, why would I have gone in?'

If what Zyazikov and Aslakhanov have said is true, it strongly implies that Putin personally used both men to influence the course of events in Beslan and, in the case of Aslakhanov, to try to gain an advantage over both the terrorists and the local crisis committee by carrying on secret negotiations. Certainly he would have known of the terrorists' demands regarding Chechnya earlier than anyone in Beslan. The head of the crisis committee had the terrorists' phone number and would have made it known to those above him in the FSB. It is therefore plausible that Aslakhanov acted independently of everyone in Beslan. The official negotiator Zangionov was aware that he was not the only person carrying on discussions with the terrorists, a fact which undermined his own role. If the terrorists were similarly aware that the people they were speaking to did not know about each other's conversations, this strengthened their hand considerably.

Other allegations, if true, suggest – like Aslakhanov's phone calls – that Putin was keen to exert secret but effective control over the siege. The experience of investigative journalist Anna Politkovskaya is particularly chilling. She had acted as a negotiator with some success at the Moscow Theatre siege two years before. Having decided to come to Beslan both to cover the story for her paper and to make herself available as a negotiator once more, Politkovskaya had great difficulty getting on a flight. Eventually, she bought a ticket on a plane going to Rostov-on-Don. Once seated in the cabin, she ordered some tea from the flight attendant; when she drank it, Politkovskaya quickly lost consciousness. After the plane landed, she was rushed to intensive care at a local hospital, where at times doctors feared for her life. She never made it to Beslan and was instead taken back to Moscow – shaken and frail – by the editor of her newspaper. She and those around her were convinced that she had been deliberately poisoned to prevent her becoming involved in the siege. Now, she has been silenced permanently, murdered by a contract killer in the lift of her apartment block in Moscow in October 2006. Needless to say, the poisoning allegations have gone unanswered, just as the person or people who ordered her death remain at large, unidentified and unpunished.

It was not just central government which sought to under-mine effective negotiations. The crisis committee in Beslan allowed many people other than Zangionov to talk to the ter-rorists by phone without telling him. Again, this would seem to make a nonsense of the assertion that the terrorists refused all offers to negotiate except with the four people they had named. The person who had most success in speaking to them was Ruslan Aushev. He was Zyazikov's predecessor as president of Ingushetia and a man generally thought to have good links to all sides in the Chechen conflict and Caucasian politics in general. Before getting the terrorists to agree to let him into the school, Aushev took steps to make contact with the most senior Chechen politician then alive, Aslan Maskhadov. He thought that the influential figure would intrinsically disagree with the terrorists' targeting of a school full of innocent children and hoped that he might be able to exert influence on them. In order to get in touch with him, he had first to speak to the rebel's friend Akhmed Zakaev, in London.

At about half past three in the afternoon of the second day, Aushev walked slowly up to the main doors into the gym. He was escorted to the edge of the cordon by Vasilii Andreev, the head of the crisis committee, and Dzantiev, the North Ossetian Minister of Internal Affairs. Though his name had not been mentioned in the terrorists' note, it was he who ended up standing in the school. Though Dzasokhov and the others were advised that to enter the school would be to sign their own death warrant, he had been allowed to go in. As soon as they saw him, many of the adult hostages in the gym instantly recognized him. The conflicts between Ingushetia and North Ossetia meant that Aushev was a regular face on their local news bulletins.

Born in exile in the Kazakhstani desert, Ruslan Aushev rose to prominence as an army commander in the Soviet Union's war in Afghanistan in the 1980s. He was awarded medals for his conduct in the conflict and became a national hero to many Ingush because of the good he had done their reputation throughout the Soviet Union. In 1992, Aushev was elected president of the newly created republic of Ingushetia. He resigned before the end of his second term in office in 2001, at least in part because of President Putin's more direct style of rule from Moscow. Though he was criticized for not doing enough to improve the lot of Ingushetia, most people were ready to admit that the task before him had not been easy. Through a variety of tactics, which included maintaining relations with the separatists, he managed to keep Ingushetia out of Chechnya's war with Russia. For this Putin despised him, reportedly telling some of those who survived the Beslan siege that Aushev had only been allowed into the school because the terrorists viewed him as one of their own.

When they saw him, most of the captives in the gym were relieved that someone had finally come to negotiate. Many irrationally saw a chance that the siege might end there and then. Aushev stayed in the doorway for no more than a couple of minutes. He took in his shocking surroundings, shook his head and went out again flanked by the terrorists. Some of the hostages noticed a horrified look on his face. Those closest to him heard him say quietly, 'I must go and negotiate with them.' The headmistress Lydia Tsalieva recalled, 'I was sitting in one of the corners of the gym. When Aushev came through the door and everyone started whispering his name, I have to admit that it gave me hope too. I thought that this was the start of us getting some help. It felt like there was something to hope for again.'

A quarter of an hour after Aushev had left the hall, Lydia was summoned to the staffroom, which the terrorists were using as their headquarters. Impressed by Aushev's physical presence and keyed up by a mixture of hope and despair, she ignored the terrorists and spoke directly to the former Ingush president. 'Aushev was standing there, tall and commanding. I said, "Ruslan! Ruslan! I beg you, please help my children. Help them! Save them! Please, don't allow a single child to suffer, I implore you. I beg you." He heard me out – I think I said a bit more than that. I remember that I started to get down on my knees to beg him, but he wouldn't let me. Then he said to me, "As soon as I leave here, I am going to fly to Moscow and tell Putin all about this."'

But when she heard this, far from being comforted, Lydia realized that salvation would not come quickly. 'I just thought to myself what it meant. He was going to have to fly to Moscow and speak to Putin. How long would that take? I almost completely lost it at that point, but I think I managed to hold myself together.' Back in the gym, Lydia worked hard to look positive. 'Of course, everyone in the gym immediately started asking me how it had gone and what had been decided. Children tugged at my clothes and asked if we were going to be released now . . . if Aushev was going to get us released. I remember saying, "We'll be released soon. Don't worry or fret. We'll be released soon."'

Once Tsalieva had left Aushev and the terrorists alone, the former Red Army commander began to negotiate in earnest. Using all his powers of persuasion, he managed to secure the release of the small number of babies and toddlers among the hostages, along with their mothers. The idea to get the babies released had probably come to him when, on his way out of the gym, he was shown a small group of breastfeeding mothers sitting apart from the other hostages in one of the changing rooms. Zalina Levina was one of those women, though at the age of fifty-one she could only pretend to feed her two-year-old granddaughter, Liza. For the first year in almost twenty, none of Zalina's own children was studying at School No. 1. Her son and daughter had both graduated and started courses at local institutes. Zalina looked after the little girl while her mother was studying. On that morning, she had not intended to go to the celebrations at the school but her granddaughter and her own nostalgia had got the better of her.

'We live right by the school and we could hear the music playing from the flat. Everyone was heading off to school all dressed up in ribbons and holding flowers. Loads of children live in our block of flats. Liza said to me, "Come on! I want to go and dance!" I still wasn't dressed but I thought about it and decided we would. I got changed out of my denim house-coat and we went down to the school. I always went to those ceremonies – the First Bell and the Last Bell. We lived so close. I spent so much time at that school.'

When the terrorists had first invaded, Zalina had grabbed Liza and joined others who were hiding in the boiler room. 'I worked out immediately that this was for real. I just kept thinking about what I was going to do with the child. She was hungry. I hadn't fed her because I thought we were only going to be at the school for ten minutes or so. I was terrified. I decided that, if they found me, I would ask them to release me because I had a baby with me. Then one of the terrorists threatened to shoot us all if we didn't get out of the boiler room. Everyone apart from me ran out and I was left on my own. I thought, "I'll ask him to let us go. We live only a couple of steps away." But then, when he came in for me – he was the thickset one with the scar and the evil eyes – he just said, "What are you doing still in here? I said I'd shoot you. Are you deaf or something?" And all of the bravery just drained out of me when I saw his eyes. I realized that he really would shoot me and I didn't say a thing. I just turned the baby to my chest, so that she wouldn't see the terrorist, and made my way to the gym.'

Late on the first night of the siege, one of the terrorists had announced that breastfeeding mothers could leave the gym with their babies. Though the concession had been welcome, like all the others the terrorists made, it was constantly liable to be withdrawn. 'There was one woman there with three children, one of whom was breastfeeding,' Zalina recalled. 'The other two kids were older. We all sat in there like that for a couple of hours.' Then, in the middle of the night, one of the terrorists had come in and seen the other woman's older children. 'The terrorist said, "Right. That's it. You'll all have to go back into the hall. I thought you were told that only babies were allowed in here, but you've brought all your children in with you. Send the other children back into the hall." The mother wasn't prepared to leave her other children alone in the hall, so she left with them. I was on my own for about an hour. I did my best to keep out of sight and I gave Liza my nipple to suck on to keep her quiet. Then other women came in to join us. After a while there were five or six of us with babies.'

On the second morning of the siege, one of the mothers had asked the terrorists to give her something to feed to her children. Zalina remembered that one of the terrorists had thrown a packet of dried milk over to them. 'It was out of date. We ripped it open on a dirty table and let the children lick it up as best they could. Suddenly, another terrorist – I think he was called Abdulla – saw what we were doing and got very angry. He asked who had given us the dried milk and picked the packet up and hurled it into the corridor. Then, after a while, the one who had given us the milk came back and we asked him to give it to us again and he did.'

More and more nursing mothers joined those in the changing room during the second day, until there was standing room only. They spent most of their time praying for salvation. When Aushev walked past the doorway into the changing room, Zalina instantly recognized him and hoped that it meant that freedom was not far away. A few minutes later, he came into where they were sitting. 'He looked us over and greeted us. There was total horror in his eyes.' Then he left again, but after a time, Abdulla came into the changing room and told them that they were about to be released. He told them that if the mothers gave the security services any assistance in identifying the terrorists, they would find out about it and would execute fifty hostages immediately. 'He told us that their deaths would be on our consciences,' Zalina remembered.

Almost as soon as the announcement was made, one of the mothers, Fatima Tskaeva, started pleading to be allowed to take not only her six-month-old girl with her but also her three-year-old son and ten-year-old daughter. The terrorist steadfastly refused, but Fatima was incapable of making such an inhuman decision and just kept on begging. At first he rebuffed her quietly but, when she fell to her knees in front of him, something changed and he became enraged. 'That's it, you stupid bitch!' he told her. 'Because of you, no one will be allowed to leave.' When Zalina heard those words, she said that 'the whole scene went black before my eyes. All the hope I had disappeared. My grandchild was slipping in and out of consciousness by this point. She was hanging limply in my arms.'

Unilaterally, Zalina decided to start walking away from Fatima towards the door. 'I didn't say anything. I just started walking out of the room. I didn't care if they shot me or not. I couldn't look at little Liza any longer. She couldn't cry or anything. She was wasting away before my eyes.' I walked down the first corridor and then turned into the main one. At each door along the corridor, two of the terrorists were standing with machine guns. I got halfway along it and one of them told me to stop. I stopped and Liza suddenly started to scream. I thought, "That's it! They'll kill me now!" But then, Aushev appeared and motioned at me to keep walking. I looked at the terrorist but he didn't say anything. So I ran down the rest of the corridor over broken glass. I told myself that everything would be okay now; that they wouldn't shoot me with Aushev looking on. They moved apart the desks they had put across the doors to let me out and I walked outside. I was the first one out.'

At the rear, Ruslan Aushev walked out of School No. 1 carrying Fatima Tskaeva's baby. The woman could not bring herself to leave her other two children behind in the school. Both she and her ten-year-old daughter were later to die there. The former Ingush president also brought with him a letter he had been handed by the Colonel on his way out of the staffroom. It purported to be from Shamil Basaev, the mastermind of Chechen terrorism.

From the servant of Allah, Shamil Basaev,
to President Putin

Vladimir Putin, you did not start this war. But you can end it, if you are prepared to be as brave and decisive as De Gaulle. We offer you a sensible peace on mutually beneficial terms according to the principle of independence in return for security. If the Chechen Republic Ichkeriya is acknowledged by you and if your troops are removed from it, we will undertake never to conclude any political, economic or military unions with others against Russia. We will not allow foreign military bases to exist on our territory, even temporarily. We will not give support or financial assistance to any groups or organizations waging armed conflict against the Russian Federation. Our currency will be the rouble and we will become members of the Commonwealth of Independent States. Moreover, we may sign an agreement with Russia, though we would prefer to be a neutral state. We can guarantee that all Muslims in Russia will refuse to take up arms against the Russian Federation for a period not less than ten to fifteen years on condition that freedom of confession is observed. We have no connection with the explosions in Moscow or Volgodonsk, but could agree to accept responsibility for them under certain circumstances.

The Chechen people are conducting a battle for national freedom, for their own independence and autonomy, for self-preservation and not in order to destroy Russia or diminish it. We offer you peace, but the choice is yours to make.

Allahu Akbar
30 August 2004

'WE DON'T THINK ABOUT HOW TO STOP TERRORISM ANY MORE'

At the end of the 1980s, the Soviet Union began to collapse. By 1991, it had ceased to exist. In many respects the vacuum it left behind is still being filled: in some places by Western values, NATO membership and the European Union; in others by new personality cults and seemingly omnipotent oligarchies. The lot of the Caucasus has been particularly hard, with poverty and unemployment being compounded by ethnic strife. Though the carefree spirit that was a feature of many Soviet citizens' lives in the late 1970s and 1980s can still be found occasionally in the North Caucasus today, it has become rare. Freer in some respects than ever before, with more choices awaiting them should they become rich enough, many people in the North Caucasus feel nonetheless that they are not in control of their own destinies and that life has lost almost all of its charm.

In 1986, the new leader of the Soviet Union, Mikhail Gorbachev, began introducing a range of reforms that were aimed at making the country more open and accountable to its citizens and more economically successful. It was soon clear that, like its predecessor in 1917, the Communist empire was not readily amenable to restructuring. Although the sworn enemy of capitalism, the country had been living for years on the credit it obtained from selling its oil and other natural resources overseas. Tinkering with the command economy didn't work, just as it was not possible to control the impact of admissions by the state that previous abuses of power had been wrong. Opening the door on the cruelty and oppression of the Communist past was like welcoming in a hurricane of destructive anger and reproach. The influx of never-before-seen Western goods and media only made it more certain that people would reject any idea of living under Communist rule.

In the North Caucasus in the early 1990s people began to talk about Stalin's deportations on television and in print. Assemblies were held by self-appointed representatives of the Ingush and Chechen peoples. In ways, they were like the new political meetings that were taking place across the USSR, many of which had no ethnic flavour at all. But the bitterness and rage that were expressed in them, especially by the Chechens, were different. While the Chechens generally demanded independence from Russia, the Ingush focused on getting their land back from North Ossetia. Their resolutions, which were covered in the press, sparked a backlash in Moscow and Vladikavkaz. Ossetian politicians passed resolutions declaring their sovereignty over the lands that had once been Ingush. The Communists in Grozny asserted themselves as the only legitimate government for Chechnya.

On 6 September 1991, Chechnya declared its independence from Russia. A little over a week later, a meeting of Ingush representatives formally declared the creation of Ingushetia as a separate autonomous republic. They claimed the land on the right bank of the Terek in North Ossetia for themselves and declared that their capital would be in Vladikavkaz. For the time being, the Ingush did not want to secede from Russia.

To start with, the government in Moscow let the Chechens enjoy (or endure) their de facto independence. The army garrisons in Grozny were emptied and no attempt was made to make national legislation apply in the mountainous republic. In part, the Russians had no choice: the rest of the country was suffering too much for special attention to be paid to any individual part. But undoubtedly corruption played a part. Chechnya, through its airports and land border with Georgia and Azerbaijan, became an entrepôt for contraband and arms dealers, and a haven for vice. By greasing the palms of senior officials and businesspeople in Moscow, the Chechen leaders were left to their own devices to act with impunity.

Not so relations between Ingushetia and North Ossetia. While Chechnya initially seemed a minor issue from the vantage point of Moscow, the land on the right bank of the Terek was an enormous and ever-present thorn in the sides of both small republics. The right-bank land, although in North Ossetia, had become home to thousands of Ingush once more, who lived uneasily alongside their Ossetian neighbours. In the dying days of the old order, the Moscow government finally offered some support to the Ingush in their claim over the disputed territory. On 26 April 1991 the Supreme Soviet adopted a law 'On the Rehabilitation of Repressed Peoples', in which it spoke of territorial rehabilitation. This was taken by the Ingush to mean that their rights over the right-bank lands had a new legal basis.

As in 1981 an isolated incident sparked off fighting, but this time there was no Red Army to put a hasty stop to it. In November 1991, two North Ossetian policemen were murdered, supposedly by Ingush people living in an Ossetian village. Another almost identical incident followed a few days later. On both occasions, the men's funerals turned to violence, and in December a pitched battle was fought between police and local Ingush residents after a roadblock was set up by the former, ostensibly to check drivers' documents.

Sporadic violence between Ingush and Ossetians continued throughout 1992 but turned to full-scale war in October and November. Each side still blames the other for starting the conflict. Fearing their neighbours, local Ingush living on the right bank of the Terek had blockaded themselves into their villages. Undoubtedly, they were receiving support from their relatives and friends in Ingushetia proper. The North Ossetian government wanted to end the blockade, which they feared might turn into a de facto secession, and allowed units of volunteer partisans to form in order to do the job. Fighters from Ingushetia entered North Ossetia on the last day of October 1992 and started to fight the local Ossetian population. Atrocities were committed on both sides, and the federal Russian government appeared to support the North Ossetians, deploying some troops on their side under the guise of peacekeepers.

The Ingush population of the right-bank lands suffered disproportionately. Many thousand were ethnically cleansed and fled to Ingushetia where they lived in camps along the border. Ingushetians say that the number was over 40,000; even liberal-minded Ossetians admit to around 10,000. Over three thousand Ingush houses were destroyed in North Ossetia. Around one thousand people were killed. There was a cessation of violence by early 1993 and some refugees returned to the right-bank lands, but no significant meeting of minds has occurred since and the feeling on both sides is that scores remain to be settled.

In North Ossetia, I was told that the backward, grasping Ingush required special handling by Ossetians, who by nature were welcoming of other nationalities. A professor at Vladikavkaz Institute of the Humanities told me, 'We are on the threshold of modernizing our society. Our neighbours in Ingushetia are not quite there yet. Whatever else you say, Ossetia is still a multi-ethnic society, whereas Ingushetia is a mono-ethnic society. That has an impact on how people live.' According to the professor, a lively little man who chain-smoked his way through our two-hour meeting, Ingush people are welcomed in North Ossetia still, so long as they leave their territorial claims at home. 'Any time I talk to an Ingush I find it easy to form relations,' he told me. 'Very easy indeed. But when they start to speak as representatives of their nation – even those who lived here or studied here – it becomes more difficult. Land can and should be returned to its owners, but territorial rehabilitation? There is no such thing in international law. The Ingush can live on their land in the right bank if they want, by all means, but they shouldn't expect it to be part of their ethnic territory.'

Conversely, Ingushetians see their expulsion from the right bank of the Terek as further evidence of an Ossetian and Russian plot to wipe out their nation. It is linked seamlessly with the deportations of 1944. Ingush I have met were always keen to remind me that, had it not been for the war and ethnic cleansing of 1992, they would have been the majority population of the right bank anyway, by dint of their higher birth-rate. The arguments on both sides are grimly familiar to anyone acquainted with the conflicts in Northern Ireland, the Balkans, Cyprus or Israel and Palestine.

In 1994, the Russian government decided to reassert its right to govern Chechnya. The campaign began with the funding and supply of arms to native Chechen rivals of the leadership but ended with the Russian army being sent into Grozny to reclaim it for Moscow. Though non-Chechens had been leaving the republic since 1991, Vadim had decided to stay in his family home in the capital. He had continued working as a plumber and welder with his small team of employees, some of whom were Chechens. In December 1994, he had left the city to visit friends elsewhere in Russia. 'When I tried to go home on 10 December, they wouldn't let me cross into Chechnya. They said, "You're mad. Have you gone out of your mind?" They said that the tanks had just gone in through Mozdok. I remember telling them that I'd left the lights on in the house and needed to get back to switch them off. I always do that whenever I go away, to make it look like someone is at home. It's worth the tiny amount of money it costs. And I had all my documents there in the house. Everything. Photographs. Albums. The evidence that my grandfather had been a hereditary noble before the Revolution was there and all of it went up in flames.'

Vadim's house was levelled in the Russians' attack on Grozny: 'When the tanks and armoured vehicles went to get the leaders in their palace, they came right through my yard and flattened the house. Everything went up in flames. I had canisters full of oxyacetylene for doing the welding and it all just exploded.' Even then, Vadim briefly returned and lived with Chechen friends, but they advised him to leave. For the last ten years the seventy-three-year-old has been a refugee.

Despite inflicting massive destruction on Chechnya, the Russians failed to wipe out the separatists and were forced to conclude a humiliating peace with them. By the time their so-called 'short, victorious war' was over, life had become much more dangerous for everyone who lived in the North Caucasus. Because of the moral bankruptcy of both sides in the conflict, the hijacking, kidnapping, bombing and murder of civilians had once again become a normal part of daily life. At least 50,000 people had died in the first Chechen war. Grozny was in ruins and ordinary Chechens had fled the small republic to other parts of the North Caucasus in their thousands. Despite de facto independence for Chechnya under Aslan Maskhadov's presidency between 1996 and 2000, most

did not return, reluctant to put themselves at the mercy of a
militaristic regime with fundamentalist tendencies. Tent-cities
appeared in Ingushetia, where infant mortality and commun-
icable disease rates soared. They had suffered so desperately
that some could not fail to be radicalized by their experiences.

In almost every place I visited on my way to and from
Beslan there had been terrorist attacks. One of the first took
place near the resort town of Pyatigorsk in 1994 when a bus
was hijacked and its passengers taken hostage. Ransom and
safe passage were demanded, but local police decided to storm
the bus instead. Five women hostages were killed. In part
because of their war with Ingushetia, North Ossetians were
particularly hard hit. In 1999, an escalation in the level of violence from Chechen separatists indicated their desire to
provoke Russia into further conflict or complete withdrawal.
Within the space of a few weeks, enormous bombs in the

The central market in Vladikavkaz

central market in Vladikavkaz and in the North Ossetian village of Sputnik had killed more than sixty people. These and other explosions and a staged invasion of sovereign Russian territory by separatists under Shamil Basaev prompted Vladimir Putin to reinvade Chechnya.

But the violence only increased. In December 2000, Pyatigorsk's central market was thrown high into the sky when two cars, filled with explosives, blew up. Seven people died and forty-four were injured. In September 2003, an early-morning commuter train travelling from Pyatigorsk to another resort was hurled from the rails when a bomb exploded underneath it; another seven people died and ninety were injured. December of the same year saw an even more effective attack, when a suicide bomber detonated a bomb on another commuter train in the area. This time, forty-four people died and 150 were injured. In the same year, fifty died in North Ossetia after an attack on a military hospital.

For all Putin's protestations that the second Chechen war had ended in 2001, and Chechnya had been reintegrated again into the Russian Federation, the violence and lawlessness have not abated. Heavy-handed tactics have perhaps made it more difficult for terrorists to act but their attacks have become more deadly when they do. One man I met in Beslan told me, 'We don't think about how to stop terrorism anymore, but about how to live with the circumstances we find ourselves in. People find that they must become accustomed to this situation.' And the security forces are often as feared as the terrorists, even by communities which are deeply patriotic.

One evening I wandered up and down Vladikavkaz's flood-lit boulevard. Like the local promenaders, I was watching the world go by. I bought a beer at a kiosk and sat down. On the boulevard, two slightly drunk young men were standing by a slot machine that challenges players to grab a teddy bear with a small winch. Suddenly, out of nowhere, a vehicle belonging to one of the branches of Russia's Special Forces drew up alongside them. The men looked frightened; the people sitting around me gasped. 'Jesus Christ! What are they going to do now?' they said. The men were dragged round onto the street and pushed up against the side of the armoured vehicle. Their hands were pushed high over their heads and they were forced to shout out loud directions to the identity papers in their back pockets.

At that moment a third Special Forces man jumped out of the back of the vehicle. He was grinning broadly and punched the two men in the side of the stomach. He lifted his hands up in a gesture that indicated the whole thing was just a joke. 'Just having a laugh! You weren't scared, were you?' All five men then embraced – the best of friends – and started chatting to one another. But they had been scared, and so had everyone else.

THIRST

Dehydration. The loss of water from the body [. . .] The commonest cause of dehydration is failure to drink liquids. The deprivation of water is far more serious than the deprivation of food [and] may result in shock and death. As dehydration progresses, the tissues tend to shrink, the skin becomes dry and wrinkled, and the eyes become shrunken and the eyeballs soft [. . .] Fever develops [. . .] When five to ten litres of body water have been lost a person is acutely and severely ill [. . .] In a previously healthy adult, death follows the loss of twelve to fifteen litres of body water. In the very young, the very old, or the debilitated, death occurs at a lower level of dehydration.

Encyclopaedia Britannica (15th edition; Chicago, 2002)

The terrorists had been visibly delighted to receive a visit from such an important person as Aushev. However, once he had left along with the twenty-six freed hostages, their mood rapidly deteriorated. A couple of hours after his departure, the terrorists were more irate and unstable than ever. There was more shooting at the roof of the sports hall than before; more threats, and more sadistic pleasure in their captives' discomfort. The prospect of release that hostages hoped for after Aushev's visit quickly evaporated, to be replaced by the realization that the terrorists had been in earnest when they said that there would be no more water for anyone.

Perhaps the Colonel and his deputies came to rue the release of the babies and toddlers, feeling that it was too great a concession, given how little they had got in return. After all, Aushev had only promised to relay their letter to Putin. There were over a thousand other people who could have taken the letter out of the school and the Russian President would inevitably have learned of its contents whoever the bearer had been. Perhaps they were enraged that Aushev's visit did not lead immediately to more meaningful negotiations. Perhaps something went awry with one of the other channels through which they were negotiating. Perhaps hunger, nervous tension and lack of sleep were taking their toll on the terrorists as they were on their hostages.

Even in this, conspiracy theories abound. One survivor, Felisa Batagova, says, 'After Aushev left, the terrorists went berserk. I personally think that Aushev had come into the school with the intention of freeing his own friends and acquaintances. He left all the other terrorists to their fate. If our authorities had been a little bit cleverer at the time, they would have held Aushev hostage. As far as I can see, they were all in it together, with Aushev as the head one. He came in and told them just to keep on doing what they were doing. And it was only after he left that they worked out what he had done. He had abandoned them to their deaths. They hadn't expected to die. If they had thought they would die, they wouldn't have bothered wearing their masks. Would they? He made sure to save the terrorists he wanted and left the rest behind.'

As dehydration began to take its effects, many of the hostages had the dubious consolation that they were less and less aware of their surroundings. Even relatively healthy people were beginning to slip in and out of consciousness. Maybe this was just as well, because dulled senses were a prerequisite for the next step in the deterioration of the hostages' situation. Sanctioned by the terrorists – who at one point even carried empty bottles and buckets past fully functioning taps and into the sports hall – but driven by desperation, the hostages began to drink their own and one another's urine.

One hostage said, 'They became so evil. They wouldn't even let the littlest children out to go to the toilet any more. Instead, they brought in buckets for us to relieve ourselves in. The adolescent boys were too embarrassed to do it, but lots of the younger ones couldn't hold it in and ran over to the buckets. We had become cattle. Grown-ups, who hadn't been to the toilet for three days, were just sitting there in puddles of their own piss, stinking. The smell of urine would have put you out of your mind. Just in front of me, there was a boy sitting – he was about sixteen years old, I'd say. I can't remember what he looked like now. Isn't that just the way? The nerves we were suffering from then must have just wiped our memories; I do remember that he had a curly head of hair. He lay down on the floor and I told him to lie on my knees instead. He said that he felt like he was going to die any minute from thirst. I said that I would get him some urine to drink. I told him that he should drink it and not worry about it being urine; that he should act like an adult. Then I got one of the younger kids to urinate on somebody's shirt – it was only the young ones who were prepared to do this. The grown-up children refused. I got the boy sitting in front of me to wipe it on his back and face. I even got some of them to suck the urine off the shirt. It was difficult. Some children would lift it up to their faces but then couldn't bring themselves to drink it.'

Many of the surviving hostages speak about the pride and reserve of the older male pupils in the sports hall, who refused to relieve themselves in front of female parents, teachers and classmates. Whether admirable or not, this shows amazing restraint in people who needed not only to urinate but, more critically, to drink the pungent and poisonous liquid they had produced. Even given the inevitable peer pressure that these boys must have felt in the hall, I know that I could never have achieved anything similar. It is in acts like this that the civilized, Western veneer – already cracked and scratched – seems to peel away entirely from Caucasian life to reveal identities very alien from those to which we are accustomed. Stubborn, clannish versions of gender identities may be moulded to fit modern life without yielding any of their irrational essence. In fact, so specifically Caucasian was this bashfulness that the terrorists appear to have empathized.

Larisa Mamitova, the doctor who brought the terrorists' first communication out of the school, recalls how, at the beginning of the third day of the siege, she went up to one of them and said, '"The men are ashamed to urinate in front of women. Won't you let me take them out of the hall to relieve themselves?" He said to me, "Okay. But only the men." There was an enormous crowd of them waiting to go. You would ask one to come with you and he would have to crawl to the exit. That's how weak and worn down they had been made by the ordeal. They were crawling along on all fours. They sat on their hunkers and waited their turn. As each one crawled through the middle of the hall, they were shouted at by other hostages: "Find a bottle and pee in it!" they would say. "Then bring it back into the hall with you."'

There were nowhere near enough bottles to go round and those who were prepared to drink urine had to find other ways to do so. Seventy-year-old Vera Salkazanova witnessed a child rolling up banknotes – utterly valueless as money in the world of the besieged school – and using them like straws to suck up her mother's urine from the floor. Vera herself had at one point been right beside a terrorist as she crouched to urinate. She looked at him and said, 'You keep saying that you need to be treated like human beings. Well, we are human beings as well.' Larisa Tomaeva watched as her friend carried a sick child through the gym. She recalls, 'The girl had a very delicate little blue skirt on and, evidently, as Inga was carrying her, she started to wet herself. Well, as she passed through the rows of people, you just can't imagine what happened next. Children started grabbing hold of the wet skirt and trying to suck the liquid off it. Can you picture that scene? Try to picture it in your head. And that wasn't the worst thing that happened by any means.'

In the Beslan school siege, people's concept of what was 'the worst' was permanently in need of redefinition. Like a number of mothers in the gym, Zemfira Sozieva-Agaeva was suckling at the time that she was taken hostage. She had left her baby at home and had ended up incarcerated with her two elder children, Aleksandr, aged eleven, and Georgii, aged nine. During the first two days of the siege, Zemfira had allowed some of the child hostages to drink her milk from a spoon. At the trial of the only surviving terrorist, she turned on the defendant and demanded, 'How do you like the sound of that, Kulaev? Did you ever hear of anything so terrible as a mother being taken hostage and feeding other people's children with her milk?' Georgii, Zemfira's own son, refused to drink her milk, thinking it too disgusting an idea, so she held his nose and forced him to. By the end of the second day, her breasts had dried up because of her body's dehydration and lack of nourishment. When Georgii started drinking his mother's urine in the early hours of the morning of the third day of the siege, Zemfira remembers that the tables were turned. This scenario was too difficult for her to bear and she ordered him not to do it, but to try her nipple instead. Slightly delirious, he refused, saying that this belonged to his little sister whom they had left at home. Georgii never saw his little sister again.

The second night of the siege was worse in every respect than the first. The hostages were more desperate and more depressed; the inner resources of all but the strongest had been exhausted. The conditions were so bad in the gym that the terrorists even made a small concession: a number of the oldest and largest hostages would be allowed to spend the night in the weights room at the back of the gym. In this way, a little more space would become available for the rest. But the new arrangement made little difference. The way it was implemented caused yet more distress to worried families.

Felisa Batagova was ordered to her feet. 'I didn't know what was going on. I thought that they were taking me out to shoot me because I was the mother of the local public prosecutor. But then it turned out that they were putting me in the other hall to free up some space. I told my grandson to take care of his sister as I left. I told him not to try to follow me.' When they got to the room, the old people discovered a bare concrete floor covered in broken glass; it was a slight improvement on the heat and stench of the hall, but not much.

Sitting in the gym, thirty-nine-year-old Svetlana Dzherieva wanted to help some of the old hostages to their feet. 'Those who could went on their own. But the rest stood up and fell down again without moving. We weren't allowed to assist them. When one of the older pupils tried to assist, the terrorists put a machine gun to his head and forced him to sit down.'

Nonetheless, the weights room filled up quickly. The headmistress, Lydia Tsalieva, who was in her seventies and suffering from diabetes, would have been grateful for a place in the little hall. 'It was a terrible, terrible night. Some people went through to the weights room. I went and had a look. I would have stayed but there was no room. When I went back into the gym, I had lost my place there as well. I ended up having to sit right beside one of the terrorists.' Along with the rest of her school, she waited for the morning. There was nothing left to do.

'WHAT THEY CAME TO DO WAS KILL'

I knew as soon as it all started that it would end badly. How much grief and pain did they bring to Budenovsk, I thought to myself. Because they'd done it all before, hadn't they? They went to Budenovsk and took pregnant women and children and sick people hostage and killed them. Now they had come to our school to do the same. I'm sure they had demands and all the rest but really what they came to do was kill. And our government should have done something to prevent that.

Kazbek Rubaev, father of eleven-year-old Khasan

No one's ever guilty of anything here. It was the same in Nord-Ost. No one was guilty there. And when the submarine sank. No one was guilty. And in Derbent, and Volgodonsk. No guilty people in the whole country, because all of the guilty people are our oligarchs and our rulers. And who's going to punish them? Are they really to be expected to punish themselves?

Zinaida Tsarakhova, mother of twelve-year-old Elbrus
and ten-year-old Victoria

On 14 June 1995, Shamil Basaev led a group of Chechen separatists into the town of Budenovsk in the south of Russia.
The population of the place, which was over one hundred
miles from the Chechen border, was taken completely by surprise. After attacking the local police station, they moved
through the town, engaging in street battles which left many
members of the security services and civilians dead. They systematically kidnapped people from their homes and forced
them to join their march. The Chechens marched their human
cargo through the gates of the local hospital, which was set
apart from the town in its own grounds. Many patients and
medical staff were taken captive as well. Basaev took control
of the hospital and filled it with the hostages from the town.
Together with his own men there were well over 1,200 people
inside.

On day two of the hospital siege, Basaev telephoned government officials to demand a press conference. When he was
refused, he started executing adult male hostages. Later he
promised to destroy the entire hospital and all the hostages if
the Russians stormed it. Tense negotiations continued, but the
Russians refused to allow the terrorists safe passage back to
Chechnya and the terrorists refused to release all but a few of
the hostages. The siege dragged on for over three days.

Early on the fourth day, the Russians stormed the hospital,
attempting to use overwhelming force to achieve a quick
result. Basaev and his men stood their ground and fought
back. A thousand hostages cowered in terror, not knowing
who had started the attack but assuming that they would
soon be dead. Suddenly, with the operation failing badly, the
Russian army ordered their troops to cease fire, and the siege
continued for another day. Humiliatingly, the Russian prime
minister became involved in negotiations to allow the terrorists safe passage back to Chechnya, which had been their
demand before the building was stormed. On the fifth day

agreement was reached, but it involved Basaev travelling back to Grozny with over one hundred hostages as security against attack. In the end, over 120 civilians died in the Budenovsk hospital siege. There were many Russian officials and politicians who promised that they would never give in to Basaev again.

On 23 October 2002, at the Dubrovka Theatre in Moscow, more than 900 people were taken hostage while watching a performance of Russia's first home-grown musical, *Nord-Ost*. Around forty terrorists, working on the orders of Shamil Basaev, had marched onto the stage and halted proceedings at the beginning of the second act. They demanded the withdrawal of Russian troops from Chechnya and threatened to blow up the building if it was attacked.

The terrorists gave some interviews and Dr Leonid Roshal was allowed into the theatre to treat some of the sick and to take stock of the situation. After a day, a few hostages were released: Muslim members of the audience, and some children and elderly people. Everyone else was forced to sit in the theatre for another day and a half. Despite the terrorists' threats, once again the Russian Special Forces eschewed a negotiated settlement and sought to bring the siege to an early conclusion. This time, however, their methods were highly original. Sleeping gas, probably a bespoke KGB-invented chemical called Kolokol-1, was pumped into the school secretly to incapacitate the terrorists prior to a rescue attempt. Though it was the stuff of *Mission Impossible* films, initially it seemed to be working.

However, when the Special Forces entered the theatre they were met by gunfire from some of the terrorists who had gained access to respirators, making them immune to the gas. Because of the gunfight that resulted, there were delays in rescuing the hostages from the auditorium. They had also been knocked out by the gas but, forgetting this, their rescuers carried them outside and left them on their backs. Around 130 of the hostages died, most as a result of the gas, many when they choked on their own tongues.

The hostages in School No. 1 in Beslan and their loved ones standing outside did their best to keep their hopes up throughout the three days of the siege. But thoughts of Budenovsk and *Nord-Ost* haunted them. It was psychologically essential for them to believe that a peaceful resolution to their own predicament was possible. The achievements of Aushev, in particular the release of some hostages from the school building, helped immensely. Nonetheless most residents of Beslan who have spoken of their feelings during the siege have admitted that they felt there was a grim inevitability about a violent conclusion. Even before it was clear, they saw the hand of Shamil Basaev at work; they knew of his peculiar ability to provoke the Russians into harming their own citizens; they knew of the grudge that the government bore Basaev. As the siege in Beslan entered its third and final day, they shuddered.

'I DIDN'T FIND MY CHILDREN'

It is a feature of all traumatic events that they are recalled differently by all of those involved. While the siege was still going on, the hostages' minds were racing, sometimes obsessive, at others distracted. Time became elastic; it slowed down and sped up unpredictably, leaving people unsure of when things happened or how long they lasted. Many hostages have even had trouble recalling the day on which certain events happened. Since the siege, trauma has been able to create new realities and has played tricks with victims' memories. As a result, the deeper I had gone into the siege and the more survivors' tales I had heard and read, the more confused I became about what had actually gone on. Though hard facts and downright lies could sometimes be distinguished, more often than not I had to accept that no single, reliable account existed.

Nowhere was this truer than in people's recollections of the end of the siege. Amid the chaos and desperation, there was no time for reflection. However, the failure to hold a meaningful inquiry into the events of the siege has left people with only these distorted memories to go on. Like everyone else, the survivors want definitive answers but none has been forthcoming. Too much vital information has remained classified; too many senior officials have been allowed to stay silent. In this vacuum, the words of the survivors – justifiably confused and often contradictory – are all that we have.

On the third morning of the siege, the situation in the gym had become unbearable. There was no solace to be had anywhere. People were drifting in and out of consciousness and many hostages felt that they might fade away altogether. Doctor Roshal had stated publicly that the hostages might live without food or water for up to nine days, but reality inside the school seemed starkly different. The terrorists had become frantic too, obviously dissatisfied by the response they were getting from official negotiations. Like the captives, they had been without food for three days. Nurpashi Kulaev says that he was told by the Colonel not to drink water from the taps in case it was poisoned. But, in general, the terrorists almost certainly had their own limited supplies of bottled water. Unlike their captives, they could leave the gym, even though the heat and stench must have permeated the entire school. Finally, they gave permission for the upper windows in the gym to be broken, but by now it made hardly any difference to the stifling atmosphere. They were finding it difficult to remain sane and control their actions.

The Colonel kept asking Larisa Mamitova if she knew the telephone numbers of any more politicians. She didn't. 'I told them, "I could phone the casualty department of the hospital, if you want. The women who work the phones are bright. I could tell them whatever you wanted and they would pass the message on."' The terrorists took her to the staffroom to make the call. The doctor she wanted to speak to was not available, but she told a shocked nurse that the hostages were suffocating. 'I told her to do something, to call Moscow, to call wherever but just to *do* something.'

A few minutes later, she tried calling again. This time she

got the doctor she wanted, but the woman didn't really listen to what she said, assuming that Larisa was speaking under duress. To convince her, Larisa started speaking in Ossetian. The Colonel couldn't understand and shouted at her to speak in Russian. He told her to invite the doctor to come to the school and see for herself, promising that she would be safe if she did. Larisa made the offer and put the phone down, unsure of what would happen next.

After a while, one of the terrorists came into the gym and ordered Larisa to go with him. She assumed that her colleague had taken up the offer. But once in the corridor the terrorist asked her if she was frightened of blood and corpses. 'I'm used to everything,' was her reply. They went to Room 16, where the floor was covered in blood. Larisa instantly understood that this was where the male hostages had been brought. 'I asked where the bodies were and he told me to look through the window.' She used a chair to climb up onto the windowsill. Looking down, she saw the corpses on the ground, flies already buzzing around them. 'I started counting them and the terrorist asked me what I was doing. I told him, "I'm counting them because, in the gym, people have been asking about what happened to their relatives."

'"There are twenty-one bodies. Now get down from there. The Ministry of Emergencies is just about to send a van to collect the corpses. When they do, you will speak to them through the window. You will tell them about the state of the children in the gym."'

The Colonel had agreed to the bodies being removed following telephone negotiations with Ruslan Aushev that morning at around 11 a.m. Apparently, Zangionov, the official negotiator, had been bypassed once again and knew nothing of this decision. This was intended to be a goodwill gesture that would rescue these formerly proud men from a humiliating resting place.

Larisa and the terrorist waited for some time but no van appeared. Just after 12.30, she was sent back to wait in the gym. Having been out of the hall for some time, Larisa really felt the unbearable heat and stuffiness on her return. Whoever was not unconscious was being driven out of their minds. 'It was airless in there. It made me cry. I shouted at people to get as close to the floor as possible. I told them they would suffocate if they didn't. I walked the length of the hall; I remember screaming at a kid to get down off the windowsill or else he would die. Out of the corner of my eye, I saw something going on in the corridor outside the gym. People had run into the passageway. I don't remember anything else. That was when the explosion happened.' It was just after one o'clock. Unbeknownst to most of the hostages, Larisa included, the Ministry of Emergencies van had just approached the school. Four Ministry workers had got out ready to begin the task of loading the corpses. The terrorists had no time to bring Larisa to talk to the officials before the explosion happened. It was followed moments later by a second, even stronger blast.

Elvira Tuaeva and her ten-year-old son Khetag were sitting in the same place they had been in for the past two days. Both were very sick. Her daughter Karina, who was twelve, was sitting a little way from them, keeping company some schoolfriends whose parents were not among the hostages. Elvira had been reluctant to let her daughter go but had relented only twenty minutes earlier. Khetag was desperate for water and said over and over, 'Mummy, I'm going to die. Please, give me something to drink!' He had an empty bottle, but there was no more urine in his system; he and his sister had spent the morning incessantly asking one another if they needed to pee. A short time earlier, they had unsuccessfully begged one of the terrorists to let them out to have a drink.

Minutes before the explosion, Elvira had felt herself losing consciousness and had asked a woman to pull her hair hard. When the blast happened, she was knocked out instantly. Her first sensation was of being on fire: 'I remember feeling like I had been set alight. I was burning. And then people started falling on me. That probably saved my life.' When she opened her eyes she realized that the people on top of her were mostly dead. For some time she could think of nothing; guiltily she confessed that it had taken time even for Khetag and Karina to enter her mind. She was badly concussed.

After the first explosion, Sergei Urmanov turned to his wife, but found that she was dead. Almost exactly two days after he had survived the bomb blast intended to kill him, Sergei had only just been reunited with the rest of his family: his wife Rita and six-year-old daughter Zalina. Though he was feeling weak and ill, the thirty-four-year-old was relieved finally to be speaking to the two people he loved the most, though their conversation was very brief. 'I told Rita that I just wished it would all end. She agreed. "The sooner, the better," she said. "I don't care whether they blow us up or release us. I just wish something would happen."' Those were her last words. Rita was dead. She had been killed by a piece of debris that had ripped through her stomach; her body was later severely damaged by fire as well. Sergei saw that his wife had been killed, but his next thought had to be for his daughter. He took hold of her and threw her into a hollow that had been created where three dead bodies had fallen. He then lay on top of her. His instincts had been right. Suddenly the second explosion happened. He saw one part of the gym was now engulfed in flames.

History teacher Nadezhda Gurieva had become aware of growing disarray in the gym in the hours leading up to the explosion. Some people had become fearless because they had lost control of their minds. 'The situation had become so unbelievably tense. People had exhausted all their internal reserves. They were past caring.' Her own three children, Boris, Vera and Irina, had been sitting beside her. It was only after the second blast that Nadezhda came to her senses and began trying to find them. 'I came to before people had started running away. No one had stirred. A pile of bodies and a film of silver dust settling over the room was what I saw. A moment later, little Irina said, "Mummy, everyone is escaping."' Nadezhda told her to run if she could, and then she noticed that twelve-year-old Vera was already dead. Irina had survived because she had been sitting behind a screen of adults who took the force of the blast.

Only now did Nadezhda realize that she was injured; she noticed blood dripping from her head onto the body of her son. As she looked at him, he began to stir. Irina had obeyed her mother; she and another girl ran for the exit. They were stopped in their tracks by a terrorist with a machine gun. They hid in a pile of the belongings which had been confiscated from the hostages on the first day. Later, Irina told her mother that at that moment she looked up and saw the terrorist take off his beard and throw it into the pile. 'At first I thought it was just a hallucination. But other children said the same thing. It would be practically impossible for several children to have the same hallucination.'

Throughout the gym, people were having identical thoughts as they came to: find their loved ones, then escape with them. For many this was impossible because of death or injury; others had their paths barred by the terrorists, who were keen to hold on to their precious prisoners. There was no time to wonder what had triggered the explosion. When Kazbek Dzarasov came round at first he felt unable to move. Then he looked for his children and their grandmother, his own mother. He found his first son, who was alive, and immediately threw him through the window which had been blown out by the blast. In the split second he took to think about it, this was the only way he knew to get the boy to safety; others did the same. His mother was able to walk and he helped her out as well.

But Kazbek stayed behind to look for his youngest son, nine-year-old Aslan. Though he didn't find the boy, he helped many other people to escape in the process, only leaving himself when the terrorists started shooting at the survivors. Aslan was dead, and since the siege Kazbek has suffered from constant and indescribable feelings of grief and guilt. He has been treated for post-traumatic stress disorder and depression but with limited results.

Twenty-seven-year-old Madina Khuzmieva was one of those who was able to get out of the school very quickly after the blasts. In the gym, she had been sitting with her son Alex, who was seven, and her sister near the double doors that led directly out into the schoolyard. Her husband Murat was already dead, though she did not know this for certain. Seconds after the bomb, she opened her eyes. She saw that the doors had been blown open. 'No one else had come to in the gym. People were still bent down. Some of them were covering their children. I lifted Alex up and told him to run through the doors. I turned around to my sister beside me. I looked but could see nothing of her except the crown of her hair. I nudged her and she didn't react, so I just grabbed her by the hair and dragged her after me. I can't even remember at what point she woke up. I don't remember taking Alex's hand either. He told me afterwards that he had waited just outside the doors for me.'

Once outside, Madina and her family found the strength in their legs to run. 'We ran the whole length of the schoolyard. We were being shot at from the ground floor of the school as we went. I remember thinking that if we could make it to the fence, we'd be home and dry. But when we got there, we couldn't see anyone. Then we heard men's voices shouting at us from the alley that runs along the side of the school, from behind the corner of the building. We ran towards them and they took us across the allotments. Then we were put in a car and taken to hospital. My sister was a bit burned and had minor injuries, but compared to what happened to those who were left in the gym that was nothing.'

Outside the school, the explosions had caused pandemonium. To everyone who has spoken about their experiences, the blasts, when they finally came, were totally unexpected. Standing in the square in front of the Cultural Centre, Kazbek Rubaev had been tormented throughout the morning of the third day of the siege by rumours that his son, eleven-year-old Khasan, had managed to escape at the beginning of the siege and was now at the house of a friend. Though he doubted the news was true, he hoped so much that it was that he could feel he was losing his mind. He wanted to go to the friend's house to check, but he couldn't bring himself to leave the vicinity of the school.

He was still playing the different scenarios through in his head when the first explosion came. 'The cloud from the blast was white to start with. Then there was all this debris flying through the air, bits of the roof and stuff. People started running for cover. Five or six seconds later – maybe it was more, maybe less; I have difficulty remembering – there was a second explosion. Then the sound of shooting: from who and from where we weren't sure.'

Rita Tibilova was in a friend's flat right beside the school, near the allotments over which Madina Khuzmieva had just run. The pain of not knowing if Agunda was going to be alright was physical, but she still held out hope. Just outside the house soldiers had gathered. Thinking back, Madina said angrily, 'They weren't real soldiers. Even when they were standing up straight, their guns were taller than them.' The explosion made everyone she was with jump in the air; they ran outside into a hail of bullets. The soldiers told them to go back and at that moment the second explosion happened. Then, from inside the house, they watched as children started to emerge from the school. 'We shouted at them to come towards us. The flats were under fire as well of course. We started giving them water through the window. A neighbour gave them all her bed linen to use to make bandages. Then I thought, 'Here I am handing out water when I should be off trying to find my own child.'

Within minutes of the bombs going off, Major-General Andreev, the head of the official crisis committee, gave orders for the forces under him to begin operations against the besieged school. It is not known whether he spoke to anyone in Moscow or elsewhere in the time between the blasts taking place and the orders being given. Officially the various troops, led by the FSB's Special Forces, were commanded to rescue the hostages and neutralize the terrorists, some of whom – mainly those who had not been in the gym at the time of the blasts – had begun to shoot indiscriminately out of the school.

Afterwards, a very limited and pro-government inquiry by the Duma (the federal Russian parliament in Moscow) described how 'the crisis committee organized the evacuation of the hostages, ensuring that they were provided with medical assistance and questioning them. An uninterrupted flow of vehicles took the injured and other former hostages from the scene.'

The realities were somewhat different. Everywhere around the school there was total disarray. Stories of the intuitive responses of members of the public to the unfolding tragedy are as frequent as stories of the authorities' inadequate and ill-conceived activities. Despite the length of the siege, and the amount of time there had been to plan for its end, the majority of the vehicles available were privately owned and the hostages were loaded into them inexpertly, in a way that could have worsened their injuries and may even have caused death in some cases.

The involvement of the crisis committee or those under its command was patchy at best. Many essential emergency personnel had been kept out of the area nearest to the school, instructed to plan and set up their field hospitals, feeding stations and other operations further away. The area along the front of the school, in Comintern Street, had been closed to everyone but the security forces. However, the effort to evacuate ordinary citizens from the cottages and blocks of flats behind the school had been much less thorough, even though these people were at risk of being hit by an attack from either side. In the event, this oversight had been fortunate, for the only people involved in the first stages of the evacuation, apart from the soldiers, were members of the public. Without them, even more hostages would have perished.

Local gardener Ruslan Bokoev, father of Stanislav, was walking towards the school, on his way back to the crowd, when the bombs went off. He had just gone home for the first time during the siege to get pills for a blinding headache. He heard shooting erupt from every direction and saw the hostages, many of them injured, beginning to escape. 'The cars on my street were being loaded up with children covered in blood. The boots were left open and their legs were left hanging out of the back.'

The manner in which the Russian government forces used their weaponry also remains a deeply controversial issue. Without candid and concerted efforts by the authorities to make the truth known, there can be no definitive answers. The Duma inquiry found that 'snipers and intelligence and surveillance personnel returned the terrorists' fire, making sure to shoot at the source of the original shots. In this way they aided the hostages' spontaneous efforts at evacuation. Terrorists trying to escape through the cordon were surrounded by the team that had been tasked to neutralize them. The streets came under fire from the terrorists and the police tried to attract that fire onto themselves [and, therefore, away from the escaping hostages] by shooting into the air.'

This was not how it looked to Taimuraz Gasiev, local driver and one of the men who had tried to shoot at the terrorists at the very beginning of the siege. The twenty-nine-year-old had heard the first explosion and had run towards the cordon. The elite Alpha soldiers had halted his progress: 'They said to me, "The terrorists are going to start firing in this direction in a minute."

'"But if we don't get in there now, they'll have all of our children shot," I told him.

'"Don't you worry about it. We're here," they said.'

Taimuraz stood there as the second explosion happened. It was quickly followed by an outbreak of automatic fire. 'I shouted at them, "They've blown the whole school to bits, haven't they?"' Though he could not see all of the Russian troops and equipment from where he was standing, he had already seen how they were positioned earlier in the day. Now he heard one of the armoured personnel carriers, which had been driven into the riverbed immediately in front of the school, firing intensely. When he saw children running out of the school a moment later, he didn't know how the two things could both be occurring simultaneously. 'The children were waving their vests and bits of rags and ripped-up curtains in the air as they ran.'

Hostages escaping from the school quickly realized that they were being shot at from all directions. Svetlana Dzherieva and her young daughter Dana managed to escape from the gym soon after the initial explosions. As they clambered across the schoolyard, she realized that they were being shot at not only by the terrorists but also from nearby roofs. 'I remember seeing my daughter's big open mouth screaming, but I couldn't hear anything.' They were running round towards the garages at the back of the school and saw that that was also where much of the shooting was coming from. Diving behind one of the garages, she pulled her daughter and another child to the ground and lay on top of them. She lay there for what felt like twenty minutes, aware that the children were lying on top of broken glass. Only then did a soldier approach and help them to safety. They were put in a car and the driver set off at high speed. A few seconds into the journey he turned around and said to Svetlana, 'You'll have to give me directions to the hospital because I don't know where it is.'

Before long, the entire world's news channels switched to cover the unfolding story live. The world began to see uncensored footage of how the mighty Russian bear had fallen. They watched aghast as the survivors ran from the school under a hail of bullets, and shook with the cameramen who were unable to stay still under the force of the explosions.

The terrorists regrouped quickly after the initial explosions. Some were dispatched to fire at the Russians from the classrooms facing Comintern Street. Others trained their guns on the internal schoolyard through which most of the hostages were trying to escape. The ones who remained in the gym began to move through the rubble, systematically ordering the survivors they found to get up and move to the school canteen. Many of the people they found were so shell-shocked and disorientated by the explosion that they offered little or no resistance, obeying if they still had the strength and ability to move.

Like many, Elvira Tuaeva had been deafened by the explosions and became aware of the terrorist's voice only gradually. 'I opened my eyes and saw one of the terrorists. Then I heard him: "Whoever is alive, get up!" I wondered whether to get up or not. I thought that this must be our forces, come to rescue us so I got up and went. I suppose you could say I got taken hostage twice.' Elvira was walking out of the gym over the top of the dead and the living when she remembered about her children, Khetag and Karina. She started to scream and wail, but the terrorist turned to look at her and said, 'If you so much as take a step in the wrong direction, I'll shoot you in the back.' 'But by this stage his threats made no difference to me. I ran back to where we had been sitting. They weren't there, but some people were still alive. I told them to get up and come with me, that we were being released. I didn't know where we were going at that stage.' Hysterical, Elvira ran to the other side of the gym but couldn't locate her children. Forced to give up, she went unknowingly to a second imprisonment in the canteen. 'I didn't find my children, but I did remember I had them.'

Nadezhda Gurieva knew that the men moving through the room were terrorists and not rescuers. But she also knew that, once they had seen someone moving, they might shoot if that person then pretended to be dead: 'Those who were alive but refused to move got shot.' The race was on for her to get away before they reached her. While the terrorists were busy at one end of the room, hostages continued to leave from the other, mainly through the double doors leading out into the schoolyard. Nadezhda wouldn't leave without her fourteen-year-old son, who was lying beside her unable to get up. She couldn't lift him on her own. She tried to attract the attention of someone else who was fleeing and might help her to lift him but no one paid any attention. She knew she couldn't drag him out on her own.

While she stood there wondering what to do, she saw a mother climbing back into the school through one of the shattered windows, presumably returned to find a child. Being a teacher, she saw many people she recognized amongst the living and the dead on the floor. Some of the ones who were still alive died later and Nadezhda constantly remembers those last looks. Escaping hostages were now being ordered back into the gym by the terrorists and Nadezhda realized that she had no choice but to follow her other child, Irina, out into the corridor and up to the canteen. As she went, she asked one of the terrorists to help her injured son. He told her that the gym was coming under too much fire from outside but that they would return for Boris later.

At 1.30 p.m. the situation deteriorated further, when yet another explosion, the largest and most damaging by far, rocked the school gymnasium to its foundations. The previous blasts had sent people and objects flying through the hall. Pieces of masonry had fallen in parts of the room and holes had been burnt in parts of the roof. There had been some localized fires. Fundamentally, however, the structure of the building had remained sound. Now, the entire roof ignited and, some minutes later, most of it crashed onto the hundreds of people lying on the floor underneath.

The terrorists had been just on the point of reaching Sergei Urmanov and his daughter as they combed the room for survivors when the latest explosion went off. Again the two of them were lucky and survived. He was unsure what to do, fearing that the terrorists were still forcing people to go with them to the canteen. 'I just told my daughter, little Zalina, to stay still. "Lie there and don't move," I said to her. I was lying on top of her. I don't think it would have been easy for anyone to tell that we were alive. I was all covered in blood. I looked like a corpse.'

As they lay there, they listened to ferocious shooting and the sound of more explosions. Sergei didn't dare look up, frightened of being spotted by a terrorist or of seeing the carnage around him, including the body of Rita, his dead wife. Eventually, he heard a voice speaking in Ossetian. It was shouting, 'Over here. Come over here.' He listened three times, trying to make sure that he was not about to make a mistake, before lifting his head and getting to his feet. 'What we saw was horrific. I had to make my way to the door by walking on a carpet of corpses and living people.' When he and Zalina got there, they realized they had been tricked. Standing there were three terrorists, one of whom was Khodov, who had grown up nearby and spoke fluent Ossetian. They ordered them to the canteen.

Many others have remembered Khodov's cruel but clever trick. Seventy-year-old Vera Salkazanova had been near the centre of the first explosion and had lain unconscious until after 1.30 when the third blast seemingly jolted her back to life. She was disorientated and badly shaken. 'I could hear helicopters flying overhead. Come to save us, I thought to myself. I couldn't stand up because Rada, my granddaughter, was underneath me. She wasn't breathing and I decided to massage her stomach to try to give her some air – to stop her suffocating. It felt like I did that for a long time and then everything suddenly went quiet. Nothing was stirring . . . Of course, it could be that I was deaf from the explosions.'

Vera became aware that someone was tugging at her skirt. It was a terrorist. He got her to her feet but she could hardly stand. She couldn't focus on anything and her only thought was for her four-year-old granddaughter, her daughter-in-law and her grandson. She made a move to go back for Rada and the terrorist raised his machine gun against her. Her vision filled with the sight of her dead granddaughter: 'Her skull and one of her arms had been blown off. Her foot had been reduced to a mush. I couldn't have cared less at that point what they did to me.' Unable to think straight, she was taken from the gym before she had time to find the rest of her family. From now on she assumed they were dead as well. On her way out, she walked over the dead body of Tatarkan Sabanov, the school's ninety-year-old former headmaster who had been a guest of honour at the Day of Knowledge celebration. At the door Vera asked in Russian where she should go. The person who replied was Khodov, once again in Ossetian. He ordered her into the corridor and told her to follow the rest. She ended up in the canteen.

When the third explosion happened, Larisa Tomaeva and her two children had clambered out of the gym and into a small room which adjoined it and was used by Alik Tsagolov and the other P.E. teachers as a staffroom. Somehow, they had managed to evade the terrorists' notice. Minutes after the explosion, she looked into the gym through a crack in the door. The intensive-care nurse was horrified by what she saw: 'The roof was on fire and it was burning very quickly. Molten plastic was dripping onto the floor. The fire was spreading through the hall so quickly, right before my eyes. I can say with absolute certainty that many, many people were burned alive: people with stomach injuries or whose legs had been severed; people who were stunned. They couldn't get to their feet and they started to burn. I saw it with my own eyes.'

Tomaeva kept waiting for help to appear. 'No firemen. No First Aid. No Special Forces. No one came into the hall at first.' After what felt like an age, but was in reality only ten minutes, Special Forces finally made it into the gym. Tomaeva remembers the first soldier she saw because he was Korean-looking. 'He had some kind of apparatus around his neck and stood in the doorway. He looked at the scene in front of him as if it was on a television screen. He had a two-way radio and now he shouted into it: "Andy! Andy! Don't shoot. It's our own people in here! Don't shoot, I said!" He repeated this a few times and then I lost sight of him.'

The doctor Larisa Mamitova had been knocked out by the first explosion and only regained consciousness after the third one. 'When I came to, I couldn't understand what had gone on. I was lying on the floor, completely naked. I had regained consciousness because my back was on fire. The burning sensation was intense. I lifted my head and saw that the gym had been turned upside down. Everyone was lying down. No one was standing.' She looked up and noted that the wires suspended between the basketball hoops and the bombs that had been attached to them were gone. She saw as well that the roof had caved in and heard the terrorists shouting at people to leave the hall.

When he saw her moving, a terrorist came over to Larisa and held his machine gun to her head: 'If he had wanted to kill me, he could have done it. Then someone started pulling my hair very hard; it made me cry out loudly. Suddenly they let go of it and there was nothing.' She assumed this had been the terrorist but when she looked behind her she realized that it was a boy in his death throes who had reached out and gripped her. His death made her think about Tamerlan. Somehow she got to her feet and saw that the armed terrorist was still standing behind her. 'He moved across to the place

where all the bags had been stacked. That was where I had been telling the children who had temperatures to go, the sick ones. I saw that the whole building had collapsed on them from above. The terrorist was pulling some of them out from under a mass of desks and things and telling them to get out of the gym.'

In front of him, Larisa felt ashamed of her nakedness and put on a shirt she found. But she felt no fear and walked away from him desperate to find her son. From the floor she heard people shouting at her to lie down. 'I have to find my son,' she told them. Dazed, she eventually found her way to the place she last remembered seeing Tamerlan. 'I started searching for him in the rubble. I'd get to a boy about the same age as Tamik and think it was him. I couldn't tell because they all seemed to look the same; eyes wide open, mouths wide open.' She pulled one boy out who was already dead, but it wasn't her son. She put him back and moved on to look elsewhere, still digging with her hands. Larisa couldn't think of a way to tell her son apart from all the others, but then remembered that he had a scar on his forehead.

Then she saw people escaping at the far end of the gym from the small adjoining hall. Larisa ran towards the room thinking Tamerlan might be there or might even have escaped. When she didn't see him, she became hysterical. She had to fight to remember what she had been thinking only a second earlier: that Tamerlan might have escaped. She had to get out there to help him. He might be injured. Larisa jumped through the window and ran over the broken glass to where people were waiting to take her to hospital. Her mind registered that Tamerlan was not there and she tried to run back into the school but was stopped by her brother who was among the local civilians helping with the rescue. He told her that Tamerlan was already safely on his way home and put her in a car to the hospital. 'Even when I was in hospital, I assumed that they were lying to me and that he was dead. I made them bring him to me so I could see that he was still alive.'

P.E. teacher Alik Tsagolov was one of the hostages to be taken in by Khodov's use of his native tongue. His ribs had been damaged in the first explosion, but otherwise he felt better than he had for some time: his adrenalin pumping, his mind thinking of the most sensible way to proceed. At first, he and a few others disobeyed the terrorists and headed for the assembly hall. Alik assumed that, in the heat of battle, they would soon be forgotten about by their captors. But the terrorists were in pursuit and forced the hostages into the canteen. According to Alik, the panic-stricken hostages were making too much noise to hide anyway.

From now until the end of the siege, the canteen became the main focus of the fighting. Although exact figures are not known, around three hundred hostages had probably been guided to the room, whose windows faced out onto Comintern Street on two sides. Having survived the explosions inside the gym, the hostages were now much more vulnerable to the attack that was being mounted on the school by the Russians outside. They were now at the mercy of both the terrorists and the government forces. If the terrorists had hoped to use their captives to blackmail the authorities into holding fire, they failed. Whatever they knew about who was inside the canteen, the crisis committee did nothing to halt a full-scale attack. The force of the Russian onslaught was massive, involving armoured personnel carriers and rocket-propelled grenades. From 2 p.m. onwards, hostages and bystanders alike, including experienced news journalists and many who had served their time in the Russian army, were shocked to hear the sound of tank shells being fired at the building.

More than half of the thirty-two terrorists were still alive. Sergei Urmanov watched as they forced mothers at gunpoint to stand their children on the windowsills in the hope of discouraging the Russians from shooting. 'I personally saw two women who were mown down as they tried to do this. I don't know which side got them, but I saw them fall. Then a shell was fired into the room. It came in spinning and smoking and burst into flames. It fell on my daughter. I was lying on top of her to protect her, but it landed between her body and the wall.' On contact with the floor, the shell exploded, burning six-year-old Zalina and filling her body with shrapnel. Sergei stood up and tried to put the fire out with anything that came to hand: tablecloths, clothes, anything. He tried to clear the burning metal from around her body but was sent to the floor by a bullet through the spine. He lay writhing in agony, powerless to help either himself or his daughter.

Zarina Daurova's younger brother Zaur was already dead. The nineteen-year-old who had popped into her old school on a whim for a few minutes three days earlier had been forced to leave her brother's blood-stained body in the gym and head for the canteen. 'When I saw the canteen, I wished that I had just stayed in the gym and died there,' Zarina said. 'It was a scene of horror beyond all imagining. The shooting didn't stop for a second. The explosions were nothing like the ones in the gym. The terrorists shouted at us to stand up and shout to the people outside that we were in there. We shouted alright, but nobody heard us. Then a girl who was sitting alongside me stood up and started to scream that we were being shot at by tanks. The canteen was a nightmare.'

History teacher Nadezhda Gurieva continued to demand that one of the terrorists go back with her to the gym to carry her son Boris to safety. Instead of ignoring the distraught woman, the terrorist hit her hard in the mouth with the butt of his gun, knocking out several of her teeth. She staggered to the kitchen, the part of the canteen furthest from the windows facing onto the street, and crouched by the stoves. Despite the danger they were in, she noticed that many hostages – children and adults alike – were standing up, gulping down mouthfuls of water from taps. After so long without liquid, most of them instantly started to retch.

Vera Salkazanova was watching this too and thought to herself that the water supply must have been poisoned after all. She looked for somewhere to hide. At the beginning of the siege she had hidden in the boiler room, now she hid in one of the stoves. She was joined by a young woman who had been injured in the shoulder: 'Every time she breathed out, she sprayed me with blood.' She heard the children shouting at the windows for the soldiers to stop shooting. 'They said, "Good people! Help us! We want to live! We don't want to die! For the sake of Allah, in the name of the Holy Spirit, help us!"'

Though they could not hear the children's shouts, there were plenty of people outside the school who sensed that the government's strategy was dangerous and misguided. They heard the constant shooting and explosions and assumed that their loved ones were amongst those being hit. When the cordons around the school collapsed, soon after the third explosion, they rushed forward but were powerless to restrain the security forces. Instead, many put themselves in the line of fire as they tried to rescue hostages from the burning rubble of the gym. Ridiculously, ordinary members of the public were able to approach the gym even before the crisis committee had given the signal to allow firefighters in to tackle the blaze. The gym had burned for almost two hours before they were given access.

After waiting for so long, by 3 p.m. the surviving hostages who were trapped in the school were beginning to be rescued. Some, like Felisa Batagova, were carried out unconscious and only realized they had survived when they woke up in the street. Immediately, worry kicked in for their families. In Felisa's case, the news was not good. Her granddaughter Alana, who was only ten, had been killed. Her sister and her sister's child were dead as well. Only her grandson Khetag survived.

Even when the rescuers started to reach them, the odds were against the survivors. The shooting continued and there were fires everywhere, the biggest of which was still raging in the former gym. One wrong step could set off a grenade; masonry was falling everywhere throughout the building. It took time for the rescuers to carry one person out and return for another; as they waited many lost the battle to survive. Each time the fighting flared up the rescue effort was abandoned for ten or twenty minutes at a time; hostages lay paralysed waiting for help that never came.

One of the first to be rescued by the outsiders was the headmistress, Lydia Tsalieva. Proudly she likes to recall the fact that her saviours were not just brave members of the public, but actually people she had taught as children. Amidst the rubble and the tangle of bodies, it was very difficult to walk whilst carrying a body. Instead, many people, Lydia included, were dragged out, feet first. This must have hurt the seventy-two-year-old a lot because she had received a deep flesh wound to the leg from one of the explosions. She was taken to hospital, where she remained for four days. Her injury was serious enough to require treatment at a national centre of excellence. She was told that because of her diabetes her leg would never heal and would have to be amputated.

In the small staffroom, Larisa Tomaeva and her children had continued to wait. Hearing the helicopters overhead, she thought that more Alpha troops would rush in at any moment. 'Like they do in the movies,' she said. For some time no one came. Then those who did were just ordinary local policemen. Larisa's son ran towards them, across the burning hall, over the bodies of his schoolmates and to safety. Her daughter remained in her arms and when another man came to take her away, Larisa grew fearful that one of them – either herself or her daughter – would not survive. She saw that her girl had made it outside and felt relief: 'Even if I were to die then, I thought, at least the children are safe.'

Larisa knew that she now had to try to escape herself. It seemed that the rescuers were concentrating on saving children. She psyched herself up to run across the gym and out of the school. 'I thought I was ready for it but found that I wasn't able to run on the corpses.' Instead she turned around and made for the showers in the changing room opposite. She had stumbled upon a secret hiding place full of terrified women and children. They were desperate not to be discovered and frantically waved her away. She went into another shower room which was less full. From there, she waited once more to be saved; but she saw that now the rescuers were coming back more often. Larisa saw the body of one of the women suicide bombers turned over and dragged out, as the men searched for the living. Outside, the fighting did not abate. Eventually, her turn came and she was led to an open window and thrown through it. On the other side, she was led to an ambulance and then to hospital. Remarkably, she and her children had escaped with only minor injuries.

By 5 p.m. almost no hostages were left alive in the gym. The rescuers reached the canteen and school kitchens last of all. Taimuraz Gasiev heard the first tank shell being fired. 'It was totally unexpected. I just wouldn't have thought that they'd use tanks. It made me jump.' 'But there are children in there!' he reminded the soldiers who were standing beside him. They told him that the tank was being used to create a hole in the wall to allow people to escape. Around where he was standing, everyone started running towards the school: ordinary soldiers, Special Forces and civilians alike. No one tried to stop Taimuraz any longer.

At the wall of the school, a member of the elite Alpha force told him to crouch down so that he could stand on his back and haul himself in through a window. While he was bent over, Taimuraz felt the man fall backwards. He looked around to see his headless corpse lying on the ground. Shocked but determined, he bravely continued into the school. Eventually, he made it to the canteen, where the bars had finally been blown off the windows. Those hostages who were still alive and able to move were climbing out. Others were being carried by a mixture of military and civilian personnel. One of the first things he saw was a dying terrorist, his hand still pressed down on the trigger of his gun, which continued to shoot until it was empty.

Then Taimuraz lifted a three-year-old child. 'He was alive. I started to carry him towards the windowsill. I heard a shot but I didn't understand who was shooting or from where. Then I felt this warm sensation against my body. I assumed I'd been hit and I just thought to hell with it. But then someone shouted at me. They asked me why I was carrying him when he was already dead.' Taimuraz put the toddler on the ground, fell to his knees and started to cry. Another tank shell exploded nearby and a piece of the school's masonry was lodged in his leg. As he lay there, he heard the Alpha troops express surprise at the quality of the terrorists' bullet-proof vests; apparently they were the very latest models which had only just been issued to Russian troops.

From her vantage point in the oven, Vera Salkazanova saw the arrival of Special Forces in the canteen. She glanced out and asked the newcomer if he was one of theirs. 'He said he was. I told him who to shoot at. I pointed out these two who were sat in the doorway between the canteen and the kitchens. I told him they had been shooting at us. He set about his task. They shot at each other for a long time. And then it became quieter.' Vera thought that now might be the time to escape, but as she climbed from the oven the fighting intensified once more and she saw pieces of shrapnel flying in her direction. At the next lull, she was able to make it to a window and from there was lifted to safety. Even then, the bullets continued to buzz all around; Vera is sure that some of them were coming from the Russian forces who were trying to get into the school.

At first Vera was taken to the field hospital, where the dead, the dying and the living had been laid out. From there she went to the local hospital. Though she seemed in reasonable health, the shock of what she had been through only hit her a few days later. The seventy-year-old grandmother fell into a coma. She was taken to a hospital in Moscow, where she spent more than six weeks recovering. The thought of her dead daughter-in-law and granddaughter, and how she had missed their funerals, haunted her.

Elvira Tuaeva, Nadezhda Gurieva and Zarina Daurova were all rescued from the canteen at around the same time. The majority of the terrorists had been killed, though it later became clear, at around 5.30 p.m., that one or two had managed to hide with their weapons. After the days of hardship, these women had endured four hours of the most intense aggression imaginable. They emerged into a world that had changed for ever. With both Khetag and Karina dead, Elvira was no longer a mother. Zarina's brother was dead too, along with dozens of friends from the school she had just graduated from a few months earlier. Nadezhda Gurieva's grief is unending: so many of her beloved students and colleagues were killed along with her eldest son and daughter. Only her youngest daughter Irina survived.

The P.E. teacher, Alik Tsagolov, lay slumped against the

wall in the canteen. He had been joined by Nurpashi Kulaev, the terrorist who insisted that he was not a terrorist. Not knowing all of the parents individually, Alik initially assumed that Kulaev was one of them. As soon as he spoke, Alik knew from his accent that he was actually one of the terrorists. Amidst all the chaos, the teacher tested him with a few words of Ossetian. Kulaev admitted that he only knew a little. Then he said, 'I haven't killed anyone. I just want to live.' After a while, the terrorist said that he could hear voices on the street. Alik told him to try climbing out. '"They'll kill me," he said.'

'Your lot showed no pity to our children, did you?' Alik replied. And at that moment he saw another child gunned down as it tried to climb through the open window: 'He was no older than six or seven.'

Kulaev escaped just before the Special Forces and other res- cuers entered the canteen. Alik recalled that the Russians entered through the kitchen and ended up shooting at the ter- rorists in the canteen over his and other survivors' heads. 'The Special Forces were very brave. They didn't blink an eye; they didn't rush anything. They were careful to take aim and only then did they fire. At some point they told us to jump out of the window.' Alik got to his feet and started to help people out, but one of the soldiers told him to leave immediately: '"You should climb out now. You're being more of a hin- drance than a help," was what he said to me.' Once on the outside Alik went into shock. 'In reality, there's nothing more to fear at that point, but somehow the fear intensifies.' They were taken to hospital in someone's car, a black foreign import, Alik remembered.

Sergei Urmanov now got his chance to escape too. Lying on the floor, covered by dead bodies, he heard someone ask if there was anyone left alive. He raised his arm through the corpses. He was dragged to the window and dropped through it by someone he recognized from the local police. Now on

the ground he was surrounded by soldiers. 'They were conscripts, I think. They certainly weren't Special Forces with
shields or anything. I lost consciousness and they must have
put me on a stretcher. When I came to they had carried me
round the corner and started beating me up. They were saying
that I was a terrorist. They were hitting me so hard that the
stretcher I was on ripped underneath me. Then I was taken to
hospital. But they came to me there as well and started torturing me in hospital. Somehow, it was explained to them that
I was one of theirs and it all ended.' Sergei was left to think
about everything he had lost in the space of three days: his
wife, his daughter and, he was then to learn, his sister and
three nieces.

Everyone started heading towards the local hospitals in the
late afternoon. It became clear that there were fewer and
fewer survivors left in the school and those bystanders who
had failed to see their loved ones escape had no choice but to
hope they had been taken to casualty. They checked first in
Beslan's hospitals and then tried in Vladikavkaz. But the roads
and telephone lines were blocked and many people had to
wait until early the next morning to hear definitively where
their relatives and friends had been taken.

For gardener Ruslan Bokoev the news was good. After
checking the local hospitals, he phoned friends in Vladikavkaz
and heard that sixteen-year-old Stanislav was in hospital
there, injured but alive. Later, Ruslan heard that he had survived because of the unusual position of his heart. The wound
he received to the torso would have pierced a normal person's
heart and killed them, but he had survived. 'His larynx had
been temporarily severed and a piece of shrapnel had lodged
in his lungs from behind. They turned out to be minor
injuries, but he still has three pieces of shrapnel in his body
even now.' Much worse were the boy's long-term psychological problems. Ruslan said, 'He's alive. He walks about. But

the problems are all in his mind. When he sees anything to do with it on television, even the trial, he starts to foam at the mouth. His hands start shaking and he makes me turn it off.'

Many other parents got the news they had dreaded. Though he had been told at lunchtime that his son had escaped on the first day of the siege, Kazbek Rubaev knew better and went to the hospital to learn the truth. He watched as a friend found his son in the morgue: 'He hugged his child and cried.' Then Kazbek searched all the other hospitals he could think of. The absence of information was an answer in itself, but the remains of fifteen-year-old Khasan's body weren't pulled from the rubble of the school for a further two days. Rita Tibilova, who had waited so patiently for news about Agunda, also drew a blank at the hospitals. 'Of course I found nothing. We looked for her in the morgues, but she wasn't there either. We kept going back to the morgues as regularly as if we were going to work there. We touched the bodies and looked at their teeth to try to recognize our own

children.' When eventually they found her, she was unrecognizable; half of her body had been completely burned away.

It is an indication of the scale of the tragedy of School No. 1, as well as of the inefficiencies of Russian bureaucracy, that accurate figures for the number of hostages and the number of dead and injured have never been compiled. However, by the end of the siege, some 330 hostages were dead; at least 188 of them were children. A further 610 hostages were injured or needed treatment; no fewer than 356 of them were children. The school lay in ruins and everywhere across the town deep wounds had been created that will never be healed.

TRUTH AND BESLAN

On 29 November 2005, a commission of deputies from the North Ossetian parliament published its report into the events leading up to and surrounding the siege of School No. 1. Having analysed a mass of information and interviewed many key players, the deputies were still dissatisfied. Many questions remained unanswered. One month later, the head of a federal parliamentary commission into the school siege held a press conference to present its preliminary findings and ask for more time to investigate important issues related to the siege. In part they were waiting for the conclusion of the trial of Nurpashi Kulaev, officially held to be the only member of the terrorist gang who survived.

On 26 May 2006, Nurpashi Kulaev was sentenced to life imprisonment for his part in the Beslan siege. After a trial lasting a year, which heard evidence from many former hostages and government officials, there was still widespread disagreement about the twenty-five-year-old's role in the events. Even those who called for a death sentence to be handed down have said that Kulaev was at most an insignificant cog in a much larger machine.

Despite the three inquiries – all of which have now produced their final reports – there is a lingering feeling that the truth about the siege remains hidden, and a growing acceptance that this will always be the case. Many people were angry that key witnesses were not obliged to be interrogated by any of these three bodies. There are allegations that people have been got at by officials and made to change their stories. Conspiracy theories have flourished. One member of the federal parliamentary commission felt unable to agree with its conclusions and published his own dissenting report, entitled 'Beslan: The Hostages' Truth'. But this and other attempts at openness cannot remove the suspicion that many lies continue to be told, and the truth about Beslan remains beyond reach. Were it not for the dead, who remain dead, the inconsistencies might sometimes seem to cast doubt on the siege altogether.

The town is a place on hold, unable to escape the event that engulfed it. The feeling that time has stood still, a natural consequence of an attack like the school siege, is exacerbated by indignation and anxiety about the information that survivors feel they are still owed. Many of Beslan's strongest personalities – the people who might carry others through this dark time – are distracted from thinking about the present and the future by an energy-sapping pursuit of justice for the past. Though the crisis continues to unite some survivors, it has divided the town's population as well.

Major questions remain unanswered about every stage of the siege, from the planning of the attack to the storming of the school; the most intractable and serious concern the end of the siege. Even when the wildest conspiracy theories are put to one side, the gaps and contradictions are astounding. Whilst accepting that ultimate responsibility for the attack must be borne by the terrorists and their masters, those left behind want to know how the authorities' actions and omissions aggravated the situation.

Crucially, many survivors and other commentators still do

not believe the official versions of the end of the siege. Thinking of how the Russian authorities have behaved in other situations, many are convinced that the explosions in the gym were not set off by the terrorists or by mere chance; they see the hand of the government and, in particular, the FSB. One influential point of view suggests that the authorities fired a rocket-propelled grenade at the roof of the gym and that this set off the chain reaction of explosions and fires. According to this version, the intention was to blast a hole in the wall at the back of the gym to allow the hostages to escape to School Alley. Perhaps they timed the shot to coincide with the arrival of the Ministry of Emergencies van in the hope that some of the terrorists would be out of the gym and distracted. Similar acts of well-intentioned heavy-handedness have been seen before. Of course, it is more than possible that one of the terrorists simply decided to bring things to a head; it may be that one of the improvised bombs that were sellotaped to the wall worked itself loose in the sweaty atmosphere and fell to the floor.

Alla Khanaeva, who lost two of her three children in the siege, is convinced that the first explosion in the gym was caused by the Russian authorities. 'I am 300 per cent certain that the first bomb was caused by people outside the school. Nothing blew up inside. There was a terrorist sat at the doors between the gym and the small training hall. When he heard the explosion he jumped to his feet and started screaming and running around. He had been sitting calmly right up to that point. If he'd been expecting the explosions you would have seen it on his face.'

Other people demand to know whether and when tanks, armoured personnel carriers and rocket-propelled grenades were used by the government forces. On this issue too there is insufficient information in the public domain for people to reach a conclusion. Many eyewitnesses are convinced that they saw this equipment being used at an early stage in the rescue operation. The government says not. Everyone agrees that it would have been cruel and stupid to fire such heavy weapons at a small building with the intention of saving the lives of innocent civilians who were trapped inside.

For young Zarina Daurova, it seems clear that the authorities basically stayed true to their policy of not negotiating with terrorists, whatever they might say to the contrary. She believes that the terrible end to the siege, including the death of her brother, show how flawed this was. 'I think that tragedies like this one will continue to happen. I understand that our authorities don't want to hold negotiations with terrorists; that they look on these people as being not worthy of their notice. They think it is better to piss in the shithouse than to try to hold negotiations in it. But this time they got it wrong. A school full of children isn't the shithouse.'

But most survivors focus on the negligence of the Russian system, which is beyond dispute and perhaps beyond description. Rita Tibilova, mother of Agunda, says, 'I just don't know how it was all able to happen. I don't know why it was allowed to happen. I think that it is not just the local authorities who are guilty, the ones who allowed them into North Ossetia. Someone directed them to us. Our government has behaved with such negligence towards us. But they don't stop to think that the same thing could happen again tomorrow to them, to their children. It's the whole of the leadership, from the district administrations all the way up, Andreev, Dzasokhov, Mamsurov included. They were all in command. They all came out and told us that they had food and water ready for the hostages, that they'd reach an agreement with the terrorists if they could.' Living alongside the police station, Rita says that she saw how little the officers did to help the hostages during the siege. 'They just spent their time sitting on benches. I even saw one of them washing his socks.'

In the aftermath, the country's creaking infrastructure meant delays of weeks and even months in identifying many of the dead through DNA tests, dental examinations and other procedures. Worse, there were numerous cases of misidentification. Parents buried the children who had been taken away from them, only to have to dig up their bodies when the remains were shown to be those of another.

The absence of convincing or honest answers to important questions has caused many survivors to fall back on conspiracy theories. These are a tried and tested solution to many mysteries in a country with a pathological aversion to honesty and openness.

Were there really only thirty-two terrorists? Many hostages are certain that there were closer to fifty in the gang; some even say there were seventy. Knowing that many escaped in the chaos at the end of the siege, the government has supposedly decided to base its calculation of the number of terrorists on the number of bodies it found.

Was Ruslan Aushev really trying to help? Understandably, given previous enmities, his achievements were too good to be true for some. He was the only person to enter the school after the siege had begun. He left it alive, and he was the only person to secure the release of any of the hostages. Seeing no reason for Aushev, an Ingush, to want to help them, some smell a conspiracy. Taimuraz Gadiev, in his seventieth year at the time of the siege, stood on the street near the school waiting for information about his two daughters and three grandchildren, all of whom were in the school. An old and sick man, he has had to accept the death of one daughter, Fatima, two granddaughters, Kristina and Stella, and one grandson, Georgii. Another daughter, Zalina, survived with shrapnel embedded in her head and brain damage that affects her ability to speak and walk.

Taimuraz's surviving daughter told him that when Aushev walked into the gym he expressed approval for what the terrorists had achieved. 'Aushev told them that they would all go straight to heaven when they were killed. He said, "Great work, boys. You've done well. You'll go to heaven for certain. God will carry your soul there instantly."' According to Taimuraz, Aushev's rescue of the babies and their mothers was simply a smokescreen to cover his own involvement with the terrorists.

Others agree. Larisa Tomaeva is also sceptical about other hostages' description of Aushev's shell-shocked expression. 'He walked in dressed in a tweed jacket and carrying a mobile phone. He had something black thrown over his head as well. It must have meant something to the terrorists. It must have been a sign of some kind or other. Why else would he have come in with it otherwise? Anyway, he came in and stood in front of us, calm as you like. I heard one woman saying he looked shocked. I for one didn't see any shock in his eyes, I can tell you. I think he knew all about it. He knew perfectly well where he was going and what he was going to see there.'

Larisa believes that not just Aushev but all of Ingushetia knew in advance about the impending attack on School No. 1. Her feelings are shared by many in North Ossetia, who believe that another day of reckoning is now inevitable with their Muslim neighbours to avenge the blood of their relatives. As she sat in the school gym, she remembered the words of a friend only a few days earlier. 'During the last days of August, all of the Chechen and Ingush patients started to check out of the hospital and go home. We're always treating loads of them in our hospital because it's owned by the railway company and it's easy for them to get referrals for treatment. We noticed the same thing happening in the run-up to every terrorist attack there's been here, and just before the Ossetian–Ingush conflict in 1992. There's no denying that they all knew about it beforehand. They always know if something's going to happen in North Ossetia and then they make damn sure to get out.'

More than a few survivors have turned on fellow hostages, openly accusing them of collaboration with the terrorists. The former headmistress Lydia Tsalieva and to a lesser extent other members of her staff have suffered most from these slurs, which hark back to the denunciations of Stalinist times. There have been allegations, not substantiated by statistics, that the teachers in the gym somehow managed to protect themselves at the expense of parents and pupils. A mixture of grudges – personal, class-based, local – has created this terrible channel for grief and guilt.

Perhaps the words of Felisa Batagova, who lost a sister, a niece and a granddaughter, give an indication of the personalized rancour which has led to this situation. Of the time just before Aushev's arrival in the gym, she said, 'The headmistress got to her feet and started screaming at everyone in the hall. "Be quiet! You make me ashamed of you. What are you acting like? Were you taught nothing when you were at school?"' Felisa was angered by the headmistress's words.

Many months after the siege, her rage was as fresh as when she first heard them: 'Taught nothing!' she said. 'We certainly weren't taught to put up with that sort of humiliation. Unlike her, I didn't give birth to a drug addict. My son was never a drug addict or a thief, and I didn't keep prostitutes either.' Felisa seemed determined to show that there was nothing special or impressive about the former headmistress of Beslan's School No. 1. She had no more right than anyone else to define what behaviour was fitting for inhabitants of the town, even in such extreme circumstances.

'I grew up in Beslan as well. We were treated like lambs to

the slaughter for the three days we were in there. And that is what we are acting like if we let her just go on living her life like nothing happened. I want her to come and sit with us and listen to our grievances and complaints.' Felisa does not just think that Lydia Tsalieva is bossy and arrogant, she actually believes that the seventy-two-year-old assisted the terrorists. 'Because of her greed, because of her negligence, our children died! She did not behave like a headmistress when she was in the gym. She made damned sure she saved her own skin.'

Tsalieva's staff did the same. 'She let her teachers sit beside her instead of making them go and sit with their pupils around the sports hall. She should have told them that their first duty, as teachers, was to their pupils. I'm not saying that they should all have died or anything. They didn't deserve to be taken hostage any more than the rest of us. But they should have been sitting with their pupils, comforting them. I hope the children I was sitting near will forgive me for comforting them with lies. I told them not to worry; that everything would be okay; that the terrorists would have to let us go because there were so many of us. You should have seen how reassured my little granddaughter was to have me with her. She was distressed, but she was reassured at the same time because I was beside her. I was at least able to try to convince her that we would be all right. The teachers should have done the same.'

Other hostages have criticized the headmistress and her staff for what they feel was a certain aloofness from parents and pupils. For instance, some are suspicious that Lydia handed over the school's master keys to the terrorists without protest on the first day of the siege. One mother accuses Lydia of doing nothing to help her diabetic son who died during the course of the siege. Another says she heard Tsalieva having conversations with the terrorists, which she describes as overly friendly.

Some go so far as to allege that the teachers and the head-mistress actually helped the terrorists to take over the school – whether through negligence or collusion. Summing up this anger, one woman says bitterly, 'She left the gym on the third day with exactly the same hairdo that she had when she entered it on the first.' The key claim is that Tsalieva mis-managed the school's annual programme of essential repairs and maintenance in the months before the siege and arranged for the Day of Knowledge celebrations to begin an hour ear-lier. The headmistress insists that during the summer holidays of 2004, as in every one of the preceding twenty-three years, repairs were carried out by the school's works department assisted by some of the teachers. They painted some walls and renovated certain parts of the school's floors where the boards had rotted away. They had been ready to collapse for longer than Lydia Tsalieva can remember. 'I had been saying these needed urgent repair for at least three years, but there was never any money to do it. Finally, I went to the local admin-istration personally and told them, "I am supposed to let the children come back to school on 1 September even though parts of the floor are not capable of bearing their weight."'

When the administration sent a civil servant and an engi-neer to inspect the problem the next day, Tsalieva stood on the affected parts of the floor, moving back and forth, to demonstrate how fragile the structure was. Money was found and the repairs were carried out over the course of a couple of weeks. Her accusers say that Tsalieva hired outside workmen to undertake the work. It was these workmen who prepared the ground for the terrorists, secreting large amounts of weapons and munitions under the floors in readiness for the attack. How else – they wonder – could so much equipment have made it into the school? How else could the terrorists have known with such seeming accuracy the layout of the building?

These allegations are often accompanied by convincing anecdote and personal recollection. Suspicious characters were seen loitering around the school in the days leading up to the attack. Sometimes there were suspicious-looking boxes as well. Language, always a key signifier of difference in the Caucasus, has also come into play. According to at least one woman, during the last days of August, Tsalieva was seen talking to some men in the school playground. They were conversing in a language that was neither Russian nor Ossetian. The clear implication is that it was either Chechen or Ingushetian. Elvira Tuaeva remains convinced that the young boy she saw talking to one of the terrorists was speaking Chechen too. Another survivor says that trees that had been growing around the perimeter of the school were cut down just before the siege, aiding the passage of the terrorists and making it easier for their snipers to fire at government troops and police.

One woman, whose adult son was killed during the first day of the siege, accuses Tsalieva of tipping the terrorists off about his former job as a policeman. Others say that the poor woman faked her injuries or lied about their severity to cover up her own role in the tragedy. A small number of victims have even tried to show that Tsalieva had been planning the siege for many years. One wants to know, 'Who did Tsalieva get to fix the stage in the assembly hall after it burned down three years ago?' Another asks whether the headmistress was the mole who informed the gang of the last-minute change in the timing of the Day of Knowledge celebrations.

Lydia has tried to defend herself against the least fanciful allegations. It was no natural bossiness that made her keep insisting that other hostages were quiet. 'It really was very noisy in the gym. Incredibly noisy. Not because of my pupils. It wasn't their fault. They are all well brought up and their parents are too. The problem lay in the room itself. It has terrible acoustics and noise carries easily. Even normally, when there was only one class using it in school time, you could hear everything they were doing even from far away. The terrorists were telling me constantly to make everyone settle down. I had to keep on telling people to be quiet and sit down.' After the insinuations, Lydia now sounds repentant for asking the hostages to be quiet.

'There was a woman alongside me with her child – both of them died in the end, I think. She tried to help me to establish quiet. She was really screaming at people. At some points, she even swore at them. My pupils didn't deserve to be sworn at. They were in a miserable enough situation. Anyway, we sometimes managed to quieten them down. But if we couldn't, then the terrorists would fire guns into the roof of the hall – two or three times in a row – and that would make the children even more frightened.' Lydia felt herself to be under tremendous pressure in the gym. Charged with enforcing the terrorists' commands, she also bore the weight of pupils' and parents' desire for leadership. 'Everyone looked at me all the time. Almost everyone in the whole gym sat with their faces turned towards me. I saw them all.' Of course, there was next to nothing of meaning that she could do for them.

There is one person whose name is seldom mentioned in Beslan, but whose part in the siege was key. President Putin has remained distant from the events. Indeed, on the basis of what is publicly known, it is hard to justify mentioning him in this book at all. Even during the attack, state television news hardly uttered his name. Showing only brief glimpses of him, they implied that he was in control but not implicated. Afterwards, he would come to Beslan to visit the injured only in the middle of the night.

But just the fact of his immense and unrivalled power in Russia means that President Putin must have been involved:

studying the options; making decisions; giving orders; countermanding those of others. To date, neither he nor any of his close circle has chosen to discuss the President's role in detail. Some people, like murdered journalist Anna Politkovskaya, see him as an aloof and reclusive figure, whose views are seldom expressed openly, but must be guessed at by people under him who want to impress him. I see it a little differently. His control is secure and his invisible hand must surely intervene wherever he chooses. In a way that is beyond the imagining of elected representatives in Western democracies, he can influence the actions of the army, the Ministry of the Interior, the local governors he has appointed, and especially the FSB at will. To use such authority beneficially, Vladimir Putin would have to be a very intelligent person indeed. Two questions arise. Do those who do his bidding win his favour? Are they beyond the reach of the country's weak and feeble justice system? If the answer to both questions is yes, then perhaps conspiracy theories are the *only* way to understand events like Beslan.

As time has passed, more and more survivors have given up trying to understand the truth of what happened to them. Even a full account of the attack would not lessen the impact of the destruction it caused. Some prefer to draw a line under the siege and guard the fading memories of their own murdered loved ones. The town has received lots of investment, both from charitable giving and long-overdue government funding. A new school and a state-of-the-art hospital are among the facilities that have come to the town since the attack, and they are welcomed. However, the good intentions of charities and well-wishers worldwide have brought problems as well.

After the siege ended, hundreds of charity workers flooded into Beslan from all over the world. They came with the best of intentions: to alleviate the pain of the survivors and help them come to terms with their grief. But the unintended consequences of their actions have sometimes been severe. One clinical psychologist who has been heavily involved in treating the survivors, Igor, told me that most of the children who had survived the siege had already been on several trips abroad. He said that so many offers of holidays had come in that there had often not been enough interest to fill the places. Though kind in spirit, these offers and other gifts (of Playstations and bicycles and expensive toys) have left children, especially the younger ones, with very mixed feelings about the events they experienced in School No. 1. Deeply traumatized by the loss of parents and siblings or the memories of what they saw, these children come to see the siege as something that had to be lived through in order to get all of the benefits that have come to them since. Igor says that the confusion this causes may affect their behaviour for the rest of their lives.

I think I could sense what he meant in a painting by one little girl who survived the siege, which was being exhibited publicly in Beslan. Signing herself Zarina B., she had painted her home town alongside the Black Sea holiday resort of

Sochi. The two were separated by a gulf of sea, sunshine and thick lines. Sochi had its own sun and a healthy-looking palm tree; it was depicted in primary colours. Beslan was a desert of sickly beige with a single blood-red tree, whose leaves were weeping like tears onto the ground.

The generosity of strangers to Beslan has been focused almost exclusively on the survivors of the siege and their immediate families. Beslan's other inhabitants have been excluded from these benefits and have come to feel like second-class citizens. Their lives have continued to be as hard as ever, and jealousy has set in amongst some of them. One local woman who had not been in the siege and did not wish to be named told me that the siege was like a currency: the more loved ones you lost the more compensation you were entitled to; the more freebies you could claim; the more sympathy you could get.

My own experience of Beslan and the North Caucasus suggest that the underlying patterns of life there – which were so much a part of the siege – have changed remarkably little. In spite of all the intense emotion that followed the attack, most people's outlook on life has hardened as a result. Understandably some people felt distrust towards me, yet another foreigner asking questions and trying to awaken painful memories. But there was also harshness towards one another that many people did little to disguise.

One woman I met in Beslan, a pensioner called Anna, told me about how her son's wife and children had been hostages in School No. 1. Her grandson had died but her granddaughter was still alive. Their mother had lain in a coma three months before coming round. The doctors had given strict instructions to family and friends not to mention the dead child for fear of provoking a relapse. But, Anna told me, it had quickly emerged that the woman remembered seeing her dead son before passing out in the gym. He had been killed by a large piece of falling glass. The woman remains in a delicate mental and physical state. Her husband, Anna's son, continues to support her, but it is unlikely that she will ever recover enough to resume a normal life. The old woman's conclusion was simple and stark: 'He should leave her and she should let him. A young man like him, in the prime of his life? He deserves to have a wife who can care for him and a family of his own. Anything else would be selfish.'

POSTSCRIPT

Before I left Beslan, I returned to the school for a last visit. Walking out of the gym into the schoolyard, I met three young boys who had just cycled up. They were as carefree as boys anywhere in the world. The oldest was no more than twelve

and they paid me no attention. They got off their bikes and went into the gym without saying a word. They sat on the floor and looked up at where the ceiling had once been. They came out again and cycled away. Once they had put a short distance between themselves and the school, I could hear them start to speak to one another. Then I heard one of them laugh. A moment later they were gone.

Though solemn and silent, the boys' attitude was straightforward. Whoever they had lost, whatever they knew about the siege, they did not seem angry or consumed with hatred. They had undoubtedly come to the school to remember, but they were not paralysed by grief. I did not know any of them and cannot say what difficulties they will have to face in the future. One day these three boys will be adults. If they can remember what happened at School No. 1 without being poisoned by its consequences – as it seemed to me that day in the gym that they could – there may yet be hope for this troubled place.

APPENDIX: THE HOSTAGES

This is a list of the people who were attacked in School No. 1 on 1 September 2004. It includes the small number of those who managed to escape before the siege began; those who were killed on the street during the first minutes of the attack; the women and children who were rescued on the second day; and those who died. Due to the difficulties and confusion I have described elsewhere in the book, it cannot be taken as a comprehensive or entirely accurate list; the statistics cited in other parts of the book are not derived from this list. As far as possible, it is arranged by the year of the person's birth. Names in bold are of the people who were killed.

2004
Alena Ruslanovna Tskaeva

2003
Milana Gadieva
Diana Aslanovna Khablieva
Ilina Albertovna Kokaeva
Madina Aslanbekovna Kudzaeva

2002
Diana Alanovna Azieva
Georgii Vadimovich Daurov
Aspar Arturovich Dzampaev
Alan Batrazovich Dzandarov
Amina Aleksandrovna Dzaparova
Alan Arsenovich Dzhioev
Diana Khodova

Ellina Taimurazovna Kubatieva
Astemir Albertovich Kundukhov
Oleg Gievich Makiev
Azamat Aslanovich Mukagov
Inal Edikovich Naifonov
Azamat Semikhov
Vika Eduardovna Sidakova
Zelim Olegovich Tebiev

2001

Albert Kazbekovich Adyrkhaev
Murat Batrazovich Badtiev
Amirkhan Avazovich Bakhromov
David Soslanovich Biboev
Valeriya Olegovna Budaeva
Alsu Ruslanovna Fraeva
Ellina Tamerlanovna Gusova
Viola Vladimirovna Khubulova
Lera Rustamovna Kokova
Sveta Aslanovna Malieva
Regina Sanakoeva
Adelina Aslanbekovna Sattsaeva
Makhar Ruslanovich Tskaev

2000

Milana Alanovna Adyrkhaeva
Alana Arturovna Albegova
Elizaveta Konstantinovna Alikova
Marat Vitalevich Ambalov
Amina Germanovna Batagova
Georgii Kazbekovich Koniev
Fidar Kazbekovich Kusaev
Amirkhan Normatov-Bakhromov
Ani Arutyunovna Rusova

Rada Valerevna Salkazanova
Dana Aslanbekovna Sattsaeva
David Albertovich Sidakov
Gleb Olegovich Tatonov

1999

Aleksandr Tamerlanovich Agaev
Mariana Viktorovna Agaeva
Dzerassa Kazbekovna Basaeva
Diana Elbrusovna Esieva
Georgii Alanovich Maliev
Soslan Atsamazovich Melikov
Larisa Atsamazovna Melikova
Lorena Kazbekovna Melikova
Aslan Valerevich Murtazov
Soslan Valerevich Murtazov

1998

Svetlana Yurevna Ailyarova
Madina Konstantinovna Alikova
Linda Aslanovna Archegova
Robert Tamerlanovich Balikoev
Alana Alanovna Batagova
Diana Aslanovna Batsazova
Alan Anatolevich Berkaev
Alina Eduardovna Bigaeva
Sarmat Vadimovich Boloev
Roma Sergeevich Bziev
Liza Kazbekovna Cirikhova
Mairam Soslanovich Diambekov
Milena Dogan
Artur Taimurazovich Dzagoev
Vika Kaspolatovna Dziova
Zaur Ruslanovich Gadiev

Dzera Ruslanovna Gappoeva
Elena Georgievna Esenova
Milana Elbrusovna Esieva
Elbrus Aslanovich Farniev
Ruzanna Kambolova
Alana Sergeevna Kantemirova
Oksana Mairamovna Kesaeva
Ali(Oleg) Kazbekovich Koniev
Dana Aslanbekovna Konieva
Zaurbek Tamerlanovich Kudziev
Luiza Makharbekovna Kulakova
Berd Olegovich Kusov
Elvira Valikoevna Margieva
Batraz Yurevich Misikov
Azamat Arturovich Murtaziev
Batraz Soslanovich Nogaev
Dzhumber Pelishvili
Boris Arturovich Rubaev
Amina Azamatovna Sabanova
Vladislav Gennadevich Sanakoev
Tamerlan Aslanbekovich Sattsaev
Aslan Borisovich Shavlokhov
Vyacheslav Garikovich Tedeev
Madina Uruzmagovna Tedeeva
Aleksandr Germanovich Tsgoev
Zalina Sergeevna Urmanova
Albina Sergeevna Zhukaeva

1997
Emiliya Alanovna Adyrkhaeva
Georgii Tamerlanovich Agaev
Asakhmat Barisbievich Ailyarov
Kazbek Arturovich Albegov
Diana Ibragimovna Alikova

Akhsarbek Borisovich Archinov
Aleksandr Muratovich Badoev
Damir Vladimirovich Bichenov
Alan Bondoevich Chandishvili
Dana Kazbekovna Chedzhemova
Oleg Alanovich Chipirov
Taimuraz Olegovich Daurov
Izeta Akhsarbekovna Dudaeva
Chermen Atsamazovich Dzagoev
Irlan Dzampaev
Agunda Arturovna Dzampaeva
Irlanda Ruslanovna Dzampaeva
Marina Vitalevna Dzampaeva
Alana Batrazovna Dzandarova
Sveta Arsenovna Dzhioeva
Dana Vitalevna Dzutseva
David Muratovich Fidarov
Amina Ruslanovna Fraeva
Alan Ruslanovich Gappoev
Georgii Albertovich Guldaev
Irina Vyacheslavovna Gurieva
Georgii Konstantinovich Ilin
Tagir Timurovich Islamov
Alena Albertovna Kadalaeva
Olga Taimurazovna Kallagova
Khetag Germanovich Karaev
Liza Yurevna Karaeva
Georgii Viktorovich Kesaev
Alina Mairamovna Kesaeva
Karina Aslanovna Khablieva
Beksoltan Batrazovich Khudalov
Madina Batrazovna Khudalova
Timur Ruslanovich Khumarov
Stella Alanovna Khuzmieva

Aslan Arturovich Kisiev
Viktor Taimurazovich Kotsoev
Dzerassa Aslanbekovna Kudzaeva
Irina Taimurazovna Kulieva
Timur Muratovich Kumalagov
Kristina Albertovna Kundukhova
Azamat Arturovich Metsiev
Alan Feliksovich Misikov
Batraz Valerevich Murtazov
Georgii Borisovich Murtazov
Madina Muratbekovna Murtazova
Alla Olegovna Nogaeva
Zarina Normatova-Ilina
Genadii Ibragimovich Pukhaev
Karina Yurevna Ramonova
Ruslan Valerevich Salkazanov
David Taimurazovich Sasiev
Ruzana Aitegovna Semikhova
Abdul Amirovich Sheikhov
Georgii Albertovich Sidakov
Aida Kostaevna Sidakova
Anzhela Anatolevna Sikoeva
Shamil Igorevich Suleimanov
Fatima Garikovna Tedeeva
Timur Elbrusovich Tedtov
Atsamaz Taimurazovich Tsallagov
Irina Uralbekovna Tskaeva
Taimuraz Anatolevich Urtaev
Albina Albertovna Zangieva

1996

Valeriya Vitalevna Ambalova
Zalina Burievna Amirkhanova
Yulya Alanovna Batagova

Dzambolat Bekuzarov
Alina Kazbekovna Biboeva
Milana Soslanovna Biboeva
Eduard Igorevich Bigaev
Zaurbek Eduardovich Bitsiev
Tamara Gurgenovna Brikhova
Chermen Aslanbekovich Bugulov
Akhsar Batrazovich Darchiev
Karina Daurova
Zarina Vitalevna Dzampaeva
Vika Lanzbekovna Dzandarova
Zalina Alikovna Dzgoeva
Mark Akhsarbekovich Dzhioev
Timur Tamerlanovich Dziov
Valeriya Muslimovna Gafurova
Viktoriya Olegovna Gagartseva
Ilona Konstantinovna Gazdanova
Azamat Vladimirovich Kargiev
Zalina Taimurazovna Kastueva
Amina Georgievna Khadartseva
Dzerassa Zelimkhanovna
   Khosonova
Ilona Igorevna Khubaeva
Azam Tengizovich Khugaev
Khetag Andreevich Khutiev
Georgii Alanovich Khuzmiev
Ibragim Kochiev
Alan Iosifovich Kodzaev
Batraz Aslanovich Kokov
Shamil Rustamovich Kokov
Viktor Taimurazovich Ktsoev
Zarina Shamilevna Kuchieva
Oleg Igorevich Kulov
Karina Kazbekovna Kusova

Slavik Kuzmenko

Zarina Borisovna Misikova

Irina Feliksovna Misikova

Atsamaz Arturovich Miskov

Artur Ruslanovich Muzaev

Artur Edikovich Naifonov

Vova Sergeevich Oziev

Atsamaz Aslanovich Parastaev

Roma Pavlenko

Elina Enverovna Plieva

Zalina Vazhaevna Plieva

Milana Avtandilovna Pukhaeva

Irbek Kaspolatovich Ramonov

Vasilii Viktorovich Reshetnyak

Anzhela Tarkhanova

Boris Taimurazovich Totiev

Anna Konstantinovna Totieva

Aslanbek Kazbekovich Tsgoev

Vladik Alanovich Tsidaev

Aslan Kazbekovich Tsogoev

Aleksei Olegovich Tsomartov

Aleksandr Eduardovich Urusov

Mairbek Batrazovich Varziev

1995

Diana Viktorovna Agaeva

David Grigorevich Ailyarov

Zalina Tamerlanovna Albegova

Zaur Andiev

Soslan Archegov

Maksim Sergeevich Avdonin

Kambolat Georgievich Baev-Lekov

Sasha Aleksandrovich Balandin

Bimbolat Muratovich Baroev

Vika Olegovna Bebpieva

Irina Vladimirovna Berezova

Kazbek Romanovich Bichenov

Soslan Emzarovich Biganoshvili

Madina Vadimovna Boloeva

Zelim Valerevich Chedzhemov

Larisa Anatolevna Chedzhemova

Luiza Soslanovna Diambekova

Dzerassa Valeryanova Digurova

Alana Seifilevna Dogan

Kazbek Akhsarbekovich Dudiev

Agunda Viktorovna Dzaragasova

Alana Ruslanovna Dzhibilova

Artur Akhsarbekovich Dzhioev

David Eloev

Elena Sergeevna Frieva

Arsen Kazbekovich Gabisov

Timur Akhmedovich Ganiev

Nina Giaevna Gigauri

Soslan Vladimirovich Guburov

Inna Gudieva

Taimuraz Ruslanovich Gusov

Diana Tamerlanovna Kabanova

Amina Dzambolatovna
  Kachmazova

Alana Pavlovna Kaitmazova

Mairbek Muratovich Kantemirov

Irmar Kashtoyan

Kristina Borisovna Kekhvishvili

Diana Arturovna Khamitsaeva

Arsen Kazbekovich Kharebov

Arsen Ibragimovich Khasigov

Sarmat Alanovich Khudalov

Ellina Eduardovna Kodzaeva

Ilya Omarovich Kokaev

Liana Kazbekovna Kokoeva

Viktoriya Taimurazovna Kotsoeva

Timur Vitalevich Kozyrev

Sergei Aleksandrovich Kryukov

Artur Sergeevich Ktsoev

Murat Eduardovich Kulov

Izeta Kazbekovna Kusaeva

Khetag Aslanovich Maliev

Fariza Arturovna Metsieva

Atsamaz Borisovich Misikov

Mikhail Gagiki Mkrtchyan

Soslan Alanovich Morgoev

Sabina Eduardovna Naifonova

Vadim Sergeevich Oziev

Soslan Aslanovich Parastaev

Zalina Vasilevna Pelieva

Chermen Batrazovich Pliev

Milena Avtandilovna Pukhaeva

Khasan Kazbekovich Rubaev

Saneta Azamatovna Sabanova

Eduard Tavasisv

Totraz Arturovich Tamaev

Diana Konstantinovna Tarkhanova

Artur Mikhailovich Tebiev

Zaurbek Olegovich Tebiev

Alina Aslanovna Tokova

Kristina Kazbekovna Tomaeva

Laima Savelevna Torchinova

Mairbek Yanikovich Tseboev

Alina Irbekovna Tsgoeva

David Soslanovich Tsirikhov

Georgii Arturovich Tsomartov

Masha Alanovna Urmanova

Arkadii Aslanovich Zangiev

1994

Vladislav Aleksandrovich Afanasev

Timur Kazbekovich Aleroev

Amina Konstantinovna Alikova

Natalya Evgenevna Arkova

Alina Kazbekovna Badzieva

Kristina Bekuzarova

Dzera Olegovna Budaevi

Regina Stalinbekovna Butaeva

Agunda Aleksandrovna Bzykova

Lyana Valerevna Chedzhemova

David Vladimiroyich Daurov

Diana Olegovna Daurova

Atsamaz Sergeevich Doev

Dzambolat Stanislavovich Dreev

Diana Dzandorova

Aslan Kazbekovich Dzarasov

Azamat Olegovich Dzebisov

Soslan Olegovich Dzgoev

Dzerassa Kazbekovna Dzgoeva

Fatima Alikovna Dzgoeva

Ulke Vagifovna Efendieva

Alan K. Fardzinov

Soslan Ruslanovich Gappoev

Georgii Gubaev

Vladimir Ibragimovich Gubiev

Bella Ibragimovna Gubieva

Zaur Vladimirovich Gutnov

Azamat Alanovich Itazov

Anna Albertovna Kadalaeva

Sergei Soslanbekovich Karaev

Alan Olegovich Kastuev

Tsara Viktorovich Kesaev

Khada Khadikov

Elina Arturovna Khamitsaeva

Soslan Ibragimovich Khasigov

Georgii Elbrusovich Khudalov

Izolda Omarovna Kokaeva

Marianna Nodarovna Kokaeva

Alana Aslanovna Kokova

Atsamaz Aleksandrovich Kusov

Dzerassa Aslanbekovna Kusova

Khasan Khazbievich Ktsoev

Oksana Gievna Makieva

Atsamaz Kazbekovich Misikov

Satenik Gagiki Mkrtchyan

Vladislav Vladimirovich Mokrov

Tamerlan Elberdovich Morgoev

Anastasiya Gennadevna Nazarova

Soslan Ruslanovich Persaev

Zaur Taimurazovich Pliev

Martin Arutyunovich Rusov

Elbrus Germanovich Tavasiev

Azam Taimurazovich Tebiev

Azamat Tamerlanovich Tetov

Soslan Alanovich Tokmaev

Albert Aslanovich Tokov

Madina Vladimirovna Tomaeva

Albina Taimurazovna Totieva

Kristina Georgievna Tuaeva

Vadim Elbrusovich Tsagaraev

Anna Petrovna Tsaloeva

Stanislav Totrazovich Tsarakhov

Viktoriya Taimurazovna
　Tsarakhova

Tamiris Valerevna Tsibirova

Kristina Ruslanovna Tskaeva

Amiran Eduardovich Urusov

Lena Soslanovna Uzhegova

Georgii Albertovich Valigazov

Georgii Avtondilovich Vazagaev

Elena Tamazovna Vazagova

Natalya Yurevna Zamesova

Madina Sergeevna Zhukaeva

1993

Zarina Tamerlanovna Albegova

Aslanbek Izrailovich Aliev

Kazbek Izrailovich Aliev

Soslan Batrazovich Alikov

Alibek Aslanovich Archegov

Atsamaz Yurevich Bekoev

Albert Bertovich Berdikov

Khasan Batrazovich Bigaev

Zaira Valerevna Bokoeva

Zarina Vadimovna Boloeva

Batraz Kaspolatovich Chikhtisov

Azamat Alanovich Chipirov

Alena Vadimovna Daurova

Soslan Mairamovich Digurov

Vladimir Sergeevich Dryukov

Kristina Kazbekovna Dzgoeva

Alan Borisovich Esiev

Alya Genadevna Fadeeva

Zhaklin Fardzinova

Georgii Andreevich Farniev

Ruslan Sergeevich Friev

Alan Sergeevich Gabisov

Aitek Elbrusovich Gadzhinov

Alina Valrevna Gadzhinova

Georgii Giaevich Gigauri
Alina Vladimirovna Guldaeva
Rustam Alanovich Kabaloev
Alan Kabalov
Zarina Igorevna Kastueva
Samurbek Makharbekovich Kesaev
Zalina Ruslanovna Khadartseva
Borislav Soslanovich Khadikov
Volodya Mairbekovich Khodov
Ruslan Igorevich Khubaev
Alina Feliksovna Khubetsova
Albina Vladimirovna Khubulova
Alina Olegovna Khudalova
Kristina Kazbekovna Kokoeva
Pavel Robertovich Kortyaev
Borik Igorevich Kozyrev
Zaurbek Taimurazovich Kozyrev
Ilona Vitalevna Kozyreva
Lyana Chermenovna Kusaeva
Alan Ruslanovich Kusov
Madina Aslanbekovna Kusova
Natalya Vladimirovna Lyubimaya
Vitalii Germanovich Makiev
Zelim Taimurazovich Mamsurov
Karina Alanovna Melikova
Alina Yanovna Naldikoeva
Elina Elbrusovna Nogaeva
Bella Kazbekovna Nugzarova
Alana Vazhaevna Plieva
Sarmat Avtandilovich Pukhaev
Madina Valerevna Sozanova
Zaur Samirovich Tebloev
Alana Borisovna Tigieva
Aslan Alanovich Tokmaev

Azamat Kazbekovich Tomaev
Diana Soslanovna Torchinova
Marina Ruslanovna Totrova
Georgii Beslanovich Tsagaraev
David Alanovich Tsallagov
Tanya Totrazovna Tsarakhova
Razita Kazbekovna Tsirikhova
Zalina Kazbekovna Tsirikhova
Akhsarbek Uralbekovich Tskaev
Alan Kazbekovich Tsogoev
Luiza Olegovna Urusova

1992

Madina Anvarovna
   Akhmedzhanova
Zarina Olegovna Ambalova
Marat Andiev
Arsen Archegov
Artur Lavrentevich Atabekyan
David Lavrentevich Atabekyan
Madina Olegovna Azimova
Zarina Mirovna Batyaeva
David Georgievich Bedoev
Soslan Olegovich Beteev
Aslan Soslanovich Betrozov
Diana Soslanovna Biboeva
Azam Tamerlanovich Bigaev
Alana Ruslanovna Botsieva
Kazbek Arkadevich Bozrov
Zarina Stalinbekovna Butaeva
Alan Aleksandrovich Bzykov
Lena Batrazovna Darchieva
Albert Dashiev
Sabina Aslanbekovna Dzakhova

Zaur Kazbekovich Dzarasov

Mikhail Albertovich Dzarasov

Azamat Akhsarbekovich Dzgoev

Alana Ruslanovna Dzhibilova

Alina Kazbekovna Dzhimieva

Zarina Aslanbekovna Dziova

Zelim Yurevich Dzutsev

Svetlana Gennadevna Dzutseva

Vladik Borisovich Esiev

Izmail Igorevich Gabuev

Elena Zaubekovna Gaitova

Zaur Gasiev

Agunda Totrazovna Gatsalova

Olesya Vladimirovna Guldaeva

Aza Aleksandrovna Gumetsova

Vera Stanislavovna Gurieva

Artur Alanovich Itazov

Alana Kadieva

Azhau Aslanbekovna Kantemirova

Inal Arturovich Kanukov

Alan Vladimirovich Kargiev

Zarina Olegovna Kastueva

Zarina Arturovna Kesaeva

Batraz Eduardovich Khabliev

Emma Vadimovna Khaeva

Islam Makharbekovich Khudalov

Alan Yurevich Kochiev

Dina Kazbekovna Kokaeva

Bella Martievna Kokoiti

Vladimir Viktorovich Kotsubei

Akhsar Igorevich Kozyrev

Kseniya Vecheslavovna
   Krosheninnikova

Madina Vladimirovna Ktsoeva

Alana Alanovna Lolaeva

Stanislav Gievich Makiev

Anna Alekseevna Margieva

Yana Olegovna Matvienko

Khazbi Tamerlanovich Msoev

Madina Tamerlanovna Msoeva

Soslan Olegovich Murtazaliev

Alana Olegovna Murtazova

Vika Muratbekovna Murtazova

Marina Olegovna Nogaeva

Madina Avtandilovna Pukhaeva

Dzambolat Feliksovich Salamov

Alan Taimurazovich Sidakov

Oganes Ashotovich Simonyan

Albina Vladimirovna Sokaeva

Ivan Petrovich Sysoev

Kristina Aleksandrovna Tebloeva

Alan Vadimovich Tetov

Sveta Teimurazovna Tigieva

Azamat Konstantinovich Totiev

Larisa Taimurazovna Totieva

Artur Elbrusovich Tsagaraev

Alan Tamerlanovich Tsalikov

Kazbek Murtzabekovich Tsaloev

Elbrus Taimurazovich Tsarakhov

Alan Feliksovich Tsgoev

Svetlana Sergeevna Tsoi

Alina Olegovna Tsoraeva

Khetag Georgievich Tuaev

Zarina Olegovna Urusova

Vika Viktorovna Ushakova

Stella Albertovna Valigazova

Edik Elbrusovich Varziev

Erik Elbrusovich Varziev

Igor Yurevich Zamesov
Sergei Aleksandrovich Zaporozhets

1991
Nikolai Borisovich Archinov
Sonya Vladimirovana Arsoeva
Marina Olegovna Azimova
Liza Tamerlanovna Badoeva
Timur Soslanbekovich Batagov
Elvira Alekseevna Bolotaeva
Vika Elbrusovna Cherdzhieva
David Sergeevich Doev
Zaur Elbrusovich Dudiev
Ruslan Lanzbertovich Dzandarov
Soslan Eduardovich Dzugaev
Dzambolat Gennadevich Dzutsev
Soslan Feliksovich Eltarov
Ruslan Sergeevich Gabisov
David Erikovich Gusiev
Diana Kazbekovna Gutieva
Viktoriya Taimurazovna Kallagova
Soslan Kanukov
Fatima Akhsarbekovna Kanukova
Anzhelika Anatolevna Kanukova
Irina Mairamovna Kesaeva
Kristina Eduardovich Khablieva
Kristina Aslanovna Khablieva
Chermen Soslanovich Khadikov
Malik Maratovich Kolchakeev
Madina Vladimirovna Ktsoeva
Khetag Chermenovich Kusaev
Khetag Alanovich Lolaev
Zamira Taimurazovna Mamsurova
Soslan Eduardovich Margiev

Zita Aleksandrovna Margieva
Maya Nodarovna Margieva
Georgii Vasilevich Peliev
Aleksandr Georgievich Pogrebnoi
Yana Sergeevna Rudik
Zarina Feliksovna Salamova
Irina Arturovna Tauchelova
Arsen Olegovich Tedeev
Alan Vladimirovich Tedtov
Agunda Vadimovna Tetova
Alina Vadimovna Tetova
Atset Alekseevna Tkhostova
Tamerlan Vladimirovich Toguzov
Atsamaz Elbrusovich Tokhtiev
Vladimir Olegovich Toptun
Madina Soslanovna Torchinova
Madina Taimurazovna Totieva
Tamerlan Totrazovich Tsarakhov
Amaga Valerevna Tsibirova
Viktor Kazbekovich Tsogoev
Karina Georgievna Tuaeva
Agunda Ruslanovna Vataeva
Zalina Tamazovna Vazagova
Lyana Aleksandrovna Yadykina
Soslan Levanovich Zangiev

1990
Aida Nizamovna Akhmedova
Alina Kazbekovna Albegova
Diana Olegovna Alborova
Akhshar Kazbekovich Aleroev
Vadim Soslanbekovich Baimatov
Khetag Soslanbekovich Batagov
Dzerassa Yaroslavovna Bazrova

Azam Yurevich Bekoev

Ruslan Kazbekovich Bigaev

Soslan Tamerlanovich Bigaev

Artur Totrazovich Bigaev

Fatima Borisovna Bogazova

Eduard Alekseevich Bolotaev

Batraz Arkadevich Bozrov

Ruslan Elbrusovich Cherdzhiev

Soslan Akhsarbekovich Dudiev

Tamara Makharovna Dzagoeva

Dzera Arturovna Dzestelova

Aslan Vladimirovich Dzgoev

Dzera Aslanovna Dziova

Alan Vitalevich Dzugaev

Zaur Igorevich Fardzinov

Diana Valerevna Gadzhinova

Emma Ruslanovna Gagieva

Mariya Feliksovna Gataeva

Roman Maratovich Godzhiev

Kazbek Vyacheslavovich Godzhiev

Boris Stanislavovich Guriev

Mariya Ivanovna Kanakhina

Alina Arturovna Kanukova

Zhanna Germanovna Karaeva

Tereza Taimurazovna Karsanova

Soslan Olegovich Kaziev

Shalva Borisovich Kekhvishvili

Taimuraz Makharbekovich Kesaev

Dzerassa Ruslanovna Khadartseva

Zalina Soslanovna Khadikova

Zarina Valerevna Khadikova

Ira Sergeevna Khadikova

Vadim Igorevich Khamitsev

Shalva Zarbekovich Khanikaev

Khazbi Soltanovich Khodov

Kazbek Makharbekovich
  Khudalov

Albina Tamazovna Khugaeva

Soslan Borisovich Kokaev

Sergei Aleksandrovich Korobeinik

Artem Vyacheslavovich
  Krosheninnikov

Azamat Ktsoev

Viktoriya Sergeevna Ktsoeva

Alan Chermenovich Kusaev

Anzhela Albertovna Kusova

Andrei Sergeevich Kuznetsov

Arsen Aleksandrovich Malikiev

Vova Viktorovich Marusich

Azamat Kazbekovich Melikov

Diana Muratbekovna Murtazova

Azamat Yanovich Naldikoev

Anzhela Germanovna Parsieva

Otari Emzarovich Pelishvili

Kristina Anatolevna Podolskaya

Yuliya Sergeevna Rudik

Vladislav Anatolevich Sikoev

Maryam Ashotovna Simonyan

Sveta Arturovna Tauchelova

Alma Beksoltanovna Tebieva

Soslan Borisovich Tigiev

Fatima Taimurazovna Tokaeva

Larisa Taimurazovna Totieva

Inga Batrazovna Tsinoeva

Zarina Leonidovna Tsirikhova

Dzhuletta Kazbekovna Tsogoeva

Zaurbek Olegovich Tsoraev

Anastasiya Georgievna Tuaeva

David Dzambolatovich Valiev
Zarina Igorevna Valieva
Malvina Vazagaeva-Gigolaeva

1989

Aslan Borisovich Ailyarov
Sergei Dmitrievich Alkaev
Inna Evgenevna Arkova
Liana Borisovna Barazgova
Diana Muratovna Baskaeva
Georgii Mirovich Batyaev
Zhanna Aleksandrovna Besolova
Alan Soslanovich Betrozov
Marina Valerevna Bokoeva
Zarina Uruzmagovna Bugulova
Miroslav Khasanovich Dzagoev
Inna Elbrusovna Dzanaeva
Aslan Soslanovich Dzheriev
Oleg Kazbekovich Dzhimiev
Madina Stanislavovna Dreeva
Boris Feliksovich Eltarov
Aslanbek Aleksandrovich Esenov
Alan Igorevich Gabuev
Alina Umatovna Galaeva
Amran Vyacheslavovich Godzhiev
Inna Grishkova
Artur Kazbekovich Gutiev
Kristina Aleksandrovna Gutieva
Alana Muratovna Katsanova
Izabella Ervandovna Kashtoyan
Larisa Olegovna Kazieva
Islam Alanovich Khadikov
Regina Kermenovna Khuadonova
Oksana Ruslanovna Kokova

Akhshar Shamilevich Komaev
Vladimir Ruslanovich Kubataev
Konstantin Nikolaevich Kusov
Batraz Kazbekovich Misikov
Timur Olegovich Morgoev
Aslan Ruslanovich Persaev
Alesha Viktorovich Ptakh
Mariana Kaspolatovna Ramonova
Ilona Maksimovna Sabeeva
Alla Evgenevna Smirnova
Akhsar Mikhailovich Tebiev
Tina Teimurazovna Tigieva
Madina Taimurazovna Tokaeva
Azamat Elbrusovich Tokhtiev
Vadim Muratovich Tomaev
Dzerassa Konstantinovna Totieva
Soslan Ruslanovich Tsalikov
Indira Sultanovna Tsappoeva
Santa Albertovna Zangieva

1988

Zaur Romanovich Aboev
Ekaterina Eduardovna Abrosimova
Stas Ruslanovich Bokoev
Tamerlan Svyatoslavovich
  Chedzhemov
Karina Soslanovna Dagueva
Irina Valerevna Dzagoeva
Madina Kazbekovna Dzandarova
Kazbek Viktorovich Dzaragasov
Margarita Vladimirovna Dzgoeva
Viktoriya Elbrusovna Dzutseva
Zalina Yurevna Dzutseva
Kristina Alanovna Farnieva

Vyacheslav Ruslanovich Gagiev

Alan Zaurbekovich Gaitov

Viktoriya Eduardovna Guseinova

Murat Batrazovich Kalmanov

Atsamaz Akhsarbekovich
  Kanukov

Nino Shalvovna Karaeva

Kazbek Tamerlanovich Khadikov

Yana Stanislavovna Khaeva

Maiya Zaurbekovna Khanikaeva

Alan Aleksandrovich Kokaev

Lena Batyrovna Kokoeva

Elina Georgievna Konieva

Zarina Georgievna Konieva

Fatima Aslanbekovna Kusova

Sabina Konstantinovna Mamaeva

Konstantin Viktorovich Marusich

Taimuraz Kazbekovich Melikov

Sergei Sergeevich Naniev

Fatima Ruslanovna Nogaeva

Alla Vladimirovna Ponomareva

S. T. Takaeva

Madina Taimurazovna Tokaeva

Zaur Olegovich Tsabolov

Alana Olegovna Tsakulova

Zaurbek Chermenovich Tsaloev

Inga Mairbekovna Tuaeva

Inna Mairbekovna Tuaeva

Kristina Uvarova

1987

Vladislav Borisovich Ailyarov

Bella Anatolevna Avsanova

Nadezhda Ruslanovna Badoeva

Karina Kazbekovna Bigaeva

Syuzanna Svyatoslavovna
  Chedzhemova

Marat Khataev

Viktoriya Norvegovna Kibizova

Alina Anatolevna Sakieva

Siranush Ashotovna Simonyan

Inna Olegovna Smirnova

Ketevan Teimurazovna Tigieva

1986

Soslan Erikovich Gusiev

A. K. Kudakov

Madina Tamerlanovna
  Kudzieva

1985

Zarina Valievna Daurova

Vyacheslav Yurevich Kasaev

1983

Diana Albegova

Alan Givievich Kachmazov

1982

Anzhela Borisovna Archinova-
  Kokaeva

Olga Vladimirovna Dzgoeva

Nelya Tasultanovna Kaitova

Nelya Yurevna Kochieva

1981

Alena Batrazovna Agaeva

1980

Madina Borisovna Badoeva-
   Khuzmieva
Madina Feliksovna Dulaeva
Irma Valerevna Dzagoeva
Inga Viktorovna Gugkaeva
Irina Tuganovna Kantemirova
Teimuraz Batrazovich Khodov
Anzhela Taimurazovna Nogaeva
Elmira Nikolaevna Tedeeva

1979

Aslan Zelimkhanovich Beroev
Marina Sergeevna Duchko
Marina Aleksandrovna Mikhailova
Zarina Ruslanovna Pukhaeva
Lalita Ruslanovna Urtaeva

1978

Azamat Borisovich Khutsistov
Lira Borisovna Normatova

1977

Svetlana Anatolevna Dryukova
Olga Nikolaevna Esenova
Alan Batyrbekovich Gadzalov
Aiteg Izrailovich Kambolov
Aleksei Viktorovich Krasnykh
Ruslan Fedorovich Makiev
Nadezhda Gennadevna Malieva
Alena Vasilevna Pukhaeva
Andrei Nikolaevich Shuvarikov
Fatima Robertovna Sidakova-
   Mamukaeva

Alena Borisovna Tedeeva-Bagaeva
Svetlana Veniaminovna Vlasova

1976

Larisa Konstantinovna Balikoeva
Ella Borisovna Bedoeva
Irina Kazbekovna Bedzhisova
Lyudmila Gurgenovna Brikhova
Oksana Elbrusovna Dzampaeva
Svetlana Dudarovna Dzampaeva
Zarina Anatolevna Dzampaeva-
   Bicieva
Edita Konstantinovna Dzhidzalova
Alena Akhsarbekovna Dzutseva
Sveta Ismalova
Svetlana Kantemirovna Kantemirova
Diana Taimurazovna Karsanova
Aslan Safarbekovich Khabliev
Albina Kozyreva
Alla Kundukhova-Khodova
Ruzana Georgievna Rusova
Alena Akhsarbekovna Tatrova
Raisa Grigorevna Tavasieva
Zalina Batrazovna Tokaeva

1975

Irina Aleksandrovna Adyrkhaeva
Sergei Vladimirovich Dryukov
Fatima Taimurazovna Gadieva
Ira Kadalaeva
Inna Valerevna Kanukova
Sveta Batrazovna Khubulova
Amalya Armenaki Mkrtchyan
Marina Anzorovna Ozieva-Zaseeva

Marina Sogratovna Pukhaeva-
   Khubaeva
Natalya Aleksandrovna Rudenok
Natalya Georgievna Sattsaeva
Ilona Vyachaslavovna Savitskaya
Luiza Ramazanovna Sheikhova
Andrei Shibaev
Marina Ramazanovna
   Tarkhanova-Kozyreva

1974

Oksana Petrovna Ailyarova
Alina Anatolevna Alikova
Zhanna Soltanbekovna Alikova
Elena Sergeevna Bekuzarova
Garik Manukovich Grigoryan
Oleg Viktorovich Gusev
Gocha Gennadevich Kachmazov
Alina Kasabieva
Anzhela Ivanovna Khablieva-
   Ataeva
Omar Kokaev
Indira Borisovna Kokaeva
Rustam Eduardovich Kokov
Artur Albertovich Miskov
Irina Timofeevna Naldikoeva
Salima Suleimanova
Inga Taimurazovna Tamaeva-Savkueva
Oksana Magometovna Tsaraeva
Fatima Borisovna Tskaeva
Natalya Nikolaevna Urmanova

1973

Marina Kazbekovna Bedzhisova
Zalina Kazbekovna Bigaeva-Karaeva
Irina Daurova
Marat Astemirovich Dzhanaev
Georgii Albertovich Guldaev
Albina Tsaraevna Kuchieva
Madina Borisovna Kumalagova
Rigina Nikolaevna Kusaeva
Leonid Stanislavovich Okruzhko
Madina Kazbekovna Sasieva
Albert Ruslanovich Sidakov
Natalya Ivanovna Sokolova
Albina Vladimirovna Tebieva
Lyudmila Ruslanovna Tebieva-
   Fraeva
Marina Kirilovna Zhukaeva

1972

Albina Viktorovna Alikova
Aida Archegova
Anzhela Valerevna Badtieva
Marina Batagova
Ilfa Alikovna Batsazova
Anzhela Georgievna Digurova
Fatima Doeva
Lyudmila Fedorovna Dzgoeva
Madina Anatolevna Khubaeva
Anzhela Georgievna Khumarova
Artur Vladimirovich Kisiev
Lyudmila Aleksandrovna Makieva
Sveta Erikovna Naifonova
Larisa Vladimirovna Rudik
Anzhela Valerevna Varzieva

1971

Anzhela Mikhailovna Agaeva

Lena Vladimirovna Avdonina

Natasha Valerevna Balandina

Larisa Taimurazovna Farnieva

Anzhela Tsaraevna Gatsoeva

Albert Georgievich Guldaev

Georgii Taimurazovich
Khadartsev

Aslan Saukhalovich Kudzaev

Vika Yurevna Kulakova

Fatima Andreevna Melikova-
Kochieva

Zalina Issaevna Msoeva

Larisa Tomaeva-Bedoeva

Marina Vladimirovna Toptun

1970

Zlata Sergeevna Azieva

**Taisiya Kaurbekovna Dzampaevna-
Khetagurova**

Albina Borisovna Dzestelova

Khazbi Khadzhimuratovich Dzgoev

Viktoriya Tuganovna Gadieva

Ruslan Kharitonovich Gappoev

Sveta Savkuzavona Kozyreva

Madina Soltanbekovna Kudzieva

Irina Muratovna Misikova

Irma Narikishvili

Svetlana Vasilevna Oros

Alevtina Aslanovna Ramonova-
Khanaeva

Anzhela Aleksandrovna Sidakova

Artur Ramazanovich Tamaev

Fatima Maibekovna Tskaeva-
Kaloeva

1969

Vissarion Vladimirovich Aseev

Vadim Valerevich Daurov

Artur Taimurazovich Dzampaev

Kazbek Khadzhimuratovich
Dzarasov

Irina Muratovna Dzutseva

Georgii Aleksandrovich Esenov

Marina Soltanovna Gappoeva

Sveta Stanislavovna Gutsaeva

Tatyana Kadzaeva

Marina Khairbekovna
Kanukova

Emma Khasanovna Karyaeva

Zalina Sozyrovna Kesaeva

S. B. Khabalov

Zalina Borisovna Khuzmieva-
Gadieva

Marina Sulikoevna Misikova-
Karkuzoshvili

Marina Nikolaevna Morgoeva

Fatima Tatyrbekovna Muzaeva

Sergei Vladimirovich
Ryabukhin

Irina Ivanovna Sysoeva

Albert Akhsarbekovich Togoev

Zalina Taimurazovna Tokova-
Nogaeva

Timur Borisovich Tsallagov

Sergei Vladimirovich Urmanov

1968
Timur Mikhailovich Albegov
Zalina Salamonovna Albegova
Albina Muratovna Butaeva-
Dzgoeva
Oksana Khasanovna
Dzaparova
Marina Vasilevna Dzutseva
Fatima Grigorevna Esieva-
Tomaeva
Fatima Vladimirovna Karaeva-
Zortova
Larisa Kazbekovna Kesaeva
Alla Taimurazovna Kozyreva
Artur Petrovich Nartikov
Eduard Aleksandrovich Sidakov
Galina Astemirovna Sikoeva
Svetlana Ivanovna Sokolova
Sergei V. Taraev
Irina Taimurazovna Tsallagova
Batraz Georgievich Tuganov
Elena Nikolaevna Yadykina
Fatima Zangieva

1967
Aslan Feliksovich Archegov
Fatima Khazbievna Bolotaeva
Tamara Ibragimovna Diambekova
Rita Mukharbekovna Dudieva
Irina Yurevna Dzhioeva-Doguzova
Elbrus Viktorovich Esiev
Ruslan Mikhailovich Fraev
Emzar Sivavich Gabaraev
Elena Sulidinovna Ganieva

Elza Akimovna Guldaeva
Anna Batrbekovna Karaeva-Tsakhilova
Lora Sulikoevna Karkuzashvili
Tereza B. Kokova
Elena Eduardovna Nazarova
Aleta Tatarkanovna Sabanova
Fatima Albegovna Tsgoeva-Biboeva
Zhanna Petrovna Tsirikhova

1966
Rafimat Makharbekovna
Ailyarova-Gaboeva
**Zara Aleksandrovna Alikova-
Adyrkhaeva**
Tamara Kizilbekovna Bichenova-
Skaeva
Albina Kazbekovna Budaeva
Eduard Suleimanovich Doev
Rita Sergeevna Khodova
Artur Izmailovich Kotsoev
Larisa Agubeevna Kudzieva-
Gasieva
Elena Pavlovna Ostanii
Naira Andreevna Syukaeva

1965
Vadim Vladimirovich Boloev
**Lyudmila Nikolaevna Meladze-
Biganoshvili**
Irina Vladimirovna Mildzikhova-
Ktsoeva
Zhureta Kharitonovna Misikova
Dzhuletta Naldikoeva-Kallagova
Rita Sergeevna Urmanova

1964

Yurii Ruslanovich Ailyarov
Ibragim Dyuletovich Bekuzarov
Irina Borisovna Bekuzarova
Zhanna Gorgaeva Dzagoeva
Svetlana Timurovna Dzherieva
Emma Lazarevna Gasinova
Gennadii Kaporin
Luiza Borisovna Kesaeva
Ira Borisovna Khudalova
Kazbek Alievich Koniev
Zhanna Islamovna Konieva-Tuaeva
Elvira Petrovna Kusaeva
Valerii Zhrappovich Murtazov
Fatima Aslanbekovna
　　Murtazova
Dinara Nikolaevna Plieva
Zemfira Mairamovna Urusova-
　　Tsirikhova

1963

Svetlana Tembolatovna Bigaeva
Sergei Romanovich Bziev
Aneta Nikolaevna Dogan-Gadieva
Sveta Muratovna Fidarova
Svetlana Nikolaev Gochishvili
Dzhuletta Georgievna Gutieva
Zoya Ibragimovna Ktsoeva
Zalina Aleksandrovna Levina
Larisa Nikolaevna Plieva-Gagloeva
Artur Borisovich Rubaev
Svetlana Tuganovna Suanova
Zalina Mussaevna Tsgoeva

1962

Zagirat Rezvanovna Berdikova
Lemma Tsoraevna Chedzhemova
Galina Izmailovna Dagueva-
　　Kudzieva
Sveta Borisovna Dzebisova
Lyudmila Ruslanovna Galachieva
Elvira Makharbekovna
　　Khadartseva-Gagieva
Marita Borisovna Khadikova-
　　Mamsurova
Aleta Khasanbekovna Khasieva
Mikhail Zelimkhanovich Koliev
Zinaida Vladimirovna Kudzieva
Tatyana Georgievna Kuznetsova
Lyubov Viktorovna Tsagaraeva

1961

Darima Batuevna Alikova
Larisa Sergeevna Azieva
Naida Magometovna Gappoeva
Fatima Georgievna Gutieva
Elmira Aslanbekovna Kabanova
Madinat Kimovna Kargieva-
　　Kastueva
Kazbek Dmitrievich Misikov
Yurii Feliksovich Misikov
Fatima Zaurbekovna Misikova
Larisa Salkazanova-Kantemirova
Olga Viktorovna Vlaskina

1960

Elena Krymovna Ambalova-
　　Gugkaeva

Sima Georgievna Basieva
Zarina Taimurazovna Dziova
Rita Aleksandrova Gadzhinova-
　　Komaeva
Nadezhda Ilinichna Gurieva
Rita Mukhtarovna Nogaeva
Anotolii Vladimirovich Sikoev
Larisa Mikhailovna Sokaeva
Tatyana Valentinovna Svetlova

1959
Indira Akhsarbekovna Archinova
Serafima Alikovna Berezova-Alikova
Fatima Khazbatrovna Bugulova-
　　Batagova
Fatima Mikhailovna Dudieva
Zara Alekseevna Gazyumova-
　　Dzutseva
Larisa Vasilevna Levchenko
Larisa Dzateevna Mamitova
Svetlana Petrovna Margieva-
　　Salkazanova
Taya Nogaeva
Elvira Dzarakhmetovna Tedeeva-
　　Kusova
Elvira Khadzhimuratovna Tuaeva

1958
Ruslan Ramazanovich Betrozov
Bella Georgievna Dzestelova-
　　Amirkhanova
T. M. Gubaeva

1957
Akhtemir Shamilevich Badoev
Anna Mikhailovna Dzgoeva
Larisa Mairamovna Kulova

1956
Sima Gappoevna Bogazova
Natalya Gavrilovna Dzhatieva
Fatima Torbekovna Khosonova
Olga Viktorovna Shcherbinina

1955
Olga Nikolaevna Soskieva

1954
Anna Uruzmagovna Alikova
Boris Nikolaevich Archinov
Svetlana Akhmedovna Balikoeva
Tatyana Sergeevna Bazrova
Valentina Pavlovna Khosonova
**Taira Beksholovna Mukagova-
　　Kundukhova**

1953
Irina Khazbatrovna Gudieva
Yurii Totrazovich Karaev
Lidiya Khazbievna Khodova
Alma Elmurzaevna Tokaeva

1952
Fatima Anzorovna Avsanova
Boris Vladimirovich Bedoev
Lyudmila Vladimirovna Gudieva
Lyudmila Salamonovna Kokaeva

Vladimir Borisovich Sagutonov
Galina Aleksandrovna Semikhova

1951

Elza Viktorovna Dzeboeva
Elbrus Dzambolatovich Khudalov
Bella Mairovna Kokoeva
Aleksandr Mikhailovich Mikhailov
Vladimir Grigorevich Mokrov
Galina Khadzhievna Vataeva

1950

Svetlana Ivanovna Kurnosova
Alik Dotaevich Tsagolov

1949

Sima Makharbekovna Albegova
Fatima Afanasevna Tebieva
Raisa Zenonovna Yuzhikevich

1948

Felisa Batagova
Inessa Patvakanovna Daurova
Zarema Kaspolatovna Digurova
Liliya Abadievna Dzusova
Valentina Ivanova Sapronova

1947

Klara Stepanova Sidakova

1946

Lyudmila Mikhailovna
    Rasnyanova

1945

Viktoriya Zinonovna Sautenkova
Tinna Asakhmetovna Tsirikhova

1943

Tatyana Grigorevna Duchko
Izeta Totarievna Tsinoeva

1942

Raisa Kaspolatovna Dzaragasova
Zaira Aleksandrovna Gamaeva
Raisa Aleksandrovna Zhukaeva

1941

Zarema Gavrilovna Gadaeva-
    Bekmurzova

1940

Elochka Nikolaevna Dzarasova
Nadezhda Ivanovna Nazarova
Tatyana Moiseevna Tetova

1939

Tina Kharumovna Dudieva

1938

Svetlana Zakharovna Alikova
Tamara Borisovna Beroeva
Roza Timofeevna Cherdzhieva
Taisiya Daueva
Rima Daurbekovna Khamatkoeva

1937
Tamara Mikhailovna Kodzaev
Zinaida Azamatovna Urutskoeva

1936
Roza Avramovna Botsieva

1935
Zinaida Nikolaevna Daurova
Tamara Savlokhovna Tuaeva
Zarema Bekzaevna
    Zusmanovskaya-Khucistova

1934
Marusya Arkadevna Kusova
Vera Uruskhanovna
    Salkazanovna

1932
Ivan Ilich Karlov
Lydia Aleksandrovna Tsalieva

1930
Farizat Aslanbekovna Fraeva
Irina Zakharovna Khanaeva
Ivan Konstantinovich Konidi
Zoya Mussaevna Zangieva-Nogaeva

1928
Rimma Murzabekovna Kusova-Ulubieva

1927
Zinaida Filippovna Tretyakova

1920
Zaurbek Kharitonovich Gutiev

1915
Tatarkan Gabuleevich Sabanov

Hostages whose dates of birth I could not find.
Zifa Aslanovna Agaeva-Sozaeva
Albina Mikhailovna Andieva
Zita Mikhailovna Andieva-
    Sidakova
Oksana Archegova
Madina Olegovna Bebpieva
Marina Maksimovna Biboeva
Zalina Biganoshvili
Inga Dakhcikoevna Chedzhemova-
    Basaeva
Taya Cherchesova
Marina Darchieva
Artur Valerevich Dzagov
Zhanna Dzandarova
Marina Kyazoevna Gabaeva
Raisa Gavrilovna Gabisova
Alla Gadieva
Madina Valerevna Gadzhinova
Zara Aleksandrovna Gaitova
Tamara Sarkisovna Galstyan
Bella Gasieva
Albina Gazdanova
Kira Islamovna Guldaeva
Nadezhda Albertovna Gusova
Rusik Gutoev

Sabina Ibragimova

Azamat Kambolov

Olya Kambolova

Yulya Kambolova

Marina Taimurazovna
    Kantemirova

Georgii Ervandovich Kashtoyan

Ruzanna Kashtoyan

Alan Kastuev

Albina Vladimirovna Kastueva

Gabulik Khadikov

Inga Kharebova

Zemfira Khodova

Madina Taimurazovna Khozieva

Tsezar Tamazovich Khugaev

Indira Olegovna Kokaeva

Zaira Kazbekovna Kokoeva

Zalina Konieva

Diana Olegovna Kubalova

Toma Kubatieva

Alina Murikovna Kudzaeva

Roza Kudzaeva

Svetlana Aslanovna Mamieva

Irina Metsieva

Zara Petrovna Metsieva

Oleg Ruslanovich Nazriev

Lyana Viktorovna Parastaeva

Svetlana Pelieva

Dzhumber Pelishvili

Vazha Sh. Pliev

Elza Plieva

Avtondil Pukhaev

Rita Ramanyuk

Alla Georgievna Sartoeva

Yuliya Semikhova

Zarema Shavlokhova

Zaur Sidakov

Dzerassa Saukuzovna Sidakova

Larisa Taimurazovna Sidakova

Iza Atosovna Tarkhanova

Rita Iosifovna Tarkhanova

Aslan Ruslanovich Tebiev

Aleksei Borisovich Tedeev

Larisa Sergeevna Tedeeva

Irina Vladimirovna Tedtova

Zina Taimurazovna Tomaeva

Georgii Elbrusovich Torchinov

Marat A. Tsabolov

Aza Besangurovna Tsakhilova

Marina Khasanovna Tsakhilova

Lyudmila Petrovna Tseboeva

Lyana Tseboeva

Valeriya Germonovna Tsgoeva

Elvira Shamilevna Varzieva

BIBLIOGRAPHY

This section has a dual purpose: to record the published sources that have been useful to me during the writing of this book, and to enable readers to conduct further reading and research if they wish.

In addition to the interviews that I carried out in the North Caucasus and elsewhere, which are referred to in the text and in my acknowledgements, I have made extensive use of the published proceedings of the trial of Nurpashi Kulaev, which took place in Vladikavkaz in 2005 and 2006. Despite some interruptions in these transcripts, they are the most direct and complete source of first-hand information about the siege. A complete copy of these proceedings can be accessed at www.pravdabeslana.ru, which contains many other important resources relating to the siege. I have also found the websites www.hilfebeslan.ru, www.materibeslana.com and www.newsru.com useful.

I have been an almost daily reader of *The Times*, *Financial Times*, *Kommersant*, *Izvestiya*, and the Caucasian news website *Kavkazskii uzel* (kavkaz.memo.ru) at various points throughout working on this book and acknowledge the role they have played in shaping my thoughts; likewise, *Prospect* magazine has been helpful. I have made use of many other reports, newspaper and journal articles, monographs, memoirs, travelogues and novels in writing this book. The following are the sources I have relied on most or would direct the reader to in exploring the subject further. Understandably, many of these sources are in Russian.

Allenova, Ol'ga, 'Prigorodnyi tupik', *Vlast'*, 2 May 2005, 12–14.

'Another Ex-M.V.D. Witness; Example of Collective Punishment Lieutenant-Colonel Burlitsky', *The Times*, 2 July 1954.

Bailey, H. W., 'Ossetic (Nartä)' in *Traditions of Heroic and Epic Poetry*, vol. 1, *The Traditions*, ed. A. T. Hatto (London: MHRA, 1980), 249–66.

Barrett, Thomas M., 'Lines of Uncertainty: The Frontiers of the North Caucasus', *Slavic Review*, 54:3 (Autumn, 1995), 578–601.

Beattie, Geoffrey, *Protestant Boy* (London: Granta Books, 2001).

Bennigsen, Alexandre, 'Muslim Guerrilla Warfare in the Caucasus (1918–28)', *Central Asian Survey*, 2:1 (July 1983), 45–56.

Bobrova, Ol'ga, 'Ruslan Aushev: "Dlya menya pros'ba materei – zakon"', *Novaya gazeta*, 16 February 2006.

Burney, Charles and David Marshall Lang, *The People of the Hills: Ancient Ararat and Caucasus* (London Phoenix Press, 2001).

Bychkov, I. A., 'Vstrecha s synom Shamilya i ego rasskazy ob ottse', *Russkaya starina*, vol. 107 (1901), 367–93.

Checheno-Ingushskaya ASSR za 50 let: Statisticheskii sbornik (Groznyi: Checheno-Ingushskoe knizhnoe izdatel'stvo, 1967).

Curtis, John, *Ancient Caucasian and Related Material in the British Museum: The British Museum Occasional Papers, Number 121* (London: British Museum, n. d.).

De Waal, Thomas and Carlotta Gall, *Chechnya: A Small Victorious War* (London: Pan Books, 1997).

Doklad deputatskoi Komissii po rassmotreniuyu i vyyasneniyu obstoyatel'stv, svyazannykh s tragicheskimi sobytiyami v g. Beslane 1-3 sentyabrya 2004 goda, sozdannoi na zasedanii

Parlamenta Respubliki Severnaya Osetiya-Alaniya 10 sentyabrya 2004 goda (Vladikavkaz n. p., 2005).

Doklad Parlamentskoi komissii po rassledovaniyu prichin i obstoy-atel'stv soversheniya terroristicheskogo akta v gorode Beslane Respubliki Severnaya Osetiya-Alaniya (Moskva: n. p., 2006).

Dunlop, John B., *Beslan: Russia's 9/11?* (n. p.: The American Committee for Peace in Chechnya and The Jamestown Foundation, 2005).

Dzasokhov, A. S., ed., *Istoriya Severnoi Osetii: XX vek* (Moskva: Nauka, 2003).

Ewart, Ewa, 'Beslan's children try to live again', *Sunday Times*, 28 August 2005.

Ewing, E. Thomas, 'Stalinism at Work: Teacher Certification (1936–39) and Soviet Power', *Russian Review*, 57:2 (April 1998), 218–35.

Franchetti, Mark, 'Beslan mothers tell Putin: stay away', *Sunday Times*, 28 August 2005.

— 'Saudi killer spearheads Chechen war', *Sunday Times*, 13 March 2005.

Funder, Anna, *Stasiland: Stories from Behind the Berlin Wall* (London: Granta Books, 2003).

Gunther, John, *Inside Russia Today* (Harmondsworth: Penguin Books, 1964).

Haraszti, Miklós, *Report on Russian media coverage of the Beslan tragedy: Access to information and journalists' working conditions* (n. p.: Organization for Security and Co-operation in Europe, 2004).

Hirsch, Francine, 'Toward an Empire of Nations: Border-Making and the Formation of Soviet National Identities', *Russian Review*, 59:2 (April 2000), 201–26.

Humphrey, Caroline, *The Unmaking of Soviet Life: Everyday Economies after Socialism* (Ithaca: Cornell University Press, 2002).

Jack, Andrew, *Inside Putin's Russia* (London: Granta Books, 2004).

Kallioma, Larisa, 'Kto zagovoril "golosom Beslana"?', *Izvestiya*, 10 February 2006.

Kaloev, B. A., *Osetiny* (Moskva: Nauka, 2004).

— ed., *Osetiny glazami russkikh i inostrannykh puteshestvennikov (XIII–XIX vv.)* (Ordzhonikidze: Severo-Osetinskoe knizhnoe izdatel'stvo, 1967).

Khamitsaeva, T. A. and A. Kh. Byazyrov, eds., *Narty: Osetinskii geroicheskii epos*, 3 vols. (Moskva: Nauka, 1990).

Khodarkovsky, Michael, 'Of Christianity, enlightenment, and colonialism: Russia in the North Caucasus, 1550–1800), *Journal of Modern History*, 71:2 (June 1999), 394–430.

Kolesnikov, Sergei, 'Nezhivoi simvol', *Izvestiya*, 26 April 2005.

Kostoev, Beslan, *Kavkazskii meridian: K voprosu russko-osetino-ingushskikh otnoshenii* (Moskva: Gumanitarnyi fond Ingushetii, 2001).

Laqueur, Walter, *The New Terrorism: Fanaticism and the Arms of Mass Destruction* (London: Phoenix Press, 1999).

Le Carré, John, *Our Game* (London: Hodder and Stoughton, 2000).

McDowell, Robert H., 'Russian Revolution and Civil War in the Caucasus', *Russian Review*, 27:4 (October 1968), 452–60.

McCauley, Martin, *The Soviet Union 1917–1991* (London: Longman, 1994).

McGahern, John, *Memoir* (London: Faber & Faber, 2006).

Malashenko, Aleksei V. and Dmitri V. Trenin, *Russia's Restless Frontier: The Chechnya Factor in Post-Soviet Russia* (Washington DC: Carnegie Endowment for International Peace, 2004).

Marsh, Stefanie, 'The buried truth', *The Times*, 14 September 2006.

Mashkin, Sergei, 'Test' prezidenta Ingushetii ugodil v dzhamaat', *Kommersant*, 29 March 2006.

Matveeva, Anna and Duncan Hiscock, eds., *The Caucasus: Armed and Divided: Small arms and light weapons proliferation and humanitarian consequences in the Caucasu*s (n. p.: Saferworld, 2003).

Meteleva, Svetlana, 'Beslan bez grifov', *Moskovskii Komsomolets*, 26 May 2005.

Milashina, Elena, 'Peregovorshchik', *Novaya gazeta*, 30 January 2006.

— untitled editorial, *Novaya gazeta*, 1 September 2005.

Muir, Robin, 'Theatre of hate', *Independent on Sunday*, 19 March 2006.

Novosil'tsev, A. P., ed., *Istoriya Severo-Osetinskoi ASSR s drevneishikh vremen do nashikh dnei*, 2 vols. (Ordzhonikidze: IR, 1987).

Page, Jeremy, 'Mother's choice', *The Times*, 20 August 2005.

— 'Streets littered with dead after rebel gunmen strike across city', *The Times*, 14 October 2005.

— 'Victims of Beslan siege found in a rubbish dump', *The Times*, 26 February 2005.

Paton Walsh, Nick, 'Mystery still shrouds Beslan six months on', *Guardian*, 1 March 2005.

Pearce, Brian, 'The Ossetians in History' in *A People Reborn: The Story of North Ossetia*, ed. Andrew Rothstein (London: Lawrence & Wishart, 1954).

Politkovskaya, Anna, *A Dirty War: A Russian Reporter in Chechnya* (London: Harvill Press, 2001).

— 'Khochetsya nemnogo rodiny', *Novaya gazeta*, 13 February 2006.

— *Putin's Russia*, trans. Arch Tait (London: Harvill Press, 2004).

Polyan, Pavel, *Ne po svoei vole: Istoriya i geografiya prinuzhdennykh migratsii i SSSR* (Moskva: O. G. I. – Memorial, 2001).

Positively Abandoned: Stigma and Discrimination against HIV-Positive Mothers and their Children in Russia (n. p.: Human Rights Watch, 2005).

Reuter, John, *Chechnya's Suicide Bombers: Desperate, Devout, or Deceived?* (n. p.: American Committee for Peace in Chechnya, 2004).

Roberts, Simon, 'Across Eleven Time Zones', *Granta*, 94 (Summer 2006), 127–59.

Russia: Country Summary (n. p.: Human Rights Watch, 2006).

Sanakoev, I. B., *Istoki i factory evolyutsii gruzino-osetinskogo konflikta* (Vladikavkaz: SOIGSI, 2004).

Satter, David, *Age of Delirium: The Decline and Fall of the Soviet Union* (New Haven: Yale University Press, 1996).

Savel'ev, Yu. P., *Beslan: Pravda zalozhnikov* (Moskva: n. p., 2006).

Service, Robert, *A History of Modern Russia from Nicholas II to Putin* (London: Penguin Books, 2003).

'Shamil Basayev' obituary, *The Times*, 11 July 2006.

Smith, David James, 'Beslan: The Aftermath', *Sunday Times Magazine*, 12 December 2004.

Snegirev, Vladimir, *Ryzhii: dokumental'noe povestvovanie* (Moskva: *Novaya gazeta*, 2003).

Strabo, *Geography*, Books 10–12, trans. Horace Leonard Jones, *Loeb Classical Library* (Cambridge, Mass.: Harvard University Press, 1965).

The Wrongs of Passage: Inhuman and Degrading Treatment of New Recruits in the Russian Armed Forces (n. p.: Human Rights Watch, 2004).

Tishkov, Valery, *Chechnya: Life in a War-Torn Society* (Berkeley and Los Angeles: University of California Press, 2004).

Torchinov, V. A. and M. Sh. Kisiev, *Osetiya: Istoriko-etnograficheskii spravochnik* (Sankt-Peterburg, Vladikavkaz: Gosudarstvennyi tsentr pri prezidente RSO-Alaniya, 1998).

Torshin, Aleksandr, 'Deistviya terroristov ne ustupayut zverstvam natsistov', *Parlamentskaya khronika*, 29 December 2005.

Truscott, Peter, *Putin's Progress: A biography of Russia's enigmatic President, Vladimir Putin* (London: Pocket Books, 2005).

Tsutsiev, A. A., *Osetino-Ingushskii konflikt (1992–. . .): ego predystoriya i faktory razvitiya* (Moskva: ROSSPEN, 1998).

Tullagov, A. D., *Istoki tragedii* ([Vladikavkaz]: n. p., 1993).

United Nations Commission on Human Rights, *Report of the Special Rapporteur on Violence against Women, its Causes and Consequences, Yakin Erturk on her Mission to the Russian*

Federation (n. p.: n. pub., 2006).

Vernadsky, George, 'Problems of Ossetic and Russian Epos', *American Slavic and East European Review*, 18:3 (October 1959), 281–94.

Whittaker, David J., ed., *The Terrorism Reader* (London: Routledge, 2001).

Williams, Brian Glyn, 'Caucasus Belli: New Perspectives on Russia's Quagmire', *Russian Review*, 64:4 (October 2005), 680–8.

Zdravomyslov, A. G., *Osetino-Ingushskii konflikt: perspektivy vykhoda iz tupikovoi situatsii* (Moskva: ROSSPEN, 1998).

Spelling

The standard British transliteration system has been used to render Russian words in the text, with the following exceptions: the Russian 'soft sign' has been omitted throughout for ease of reading; proper names which have close equivalents in English ('Lydia' rather than 'Lidiya'); and Russian words with established English spellings, such as 'Moscow' and 'Grozny'.

ACKNOWLEDGEMENTS

This book has taken over two and a half years to research and write. In that time, I have benefited from the help and insight of a great many people at home and abroad.

I want especially to thank George Miller, who had the original idea of publishing a book about the siege, and Catriona Kelly, who guided my earlier researches in Russian and Caucasian culture and put me in contact with Granta. George has been a wonderful editor, patient and wise, understanding and trusting throughout. At the BBC, I am very grateful to Fiona Blair, Jonathan Brunert, Fiona Gough, Ewa Ewart, Leslie Woodhead and their colleagues for the opportunity to work with them on a number of excellent documentaries about Beslan. I thank Luisa Calè, Richard Caplan and Federico Varese for important insights at an early stage. I thank Vegar Jordanger for taking the risk of inviting me to interpret at the conference on Chechen culture in Trondheim. Bella Shand calmed me down at a crucial moment. Thelma Holt and Robert Sturua gave me my first opportunity to visit the Caucasus.

In Russia, I thank particularly all who spoke to me so honestly and generously. As well as those who have asked not to be named, I thank Aleksandr Dzadziev, Alan Pliev, Inal

Sanakoev, Sergei Shtyrkov and Zhanna Kormina, Roman Igorav and Igor Dulaev for helping to make my visit to Vladikavkaz and Beslan as rewarding and useful as it was. For hospitality in Moscow and Pyatigorsk, I am grateful to Nick, Susie, Holly and Miles Latta; Dmitrii Katsera and his family; Oleg Chursin and Yuliya Lyapina; Nadia Frolova; Natalya; Loren; Jamie Khan, Natalya and Felix.

Though the book was drafted almost entirely in London, it had many homes in that city whilst I searched for my first flat. I offer special thanks to those who put it up and put up with me while I wrote it. Many of the ideas expressed in these pages owe their maturity to the conversations we had: Mernie Gilmore; Tania Gault; Victoria Sowerby; Harry Wallop; Ben Wright; Yasmin Khan; Marion Turner; Elliot Kendall; Annie Crombie; Hilary Spencer and Chris Clements; and Judy Blackwood. The Egyptian House in Penzance was a wonderful haven for a week.

Friends, family and colleagues have been a vital source of support and relief throughout the sometimes troubling process of trying to understand this atrocity. They have asked kind questions and provided diversions in just the right measure. I thank Wendy and John Phillips; Susan Phillips; Pearl and Samuel McCutcheon; Ruth and John Bale; Nini Rodgers; Isabel Davis; Barbara Davidson; Sam Fleming; Beccy Loncraine; Ben Brice; Naomi and Hugo Foxwood; Rachel and John Wevill; Jane Garnett, Gervase Rosser and Cecilia Rosser; Kirstie Blair; Matthew Creasy; Ceri Lawrence; John Hayes; Susie Mesure; John Shields; Minna Rauhansalo; Anna Ingram; Masha Unkovskaya; Emma Calvert; Conor Mitchell; Karen Jackson; Mark Parrett; Helen Anderson; Mark Andrews; Andrew Denney; Dan Jenkins; Ffiona Kyte; Kirsten Payne; and Kevin Summersgill. Finally, I thank Anthony Bale, whose belief in this project has been constant since its beginning and whose insights and support have improved the book beyond measure. All this notwithstanding, any shortcomings or errors are my own.

On the morning of 1 September 2004 the children of Beslan were excited about the start of a new school year. At School No. 1 in the southern Russian town many proud parents had also turned out to enjoy a day of traditional celebrations. Suddenly, as the festivities got under way, a band of heavily armed terrorists stormed the playground and these ordinary lives were changed for ever. In the space of a few minutes, more than 1,200 hostages – mostly women and children – were herded into the school gymnasium, beginning three days of unimaginable terror and suffering . . .

'It is the frankness of the participants that makes this such an important work for any reader who wishes to understand what is happening in the North Caucasus. From the mass of information at his disposal he has woven a many layered but accessible tapestry of life in one of the most complex and explosive regions of the world' *Guardian*

'Skilful and sensitive . . . In this impressive book, Phillips manages simultaneously to offer a detailed account of the historical context of the atrocity, as well as the personal details of individuals caught up in the events . . . excellent' *Independent*

'Timothy Phillips has done a heroic and, one might have thought for a foreigner, impossible job: he has reconstructed from the testimony of many hundreds of witnesses the hellish events of that September . . . His work is a fitting memorial to the dead' *Literary Review*

'The claims, counter- surrounded the tragedy mean there is a need for a book which describes the events themselves, their chronology, and the facts and figures. This book does more, including giving insights into possible divisions among the terrorists and highlighting the still unanswered questions . . . [it] lays bare the dysfunctional state of modern Russia, and the Caucasus in particular' *Scotland on Sunday*

Current Affairs • £8.99 • www.granta.com

ISBN 978-1-86207-993-9